JUMPING OFF CLIFFS

JUMPING OFF CLIFFS

Dilene Hinton

To order additional copies of this book, contact:
Xlibris
1-800-455-039
www.Xlibris.com.au
Orders@Xlibris.com.au
788916

CONTENTS

Dedication

I dedicate this book to my earth angel for choosing me as her mother, for enhancing my life and allowing me to be myself, for accepting me unconditionally and becoming her own woman. To you, my angel, I will be ever grateful.

Acknowledgements

To all the friends that have come into my life and those that have moved on, you have been very special. You came in when I needed you most and allowed my journey just because I knew you. To those that have stayed, I thank you, because you are blessing my life with your acceptance of me.

To all the men that I have had relationships with—and there have been many—I have nothing but appreciation, because you have been my mirror. You have allowed me to see my reflection in you and make the changes that I needed for my self-growth, to achieve my soul's purpose and, in doing so, find my joy and the wisdom that came from that.

To those that have brought challenges to my life, you have allowed me to see the opportunity in those challenges.

To all the authors of books (they are countless) that I have read, there have been too many for me to mention. I did not randomly choose those books, but rather, I specifically chose them at different stages of my life; they have been inspirational for my change. Sometimes the books chose me. I am so grateful for the volumes of good reading that have changed my life. You, the authors, have been there as a stand-in for a friend that could not be there.

For all the good conversations I have had with strangers and friends, the learnings that have come from those, and above all, those unknown yet genuine smiles I have received from strangers, you have made my day. Every genuine compliment that I have received was much appreciated, and I felt humbled by them.

To beautiful Australia, my country, the ability to travel your rugged outback, your spirit, and your magnificent vastness has been a major contributor to my spiritual growth, especially your indigenous people, for their inspirational stories, their courage and generosity to share their land, and their struggle to protect it and keep it pristine.

I acknowledge everyone and everything with much gratitude, because without you, I would not have had this tremendous journey. You have travelled this journey with me, and I hope your journey of self-discovery is blessed.

Summary

This is the story of a girl growing up between two different cultures in a country immersed in its own culture, living as an outcast, and amid all the rubble, going on a journey to excavate her authentic self. It is no greater or lesser than anyone else's story. It is brutally honest.

It is about courage and strength, which is a choice, however ordinary the situation is. It is not everyone's choice. You can climb a cliff, and when you get to the top, you can make the decision to just walk back to what is familiar. You have travelled that journey. Or you can look down, not really sure of what lies at the bottom, and you can just jump off. Falling to depths or trusting that you will have the wings to fly in life. It will sometimes allow you to crash, and at times it will lift you up on wings. To make the choice is to gain the experience. Life is full of choices. Sitting on the fence is not living but existing; taking chances is what brings experiences. Life is more about experience than any other mundane reason. This story is about choosing to experience and how sometimes the experience chooses me.

It is a girl's story about getting hurt, loving hard, breaking hearts, and getting her heart broken. It is about her search for happiness and how she found joy instead. It is about her trusting that the universe has her back no matter the tragedies. It is a story of a spiritual experience rather than a human existence. We need to trust that we have the ability to deal with anything that is put in front of us. Make mistakes and have failures and finding ways to best handle situations she never knew she was going to encounter. The universe is not going to carry us on its back, but it is going to support us if we put in the hard work.

It is her journey to find her authentic self amongst the masks of family, culture, country, and conditioning. It is about her having the courage to be that person so others can have the choice of whether to walk away or draw her into their inner circle. It is about her shedding the skin that does not fit her any more and growing the skin that fits. It is about her discovering who she is not before she can find who she truly is. It is about embracing change and challenging comfort. It is about confronting the self, but it is also about knowing that we all have the ability to create our own joy.

If I asked you who you are, would you be able to tell me? This is a story of finding the 'I am'. It is about the realisation that not everyone is going to like you, but if you do, then that is all right. She had to work to get to a stage in her life that when she looked in the mirror, the eyes looking back at her approved of who she was. She needed to find the courage not to fit into the normal mould.

When you shake off all the fluff, what remains? How many of us have the courage to experience all that we want in life, simple or extravagant, and embrace that person? It is her story about emerging from confusion and arriving at her place of peace. It does not intend to target any particular person or persons but only serves to tell a story. I hope it allows you, the reader, to see yourself in her story and relate to some of the experiences or want to try some new ones.

It is a story about cultures, immigration in the seventies, and experiencing the challenging parts of life; but above all, it is written with the hope that people, especially women—even if it is just one person—will realise that they have this enormous power, the inner strength to dig themselves out of any unhappy situation and empower themselves to be respected and to respect in return. We are all no different; we might try things differently, and if not for our failures, we would not arrive at so much success. To love your beautiful self before you can love others encourages exploring the self and breaking those boundaries, although the intent is not to hurt.

It is not about the girl restricting herself to goal posts which only allow her one direction to aim. It is about self-healing, self-love and self-discovery, and being fearless in the attempt to excavate the self and bring who she truly is to life.

In life, we have family, friends, relationships, and intimate relationships. They all form some part of our lives for some time, but how well do they really know you? Yes, truly know you.

HISTORY OR DEPTH?

History is not a choice, but depth is. History gives us the ability to relate to who we are. Depth gives us the understanding of who others are.

We all have history. To some of us, history is important. To me, history is just my past; it has created who I am. But depth is a journey of an intimate discovery of the self and others that only serves to enhance relationships and communities. Depth enhances; history defines.

When I was growing up, the only way to communicate was by writing. It was before the age of serious technology. I have always loved to write just for the sake of writing. But writing to be read is quite intimidating, especially as I know that if I pick up a book and if it does not capture me in the first few pages, I will not read it. I research a book before I buy it so it is not a useless purchase. If I can't take away something from that book to enhance my life or provide food for thought, I will not buy the book. It will not find a place on my bookshelf. When I was a little girl, writing letters was the only way to communicate. When I did not have anyone to write to, I had pen pals (appropriately named, because that was all we were—pals that just wrote to each other). Sometimes this would develop into people being more than just pals. Names of people that wanted to correspond with others appeared in magazines and newspapers with a brief description of who and where they were, to encourage others to write to them.

I wrote letters to family, and later, when letters to family were few and far between, I transferred that writing passion to journals. Writing somehow formed the expression that spoken words could not. But that was not what fanned my desire to write. Most of my life, there was never the opportunity to share on a deeper level. I could tell my diary that my sister sucks, but I would not be able to tell her that to her face. I could tell someone how I felt about them or convey news between us by writing. But there is a brutal honesty that private journals give you permission to engage in. I grew up hiding my feelings because no one was interested in knowing how I felt. I was not interested in hearing how others felt. I did not have or use my opportunities to find depth with a person so I could confide in or talk honestly—brutally honestly— with them. I was always afraid of being judged. All my life, I felt I did not fit in, so I had to gain the courage to discover my true self and strive to be authentic. It was my journaling that helped me do that.

I had journals for my thoughts, my goals, my attempts to change my life, my emotions, my gratitude, and excavating my true self. I had journals in which I wrote inspirational words and paragraphs from books I read, which became my-motivation, so I had wise words to reflect on when there was no guidance. Even in this age of technology, I still love writing. I write in my diary, I write notes to myself, and I write things I need to do and buy. I write my thoughts; I write what I am grateful for. I just write. When I put something down on paper, it confronts me. I have a reason to go back and read those words, and they do have an impact on me. I am able to use it positively, and I have. I have always been able to better express myself when I write; I can be brutally verbally blunt.

History is a record of my past. It does not define me. It is important in that it allowed me to find myself outside of that history, achieve the depth I wanted, and consequently go in search of those that I can find depth with. We can all be shallow; that too is a choice. But it is for those that do not want to be known on a deeper level.,. I can sit and listen to a million stories about your history, but at some time in that process, I want to know who you truly are. For that, I need to invest in you, and if I have not invested in myself, I have no right to find that depth in you. Conversations about history come easily. Every day I hear conversations about people's history but very rarely about how they are truly feeling and who they authentically are. I went on that journey. I had the history, I changed my history, and I found the depth in myself. In my search for depth in others, it has cost me family and friends, but it is a small price to pay.

Today, when I am surrounded not by many but by those that truly embrace and accept me for who I am, I am happy and grateful to have them in my inner circle. That is more than happiness—that is pure joy!

PLANET ECSTASY

The human body is the shrine where the soul abides.
We are more spirit than human.

It is the perfect place. Everyone feels and looks young. There is no focus on appearances but on energy and wisdom. The energy is beautiful. There is no such thing as names or who anyone is. We are all perfect, positive energy, and that is the only way we relate to and know each other. The weather is always perfectly moderate, and whilst we experience all types of weather, it is calm with its changes and asks nothing but for us to enjoy it. There is a total sense of acceptance.

There are animals, forests, stunning flowers, and trees. Everyone and everything knows what they should be doing, and they work together to keep this planet in perfect alignment. There is so much love, kindness, and the feeling of what family is truly supposed to be. Family is not restricted to groups but rather the whole. There are no roles on this planet; everyone has the capacity and capability to do whatever is necessary to support each other. Children are loved and treasured and are ecstatically happy; there is so much outdoor activity, and they are self-sufficient and nurtured to be resilient and loving. There is no control but absolute freedom. There is a sense of joy, not just happiness.

Food is in abundance, produce is fresh, and survival is simple. There is an abundance of health, whole food, clean water, and comfortable housing. Everyone takes care of each other, and we are all brothers and sisters—one big family. Animals are treated no differently from people. It is a planet with an open heart and no judgement, just unconditional love of self and others. Everyone is their authentic self. This is one massive loving community, and everyone is equal. There is so much love and trust, and the pace here is very slow. We tend to spend a lot of time in nature, and nature is part of the living space. This is the planet of love and living in the present moment.

Why would anyone want to go anywhere else? Whilst we are here, nothing is difficult, challenging, or conflicting. All is well, and all is in flow. This has to be the best place in the universe—Planet Ecstasy.

Whilst there is no worry, fear, or limits, everyone has the opportunity to extend themselves as much as they want, and every single person has the support that they need to achieve this. All focus is on the present moment, with no reflection of anywhere else but here and now.

This is a planet of souls—everyone is a good person, behaviours are good, and there is the choice to stay just as sensitive energy or take on any appearance that we want by using our thought.

For some souls, this is their permanent place of rest; they have earned that because they have accomplished the journey and grown into mature souls, and they will be on this planet for the rest of their existence. For some of us, it is just a transitional planet. Some of us are here to rejuvenate, reflect, rest, enjoy home, and receive guidance to allow us to understand whether we have grown as souls or need to take on another journey to earn the right to rest here permanently.

Guidance on this planet is so nurturing and caring everyone feels supported when it is time to leave this planet and return to accomplish further growth if they need it. There is a special room on this planet where souls are summoned to when it is their time to take on existence outside of this planet for further growth.

When a soul is summoned to this room, there is no feeling of threat, just love and a feeling that this is their choice and not the choice of the planet. This room is pink and full of warmth and gives one a feeling of being hugged and comforted. When one is in this room, you are surrounded by a group of support angels, and there is an understanding that it is time for a journey, as there are more lessons for the soul to learn. Everyone has a hunger for learning. There is involvement in the decision to return and how this mission of self-growth will be accomplished.

This journey can only be accomplished by returning to Planet Earth and taking on a human form. The return is done as a child, and whilst in the early years there will be a connection with spirits and angels for support, once the transition takes place, the onus is on the human being to maintain that spirit contact, because you take your soul with you so it can experience what it needs to on this new planet. The body you choose is sacred because it carries the soul and allows the soul to experience its journey.

There will be loss of memory of the soul's planet but not the connection; there will be no attachment except connection. There is the right to choose in which part of Planet Earth the soul will take on its human existence and the right to make all the decisions as to who its parents will be and whether there will be siblings. Every soul decides and agrees on how its journey on this new planet will be orchestrated.

This is only an experience; the journey is about the happiness of the soul—*joy*. Everyone on this peaceful, embracing planet is a good person. There is no bad behaviour, because all of us are surrounded by good energy and divine guidance, and there is no place for evil to exist. Evil transforms once it has entered this planet of supreme love. Unconditional love is the healing energy on this planet.

And with all the love and farewells, I was ready to leave this amazing place I called home. I was about to take the plunge. I turned around, and there was this supreme higher being at my back, giving me a sense of love and support. I made one request before I left. 'I know the journey in this new place that I am going to is going to be a challenge. When I am struggling with things, as is normal on Planet Earth, and when I look up into the sky, will you be looking down on me with love?' 'Of course' came the answer. 'Trust that your request is granted.' And with that assurance, I plunged into my journey of an earthly experience.

This is my knowledge of where all souls come from, to take on their human existence to gain the learnings and experience that they choose to, for wisdom and growth of spirit. Life is an experience; death is a transition. To live a full life is a choice. Death is inevitable, so what have we got to lose? Take risks; stop sitting on the edge. Just jump off and wait for those wings to carry you. Love as much as you can even if it hurts. Give without expecting. But more than all this, we need to be true to who we are. That is the journey our spirits inherit in the body of a human.

If only we could keep this memory when we reincarnate. What a better world this would be if we kept our sense of spirit. .

My younger grandson asked me one day, 'Where will you go, Oma, when you die?' I said, 'Planet Ecstasy,' and it was as if he knew that such a planet existed.

BUTTERFLIES

Life is too short; we need to show our true colours.

The travel from the womb to the harsh reality of human existence was terrifying. As a foetus, I had spent my time in the comfort of the womb, getting fed and staying warm, but I could not stay there forever. I had chosen a human existence for my soul to experience life lessons and nurture the growth of my spirit. Some of these lessons would have been discussed on Planet Ecstasy, but I do not recall those discussions or the comfort of my soul's home. This was real; I was thrust into this world, here to play my part on the stage of life. An actress on the stage of life, I would play numerous roles. I would encounter as many exits as I would entrances.

My name is Prajna (the *p* is silent). I had chosen the mother that I would be born to, the family that I would grow up in, and the experiences that I would have to assist with the growth of my soul. I have no reason to point the finger at any person or process, because this was my soul's choice—but my human self would not come to terms with that until my adult years. I do not recall much of my experiences as a toddler, but photographs confirm that I was a chubby and cute baby. I was loved for what I looked like. I may have hung on to the chubbiness, but I ditched the cuteness very early on in my life. I was always a big girl and struggled with my weight, not because I carried it but because it weighed on my family and friends. However, staying cute would not have allowed me to fight the battles that I needed to in my early years.

For most of my younger years, I was brought up by my grandmother on my mother's side. I do not even remember what she looked like, but I do remember how she treated us. I think we remember people more for the way they treat us. Yes, I certainly remember my grandmother for the way she treated me. The reason I was brought up by my grandmother was that my father worked along with the British, and part of his work required him to be away at remote villages, building factories for them all over India. My mother was required to accompany him wherever he went because that was what wives did. On very rare times and mostly during school holidays, we would accompany her and spend some time with my father at some of those remote villages. Those were always fun times for me as a child because my father had a way of spoiling us. He was a giver. Being away did not give him the opportunity to spend a great deal of time with us, so when the opportunity arose, he had no hesitation in being very generous with us. That was who my father really was. He was kind, compassionate, generous, and very real.

I was the youngest girl. I disliked my grandmother; she was a tyrant, and there was no feeling of nurture or care, just rules that, if not obeyed, had severe consequences. I am sure that my dad would have given her enough money to provide very well for us, but she always kept things to a minimum. We had electricity but always studied under the light of a kerosene lamp. Food was always just enough and very basic; there was no excess. I was glad when my grandmother passed away. I could not work out what all the fuss and tears were about. It was as if my torture had come to an end. I was no different from any other little girl; it was all about me. I had no empathy in my early years for how devastating it is to lose a mother. It was my very first experience with the death of a family member. It was not that I was not sure how to feel, but I did feel a sense of relief. I did not like how she cared for us—I could barely call it that. I do not remember ever getting a hug or having anything of value said to me. Even as I would wait for the arrival of my parents, it was not a pleasant experience because Nana would be at the front door before us to tell them what a pain in the butt we had been. This would result in consequences. It was at this very early stage in my life that I formed a dislike for the word *nana*, and I decided no one was ever going to call me that. If I would ever have grandchildren, I would be very happy for them to use my first name. What they would call me is irrelevant as long as they respected me, and I would give them reason to.

She was in her bed at home, and whilst she was taking her last few breaths, I was huddled in another room with my younger brother, not wanting to be part of all the howling and crying of her children. Most of them had come from different parts of India to be with her when she was dying. Being Catholics, my mother and her sisters were reciting prayers close enough to her ears. Was she hearing anything? They believed that this was her last chance at salvation and that if she was going to move on, she might as well go on a wave of prayer.

I was so distant from their emotions. They must have known a different side of her than I did, for all the tears that were being shed for her. There were a lot of family members around her bed, most of them her children and their partners. Where were they before this? Crying now that it was her last few minutes, did they give a shit about her before this? I had to believe that she meant something to them, because all of them were in deep throes of sorrow. Then came the final scream, and that was an indication that she had taken her last breath. That was the end of her life.

The whole death thing was a long-drawn process. There were no funeral parlours in India, so the bodies of the dead would be dressed and presented in a coffin when that arrived from the local carpenter. The coffin had to be just right so the body fitted in, leaving no space around the body. Spaces around the body and the coffin superstitiously meant that there would be the loss of another family member sometime soon. She was laid in the coffin, and it was placed on bags of ice to keep the body from decaying until the burial. Home was the funeral parlour. Burials always happened as quickly as possible because the temperature was hot and humid for most of the year and decaying of the bodies was a possibility. If anyone was going to be present before the dead were buried, they would have three days at the most to arrive or else they would be left out of the ritual.

Then there was the ritual. The body would be laid out in the lounge, hands folded over the stomach, coins on the eyes to keep the lids down (God forbid them from opening, because that would be horrific.). It was to give neighbours and those within the village the chance to come over and pay their respects. They surveyed the body with so much emotion. Would Nana have witnessed so much emotion when she was alive? The worst thing was that we had to take turns sitting with the body through the day and night. There was again some superstition around this, but it was not a question I asked at the time. There would be shifts that were shared by everyone, filled with tears and stories of her life, and there were always good stories. Surely there must have been some bad ones. Why do people feel the need to only speak well off the dead? I could not think of any good things to say about her.

At my shift, I had my aunt, my mother's youngest sister, sharing it with me. Whilst she seemed to be in deep mourning and contemplation, the night was quiet, and all were asleep. I sat there absolutely petrified that Nana would wake up in the middle of the night; those coins would jump out as she opened her eyes, and all my torture would start all over again. It was a very traumatic experience for a little girl, but there was some bizarre reason for sitting with the dead, with no explanation why. Was it because they were not sure whether she was dead and thought that at some stage she would wake up and sit up in that coffin and scare me to death? I did not feel like I had the permission to show any fear.

She had to be carried down the street with a procession of people behind her, and there were prayers, tears, and songs along the way until we got to the church and then to the hole in the ground, close to where previous family members were buried. The coffin was lowered amid a lot of howling. After prayers at the church and a sermon by the priest, everyone returned to our home for drinks and some food and to share a lot of stories. Lenny, my youngest brother, and I just huddled together and found our own stories to laugh about whilst everyone else was in deep sadness. Every time a family member walked by with a sad face and a hanky in their hands, we both would pull on our sad faces too, if only for those few minutes, and then get back to our happy selves.

The graveyard was only for the Catholics and was adjacent to the local church. There were monuments built over these holes in the ground, and a lot of work was put into the marble work and structure. The structures were covered in brightly coloured flowers and candles. But these graveyards were only for the Anglo-Indians, a term used for those that were mixed breed like us, one parent being of British ancestry. Family members were buried in the same hole in the ground, so long as the death was not recent.

Every time we attended church, it was an opportunity to visit the graves. It seemed weird to me, even as a little girl, to stand staring at a monument and reminiscing about when they were alive. It is just brick and mortar and perhaps just human bones in the depths of the ground. If only humans would get the hang of this. The soul within that body has flown away; it has started its next journey or gone to that planet of ecstasy. Would it not make better sense to sit in silence and feel their presence? There is no one in that graveyard that went to hell; the common belief is that they are in heaven, and so they are. Those stories of hell are only told by priests to frighten people into being good. Every soul, irrespective of who they are, goes back to a place of peace. It is a place reserved for all souls, good or bad, because as souls we are only perfectly good. We take up a body to have our experiences as human beings, and I know we create our own heaven or hell on this earth.

The majority of Indians were either Hindu or Muslim, with a small minority of Catholics who perhaps were convinced by the church that it was a better choice. Religion—it always tells you what to do. But I thought we already had a conscience for that. Conscience is a religion in itself and does not need a church or priests for the upkeep of its beliefs. There are a lot of despicable things done in the name of religion. Those Indians that were not Catholic did not bury their dead; they burnt their bodies, and their burials were conducted a lot differently than ours. We saw death as an end; they saw death as a beginning, a reincarnation into a new life. I found their celebration of the dead a lot more fun. It was colourful, and they had drums and dancing as they carried the bodies down the streets to the burning grounds, which were far out of the village, where the bodies would be burnt on mountains of dried sticks for those that wanted to watch. There was no moaning and groaning but singing and brightly coloured people and flowers. It was a more uplifting way to celebrate death.

With the death of my grandmother, my mother now had to play an active part in our upbringing, but she had paid help to do so. I always loved the arrival of my dad, because he always had a lot of little presents for us. It was not much, but I know it was given with a lot of thought and spoke very loudly of his love for us, even though I do not once remember him saying the word *love*. What I especially looked forward to were the bags of lollies he would bring home for us. This was a special treat, as those lollies were very different from what we could buy in the shops. They were British-influenced lollies, and even the wrappers were a treat. I loved collecting the wrappers and making garlands with them or sticking them together on sheets of papersheets of paper to create artwork. The wrappers were as intriguing as the lollies, and I treasured them very much after the lollies were consumed.

The British company my dad worked for manufactured pottery, but they also made exquisite confectionery as well. India had a lot of sugar cane fields, and one way to use that cane sugar was to produce lollies. I can still taste the sweetness of the sugar cane sticks as I chewed through them—a dietician's nightmare! We had exquisite crockery at home that was only brought out on special occasions and locked away in a display cupboard until then. They had a distinct indication of having been manufactured at these British factories.

I loved that they manufactured lollies and chocolates as well. Each bag of lollies was specially selected by my dad for each of us. They were all very different in each packet. It was a very big offering because no other children that I knew got the same thing. We had our own little bags of colourful sweet treats that lasted a long time. It was rationed out by my mother. Nonetheless, we were lucky to have that. I would hold my bag of lollies in my hand and fondle it for a long time and look through the colourful transparent bag that held them. I would look in amazement at the wrappers before they were snatched from me to be put away for later. We were only allowed a couple once a day, so that was something to look forward to.

My relationship with my parents was always distant, and with me being further down the line of siblings, this was even more so. I know my parents cared for me, because I got what I needed, but I did not feel the love. I was never told by my parents that they loved me. I do not remember them being proud of anything I did—not that I did anything to make them proud! It did not bother me very much at the time, but it would haunt me in my growing-up years. I struggled to be loved, and I craved for care and nurture. From a very early age, I learnt to just take care of myself and to not dwell on things too much.

I grew up with parents that believed, like all other parents in their time, that discipline could only come from beating a child. There were very strict rules—and I mean rules—that were set by my parents, and there was no compromise. If those rules were broken or if behaviours were not in line with their expectations, there was no room for discussion—the cane was the discipline they knew. Like every other essential in the home, the cane was no different; most families had this as an essential item around the house. How was I supposed to wrap my head around the fact that I had chosen these parents for my growth? What parents care for and nurture children through illness and brutally beat them in the name of discipline?

Throughout my early years, I got severely beaten by my dad. It could be because of my getting bad results at school, talking back, fighting with my sisters, disobeying rules, or sometimes even talking to those who they regarded not good company for me. I can empathise that sometimes children can get frustrating, but it is an absolute cop-out to feel that an adult, especially a big strong man like my dad, has the right to put a hand on a child. It had a very damaging effect on my life, and consequently, I challenged any form of control or abuse all my life. Even now in my adult years, it is so easy to remember the times I would be screaming under the pain of that cane before the next strike came, my face covered in tears and the shame that came from the whole painful exercise.

I went to school with my back marked with the bloodied impressions of the cane, the swollen skin raw from the beating, and I would be in pain for days until it healed, having to keep the beating a secret because it was too embarrassing to tell anyone. I had to suffer the pain in silence. I never once saw my mother use the cane on us, but she would always pressure my dad to discipline us. Her way of doing that would be to repeat the incident numerous times to him until it frustrated him to the extent that he would be prepared to just get on with it. It was as if she wanted to see us being beaten so she could feel better about being a disciplined parent but could not do the task herself.

Parents, however well we try to do our job, we damage our children in some way. It can be the beating, the smothering, the spoiling, or the tolerance, with no consequence for bad behaviour; sometimes just getting on with our lives can be damaging to a child. I took my beatings with resentment, but it was the day that I saw my father beat my sister Laurina, for no fault of her own except that she had gone along with what my other sisters wanted to do, that I hated him for doing that. I know *hate* is a very strong word, but at the time, it was the only word I knew to describe what I did not like. Laurina was challenged in her hearing, and consequently, in her speech. Her scream was the most painful thing to hear. What parent does that to a helpless child? I did not forgive my father for this act until after his death. But there were a lot of lessons I would learn from him, which influenced my growing up.

Should parenting be a fine line between unconditional love and consistent discipline; open guidance rather than strict rules; talking, cultivating communication, and not yelling; and dedicated time, especially in those vulnerable young years? Then there is a time you should stop parenting, stay connected, and hope you have built up a strong connection that will hold up amid the challenging times. Detach so you can see your children for who they really are, and always be a support rather than conducting their lives. Our children will eventually choose their own journey. It may not look the way you expect it to, but it is their journey; they will travel it depending on the strength of your parenting and the love that they are surrounded with.

You will never be the perfect parent, but do your best. If your best is not enough, then accept that and do what is in your power to support them. Parenting is one of the hardest challenges; you only have a window of opportunity. We have the care of our child for a very short period before they are in control of their lives. Make the most of it. Most times, we all do the best we can at the time with the knowledge that we have. Our children can only reflect who we are; give them a strong foundation and allow their challenges so it builds resilience. A little trick is to reconnect with your childhood when you are struggling with parenting. Both parents need to be present for a balanced childhood, and both parents need to be on the same team. But as parents, it would be pretty naive to think that only we have the responsibility to bring up that child; it is the neighbourhood, the community, the schooling system, and most of all, who they are surrounded by that will influence their growth. They will be surrounded by good and bad people; we have to trust that our parenting will allow them to make the right choices.

We do not have to inherit the behaviours of our parents. So if there is something we do not like in our children, it is important to take a good look at ourselves as parents. A child is just that—a child. They need guidance with love, discipline with care, and a lot of nurturing so they recognise that they can be whoever they want to be; that is good enough. My daughter has always challenged me from very early on in her life. There were times that I found it very hard to be a parent; I would have rather been just a mother. I was not the best parent but tried very hard to parent differently than how I was parented. I brought her up to have her own views, to be whatever she wanted to be, and to challenge what she felt was unfair and not right. Of course, it came back to bite me in the butt, but I have no regrets because that was what I had instilled in her as a parent.

Not all parents nurture their children to be who they want to be. My childhood was so controlled I did not have the opportunity to challenge or spread my wings. There was no chance to show my true colours. But I was determined not to let how I was parented influence who I wanted to become or deprive me of what I wanted to experience. How often have we felt that we were reverting to the behaviours of our parents? Well, that is the time to make changes to fit in with who you are, what is appropriate, and what your intuition is guiding you to do.

As a young child, I was not able to show my true colours. I felt like a butterfly with no wings.

Discovering Our Tribe

*It is not just biological; it is not flesh and blood. It is a group of people
with the same values. We choose our biological family for self-growth,
and we get the opportunity to also create our real family!*

Family holds all our challenges and all our learnings. Challenge family and
learn your lessons, and life should be an easy ride. Most times, we do not challenge
family; most times, we are not allowed to. Most times, we think we need to follow.
Consequently, these challenges get carried into our adult life and resurface in our
relationships with others, especially in intimate relationships.

My family was very dysfunctional, but then again most families do not function
perfectly. My dad's background was not spoken about very much when we were young.
All through my upbringing, I never once saw anyone that was a relative on my father's
side. If it was not spoken about, you did not ask questions. I just grasped things, half
from conversations that I would pick up, some from observations. He was Sri Lankan,
and for most of his adult life, he lived and worked in Ceylon (the old name for Sri
Lanka). His looks certainly matched that, and his values and the way he conducted
himself around people indicated that he must have come from a very challenging
background. We were never encouraged to ask him about his family. My mother was
of British descent. She had the looks and behaviour to support that. My impression
of the British was that they were pompous, pretentious, and of course, better than
everybody else. Our parenting was based on that, as my mother influenced most of our
upbringing. Anglo-Indians used their Western influence to bring up their children.

Living as an Anglo-Indian in India was confusing because it was a struggle to
be either Indian or British. To me, the word *Anglo-Indian* always meant rejects, left
behind once the British had fled India, taking their own and a lot of ours with them.
We were the half castes. But try telling an Anglo-Indian that. To us, being Anglo-
Indians meant that we regarded ourselves superior to the Indians—at least, that was
what we were given to believe growing up. To the genuine Indians, we were a laughing
stock; we were the pompous half-breed people that dressed funny. Yes, some of the
Indians depended on us for their survival, but I am sure they had a lot of unpleasant
things to say about us when they were amongst their own. We surely deserved that.

Who am I—grounded, as most Indians were, or superfluous like most Anglo-Indians? That would be my lifelong journey of self-discovery and excavation.

As a little girl, I remember the comfort the Indians felt just being themselves. We, of course, pretended to be who we were not. I have memories of moving from village to village, but those memories are not very clear. My vague remembrance is that we had money; we had a good life and the best of everything. Working as an engineer meant that my dad was prosperous and that we had a better life than a lot of others. A lot of the homes we stayed in were provided by the British, as that was part of the benefits my dad received for the services he provided for them. He was also paid very well. The Indians had a sort of love—hate relationship with the British. They brought some good to the country, but at a price.

Whilst we ate well, dressed well, and had the best in life, rather than giving us a sense of gratitude, this only made us feel we were better than everyone else that did not have the same things. Our homes were always very comfortable, and we had lots of servants to do what we wanted them to. My dad was very grounded, so his values were based on trust, respect, family, and equality; meanwhile, my mother's values were very superfluous, discriminatory, pompous, and very British! I grew up with confusing values.

Most of my young life, I just went along with whatever seemed right for me at the time. I tried very hard to fit in. I loved my servants, and every moment of the day I got to be around them, I tried to. There was always a separation between our servants and us, and other than what needed to be exchanged in communication, we had to keep contact with them to a minimum. I liked their simplicity. My parents had their roles: my dad earned the money, and my mother managed the home, which was not much different from any other family at that time. Sometimes our servants stayed with us for decades and became so much a part of the family. They, however, had their place within the home, and it was as if they were geared for that because they sensed that line even though it was invisible.

I was the youngest of five girls, and my brother was the youngest in the family. I remember the standard dad joke: 'I only needed to come close to your mother and shake my pants, and she would be pregnant'. Most of the families in the village were large. It was sort of an insurance policy. As there were no nursing homes, families supported their elders; therefore, the larger the families, the more the task could be spread around amongst them. Most of our elders lived in family homes until the end, and they were looked after by family members. There was no question of whether you liked your elders or how difficult they were; it was just an accepted fact that they would be looked after to the end. There was a sense of respect for the elders, and that was a good thing. Children, regardless of age, were never allowed to leave home unless they married or had to move away for further study. So most homes were full of family—sometimes generations of family. Homes were nursing homes for the elders, as well as funeral parlours for the dead.

My youngest brother and I were very close. He was my saviour during my time with my biological family. There was a disconnection from my father's background, and more attention was put on my mother's values and her way of life and her family. There would always be large gatherings of her family at our home, sometimes over thirty of them—men, women, and children. My father would go to all the effort to make them welcome and comfortable in our home. I loved it because it gave me a chance to run around with our cousins. When the house was too cramped, our neighbours would be requested to provide whatever extra room they had for some of our extended family. They would always be compensated by my dad. Everyone in this little village knew each other, which was not such a good thing because everyone knew about each others as well. If it was not families gossiping about each other, it was the servants. Amid all that family, not once during my childhood did I ever question why I did not see anyone that had any relevance to or was related to my dad.

Servants had enough access to homes to know a lot of what was happening—the abuse, the affairs, the secrets. It was very much up to their integrity that not much was said, but it could not be policed. Growing up, I just accepted that my mother's family was my father's too. My dad was a good observer; he just sat in his favourite chair and watched, and a lot of things would churn in his mind. He was a wise man and never said much until he had something useful to say. One of my regrets today is that I was not able to get to know more about my father's background. Instead we were immersed in my mother's side of the family, which was extremely dysfunctional. Whilst it looked like we were the perfect family, there were a lot of cracks which we tried very hard to hide so we could look perfect to the outside world.

It was normal for young eligible men considering a life partner to approach a convent, where there were a lot of single women hiding away on the pretence that they would become nuns one day. Eligible men would approach these convents to ask for the hand of one of them in marriage. My dad, after establishing himself as a self-made engineer, walked into one such convent and asked if there was any woman eligible for marriage. He had to prove to the nuns that he had a home, a job, and enough money to be able to keep the woman in comfort.

My mother was one of the single women left behind by the British. Her mother had left India with her British partner, and once her husband died, she eventually returned to the home she left behind and lived with my parents until her life ended. Whilst my grandmother, when she did return, was dependent on my father, it worked well for him because it meant that he could take my mother on his travels, and my grandmother would be with us whilst they were away. When the British were driven out of India, most of them left and took their women and whatever they could of the country with them. The single women, of course, like my mother, were left behind to fend for themselves. My mother was born in India; to leave India to live in a Western country was a very complicated process, so there was no possibility of her leaving. I guess that was the reason my mother put herself in a convent, hiding away from reality. There was also a reputation amongst the Anglo-Indians: Instead of arranged marriages, they would marry into the family, perhaps with cousins, as they knew their backgrounds very well. So long as that was not on the father's side of the family, apparently that was OK.

My mother was offered to my dad when he knocked on the convent door. She was a very tiny reserved woman and was quite light in complexion because of her background. She was an attractive woman. My dad was very dark in complexion, being Sri Lankan; he was tall and very intimidating in his looks. At first sight, that did not make him very attractive to my mother. Whilst she may have thought that she had convinced the nuns that she was there because she was going to become a nun, she did not fool them. They soon turfed her out to my dad, and I will declare that that was the luckiest day of her life.

She gave the orders; my dad obeyed. I think she had a way of making him accountable for her agreeing to marry him. He let her think she was in control; he was outnumbered anyway. But there were also times that she had to compromise. She did not have to work a day in her life. She was very talented; she was a musician and a teacher, could sew perfectly, and had a great singing voice. But she did not have to use any of her talents to earn an income. She was financially dependent on my dad, and he provided for her very well. I was very little at the time, but even then I could see that he loved her very much.

I have no recollection of my grandfather on my mother's side. I think there was a framed photo of him that hung on our wall at home, but I did not take any particular interest in it. Not soon after my parents were married, my grandmother came back to live with them. She had left behind an old house in a remote village in South India, and on her return, her intention was to stay in that house. As soon as my parents were married, her expectation was that they would move into that house and refurbish it so it would be a lovely home, which my father did. This became the home where she also lived with my mum and dad, and it became our family home.

I always thought it was the best house on the street; it was our home. In the days when carpets were a luxury, we had a home that was carpeted, but of course, we, the children, were the vacuum cleaners, as there was no such invention at the time. Every weekend, we would go on our hands and knees, and pick up every bit of scrap from the carpets; that would take up most of the day. The furnishings were made by my mum and my sisters, and so were the curtains on the windows. They were pretty and matched the cushions and everything else. Everything was clean, tidy, and polished. The home was well maintained, and we had servants to tend to the gardens, cook, and clean. However, we, as children, were expected to clean up after ourselves and play our part in keeping a clean and tidy home.

It was on a large property with a natural well for water and two toilets, which were on the outside of the property. There was no running water to the house, but that was common throughout the village. Most of the homes in our village had outside toilets. They were the primitive toilets which were holes in the ground, and they were cleaned daily, as were the others in the village. The smelly crap was taken away in large trucks, and for an hour after it left, we could still smell the stale stench. But that was normal procedure in the village for disposing of waste.

We had a basic kitchen. It was certainly not the family hub but a place where only cooking took place. It had open fires and terracotta pots that were treated so they could be used over open fires. It added a certain special flavour to what was cooked, not taking away from the talented cooks that our servants were. It always smelt of spices and sweets, and our cooks spent most of their time just cooking to feed us. We had four meals in a day. They were always cooked meals, so that kept the servants very busy. All the dishes were hand-washed with water that was drawn from the well. Because there was no running water to the house, water was always heated for our baths. My little brother would stand beside the well and draw the water to have his bath. All the men around the village did that. Even though the water was cold, the weather was warm, and in the heat of the sun, it was very refreshing to have cold water on the body. There were no such things as showers and hot water. If, for a good reason, hot water was needed, it was heated in the kitchens and poured into buckets for use in the inside bathrooms.

The storeroom was massive, and it was dark to allow whatever was stored in it to last a long time. All our spices and fruits from the garden were stored there with large amounts of rice and pulses and other food requirements that were purchased in bulk from the nearest town. All the produce were ordered and were delivered to our door to be stored. Everything was grown around the region, and there was no processed or packaged food locally. Any fresh produce were bought from the open markets. We did not own a fridge, so whatever was bought would be used for the day; our servants would go out every day with instructions of what was needed for the day's cooking. Everything was cooked fresh, and whatever could not be eaten soon enough was pickled or preserved for use whenever needed. There was absolutely no wastage of food, as any leftovers were fed to the animals. All meats and vegetables were sold in fresh markets every day. Most of our diet consisted of vegetables, and there was a vast variety of that. We had a beautiful veranda in front of the house, with plenty of chairs to sit and relax on; there was also a table with chairs, so we could sit around and do our homework after school.

We had a pantry that ran off the massive dining room and that also had an old-fashioned water filter for our drinking water. There was a large dining table that could hold an entire family, and most of our family meals were around that table. Off this dining room ran two bedrooms on each side, which were large, with dressing rooms attached—an Indian version of a walk-in wardrobe but much bigger. At the front of the house was a massive living area with a whole lot of chairs and other nice furniture and things on display. There were a lot of large photographs on the wall, most of them relatives that had passed on, but what took centre stage was a huge photo of Jesus in a massive frame on the wall and an altar with candles that were lit every night at prayer time, which was sometime between after we had dinner and before bedtime. Off the lounge was a bedroom for my parents, and there was also a space in there that my dad used as an office at home.

My parents were devoted Catholics, and every night we had to kneel and say the rosary. We rattled off the prayers, and most of the time, I would either doze off or think of anything and everything except what I was rattling off and wait for the time I could get off my knees, which were sore with all that kneeling on the carpet. My mum and dad got to sit down through it, I guess because of their age, but us children had to get on our knees and stay there until prayers were over. We slept on the floor in the bedrooms, the youngest in one bedroom and the older ones in the other. There were only a couple of beds, which were shared, but for most of the time, I slept on a mat with a sheet and a pillow on the floor.

We did not have a winter at all. There was a cool period in the year, around December to February; the days were hot, but the evenings were pleasant, as we lived close to the ocean. This was followed by a very hot and humid summer, and after that, the monsoon season, which was very wet. It would rain and rain for days; our whole backyard would get flooded, and we would have to wade through the water to the outside toilets. It was great fun paddling around in the water, and there was no thought that it could have been polluted in some form. We did not own any warm clothing because there was no need for it; it was always warm enough for comfortable clothing. It was a very pretty little village.

The garden was very manicured, and we had a lot of fruit trees, with fruits that were only restricted to that part of the south of India. There were several types of mangos, roseapples, gooseberries, breadfruit, guava, jackfruit, and coconut trees all over the property. There was a massive shed outside for the dog, and for some time, we even had a cow. The garden was beautiful, with plenty of lovely colour with the flowers and greenery, and we had a home-made swing roped on to one of the strong trees. There were numerous times I fell off that swing and landed in the deep gutter that allowed the excess water to flow where it needed to go from our property. The property was fenced; there was a massive gate at the front of the house, and it was always locked. The walls around the house were very high, and that was to keep out the nosy neighbours. To me, it felt like a prison; all the good life was beyond that gate, and that was where I wanted to be. The gate was only opened when we were leaving or coming back home, and most evenings, it was a routine to leave the gate open so we could see the comings and goings on the street.

My mother supervised the purchase of the food, the storage and use of the food, and the cooking. My dad was not involved in the home affairs; he just earned the money to keep it functioning the way my mum wanted it to. Having servants was not meant to indicate that we were in the lap of luxury; it was an accepted thing that British women chose not to do housework but to supervise the household, and that meant getting servants to do different types of work. It also helped the less-educated people earn money so they could look after their families. Schooling was not compulsory, and as a lot of Indians could not afford to send their children to school, they ended up working when they were very young and taking on jobs that did not require an education. It was all learnt trade, but they were very good at what they did and were very resourceful people.

We had a servant for each line of duty—one to cook, one to clean, one to clean the bathrooms and toilets, and even outside staff that worked on keeping the gardens looking good. Whilst my dad was around, every servant was treated with the highest respect. As children, we were expected to treat them as such too. There was a remarkable difference in how the servants were treated by my dad and by my mother. We, as children, owed a lot to those servants for their loyalty and care. There was a sense that my dad felt very much a part of them, but my mother saw them only as servants.

We lived on one of the two main streets in this little coastal fishing village, which was a short distance from the main town. I did not appreciate it at the time, but it had two of the best English schools on each street. One was the boys' school, run by priests, and the other was the girls' school, run by Carmelite nuns. It was a village surrounded by the ocean, with coconut palms and hardly any motorised traffic. Transport was, bicycles and rickshaws, and most people walked or rode a bike. The local people were, of course, forced to move from the village to the beaches, and as most of them were fishermen, it was natural for them to build little shacks to live in on the beach. Most of the homes in the village were owned or lived in by Anglo-Indians.

The village was agricultural and very green, and they grew a lot of rice, tea, and other grain. We had our own chickens and ducks, which were fattened up for special occasions, and we killed them at home before we cooked them. We had the best and ate the best, which was very fortunate. I took this for granted in my growing-up years, but today I feel so much appreciation for my father for providing for us all through our early years. How you were seen in this village was dependent on how you dressed, how you ate, and how your house was run. Most of the Anglo-Indians were try-hard Catholics. The rest of the village were either Hindus or Muslims, and everyone respected each other's religious beliefs and celebrated everyone's festivals.

I loved the Indian festivals; it always seemed like so much fun. If they were not throwing coloured dust at each other, they were dancing on the street, the women in their brightly coloured saris and the men in their traditional dresses. They would bring us their food to share, which was delicious. We celebrated their Diwali, Holi, Ramadan, and any festivals and customs that were not Catholic, and they celebrated the Catholic festivals as well. All our servants, irrespective of what religion they were, came over to our home for a meal at Christmas. My dad always insisted that they got a little gift, which would be an item of clothing or money. When the paddy fields were harvested, there would be a festival that was called Onam. It would go on for days, and there would be a stage in the fields at night, where my dad used to take us to watch Indian dancers and actors tell stories of history in colour. At the end of the festival, there would be fireworks. This was the highlight of the Onam season and a celebration of the harvest of the grain. Groups would compete with each other using fireworks, so the effects were stunning. I have witnessed a lot of fireworks since then but have never yet seen one that was anything like the Onam fireworks. It was my dad's way of keeping us in touch with his background.

My mother was very clear about who we were allowed to associate with. Any family that did not fit into her idea of what a disciplined family should be was not good enough for us. We only had a choice of very few people that we could visit or be in touch with, and we had to be self-sufficient as a family for our social needs. All that changed once I was in charge of my life. Anything that was restricted became a conquest. There were very few people that she approved of.

I was never comfortable within this family. I existed, played my role, and always looked for a way out, and that made me a very lonely child in the middle of such a big family. Were they just my tribe, not necessarily my family?

My dad was a very educated man, but he was educated in a non-English school. Even though his English was fluent, he loved using some Indian words in the middle of his conversations, much to my mother's disgust. He was a self-made engineer and had had enough money and a reputation to find himself a wife, which every man needed to do in those days. He had to have some monetary standing. He was a very reputable engineer for the British and consequently had to travel all over remote India to help build a lot of the factories that the British built around the villages. The British homes were extravagantly styled in comparison with the simplicity of the Indian homes. But I loved the simplicity of the Indian homes, even though they were little shacks built out of natural material like cow dung and coconut palms, with mud floors. They always looked so clean, tidy, and cosy. My father was respected by the British, but I am not sure if the feeling was mutual.

Some of the villages that he had to travel to and live in for a while until the job was near completion were so remote, but what I always noticed was how well-liked he was by the local people. He mingled with them and spoke their language, and his humility resonated with the villagers. He never did say very much, but when he said anything at all, it had an impact. Some of those rarely spoken words had a massive impact on me even as a child. He loved to smoke a cigarette and sit back and observe. I was very frightened of him as a child. I was not one of his favourites. I was not concerned about being his favourite; I was happy to stay away from his attention.

His position on the British was very mixed. He knew he needed them for his monetary survival and the wealth of his family, and he had a lot to benefit from that. Our lives defined that. We were not wealthy, but he provided us with everything that we needed. He hated the fact that everything was so pompous and pretentious. The British had a need to call everyone that worked for them by their surnames; consequently, my dad could not hold on to his long and complicated Sri Lankan surname and had to change it to something that was easily pronounceable for the British. He had also changed his first name, which was incredibly long as well. We were never told what his family name was. The Indians were visibly very submissive to the British. It seemed that they always felt slightly inferior.

Once my dad had established himself monetarily and was in a position to provide for a wife, he did it the only way he knew and was available to him at the time. There were no Internet dating sites or social networks; my dad had two left feet, so dancing his way to meeting a life partner was crossed off. He used the best traditional method available to him.

Whilst most Anglo-Indians married their own kind, as they felt everyone else was below them, I think it was a very radical move for my parents to have made. But my mother made it work for her. Secretly, I think that whilst she loved my dad for the way he provided for her, it was hard for her to come to terms with his background. It was as if he could have been the perfect person for her if only he had been Anglo-Indian too. Every country has its racist history, and India is no exception to that. We could live another hundred years and human beings would still see each other not as people or for who we are but for where we are born and what the colour of our skin is—or, as in India, what caste we belong to.

Mum always had the final word. She cared for my dad, and the affection and respect they had for each other was obvious. They had their roles: she did what she had to do as a wife, and he treated her like a princess. My mother did not have a bad day in the times that my dad was employed, and his wages kept the whole family comfortable—that included her family as well. I am sure they had a lot of differences and, consequently, a lot of domestic battles, but we were never put in a situation where we witnessed anything but respectful behaviour between them.

My mother always looked perfect from the time she woke up in the morning, with her specially made nightdress, house slippers, and housecoat, which was sewn by her or my sister Laurina. She was always in a dress during the day, looking fabulous, and when she went out, which was most times to church or when visiting cousins and friends, she was nothing short of looking like a queen, with her perfectly glamorous dress, hat and shoes to match, and the appropriate handbag. You could take a picture, frame it, and put it with all the other royal pictures that hung on our wall, and one would think she was part of the royal family. Most of what she needed to look good had to be ordered, professionally tailored, or specially sewn by her or Laurina. My mother had the most beautiful smile. When she was serious, we knew it, but when she laughed and smiled, it lit up her face. It was just beautiful.

Anglo-Indians gave their children English names. It made them distinctively different from the Indians. This became a pain in the neck. We were recognisable not only for our names but also for the way we dressed, because my mother insisted that there would be no trace of Indian clothing within her home.

Even though I was very tomboyish growing up, I still liked Indian saris and the other clothes that were worn by the local people. At a later stage in my life, when I was older and living away from home, staying in a hostel whilst studying to get my certificate in secretarial studies, I went out to a dance with a group of my Indian friends. They were all going to wear saris, and I decided to borrow one of their saris and get them to dress me in their clothes and accessories. It is a special feeling to be embraced by those six metres of material, which is silky and good to the touch, and when it is complete with the rest of the accessories, it can transform anyone into an Indian beauty!

With it being a six-metre piece of beautiful material, the requisite to hold it to the body is to wear a long skirt with a drawstring waist. This is tied tight on the waist, and the material is dressed into the skirt, which helps hold it together. The material and colours of these saris fascinated me because they were amazing. Every sari has a bit of spare material at the end of the six metres that can be separated and tailor-made into a choli, which is a little midriff top that is worn with the sari. It is a little blouse with sleeves to the elbow and buttons in the front, and it reaches to just over the navel. Most of the belly is exposed. It is quite acceptable to show off most of your belly wearing this traditional dress, but it is not respectful to show a lot of leg—figure that! The women always looked so beautiful dressed in their saris and with the accessories, right up to the bindi and traditional slippers. I loved the colours and how the women put unusual colours together; it just worked. They looked magnificent. I borrowed a choli and a sari from one of my friends and wore it that night.

I did not have a long drawstring skirt to hold it together, so I decided I would dress it into my underwear. I felt so Indian in my sari and felt I was one with the group of friends I was with. The music was loud; everyone was dancing. We had a few drinks (these were some of the best days of my life), so a couple of us decided we would get up on the table and dance so we could see the band. I was loving the mood, the freedom of being out with my friends, the freedom to behave the way I wanted to and dress the way I loved to, the freedom of being away from the grip of my family. I was enjoying the moment, dancing on the table, when one of my girlfriends, in an attempt to get my attention, pulled my sari. The whole friggin' thing came apart. There I was, standing in my granny panties (there was no such thing as sexy underwear in India). That was not funny at the time, but I thought it was! So before I became the act of the night, I rushed off into the ladies' room and got myself decent again. I had mastered the art of dressing in a sari. Hell, I had even danced in one! I was reborn for a short while; I was Indian for a small time.

On rare occasions, my mother had to go shopping in town. It was an hour's ride by cycle rickshaw from the village we lived in. It was a big town, and there were a lot of shops there. One of us would accompany her on the trip. It was a very special experience because she would take us to the material shops to purchase material for our clothing, which she would sew herself. We would always get a new dress for our birthdays, and my brother would get a new tailor-made outfit for his. The shops were a bright mass of colour and texture. There were mountains of stuff, and you could purchase anything and everything that was needed for the house. The shopkeepers' voices were loud and intended to attract buyers. There was a lot of bargaining for prices, and as my mother would always purchase a fair bit of materials, it would always be reduced to a price that was acceptable to her before she left the shop. The little man that ran the store was hardly visible in the mountains of rolls of material, sitting in his lotus position. How he managed it for the whole day I would never know.

We would then stop over at the grocery store, and there would be mountains of rice, pulses, spices, and other food items that she would purchase for our needs. They were all held in large barrels and could be bought by the measure. The smells were so tantalising; we could smell it all over the street. We would get a little treat during these trips. It would be either a drink, an ice cream, or sometimes even an Indian meal at one of the little coffee huts. We would come home laden with all our needs, until the next time we had to restock. These trips were very rare, but when it was my turn, I always looked forward to it. Sometimes she would take my brother and me along, and it was always fun having my little brother come along.

We would travel from our little village through colourful streets and crowds of people, past temples and little shacks and open roads, to get to the town. The town had a cinema and other entertainment, and occasionally, we would go as a family to the cinema. That was always a treat when my dad was down for the holidays. We would go out to the movies, especially when there was an English film showing in town. My dad would always take us all out to dinner after. *The Ten Commandments* and *Chariots of the Gods* were a couple of the movies we saw as a family.

I had a very distant relationship with my mother, and there were no tender moments between the two of us. I was just there. She took care of me, but we had no connection at all. I tried very hard to make her laugh and sometimes succeeded, but most times I felt ignored and just had to get on with it. I just fitted in and never expected or knew what love or affection meant, so it did not bother me at all.

Very early in life, I knew I had nothing in common with any of them. It feels like I just existed within it rather than being a part of it. With me being the youngest girl, everyone had the opportunity to control me, except for my younger brother. I was a free spirit, but within this family, I felt like my wings were broken. Fixing those broken wings was a continuous job.

All our life lessons are learnt within the family. As we were very emotionally connected and aggressively controlled, it was hard to challenge all those lessons. Consequently, as I grew older and detached from the family, life did not allow me to avoid those lessons. It appeared with different faces and different challenges. One of the good things, however, is that life will allow you to create family, people who will present themselves in your life who could be an older sister, a brother, a mother, or a father you did not have. You just have to be aware and use the opportunity when it presents itself.

I am who I am because of the challenges I had within the family. I realised from very young that we did not have the same values. My family was dominated by my mother's values more than my father's, and even as a little girl, I always felt confused getting my head around how I wanted to and was supposed to behave. It was the cause of a lot of dysfunction in my life, as I struggled to strip off what I was not and to grab the values that described me most.

I gravitated towards my dad's values because I related a lot better to some of his words, which were rare but wise. 'Never treat a beggar disrespectfully, because one day that could be you.' 'I will do my best to give you the education and support you need, but you need to become an independent adult and never depend on a man to support you financially.' My life was a struggle between shedding my mother's pompousness and using my father's few words to guide me to authenticity.

Collette trained to be a teacher. She was skinny, very obsessed with how she looked, and always thought she was better than everyone else. She taught at the local girls' school that I eventually went to. She spent a lot of her time focused on her beauty. As I was growing up, she was the sister that taught me after school, trying to bring me up to the standard that was desirable to them. It was not a positive experience at all because I did not get any better in learning. I feared her tutoring because if I got something wrong, she had a wooden ruler with which she would hit the knuckles of my fingers. It was the most painful thing for a little girl to experience. Tears would flow down my face; no substance would get into my head, as I would wonder when the next blow would come. My knuckles would be so sore, and for that moment, I would feel so much dislike for her. That was very damaging for my learning. She was very outspoken and never hesitated to pick battles with anyone she felt was not doing the right thing by her. As a child, I dreaded learning with her, because most times it would end in a lot of bitter tears and no learning absorbed. I always managed to escape into my play, which was very imaginative; I could disappear into that world.

Laurina was the most beautiful person. She was born with a hearing problem, which affected her speech. That must have been a good thing, as she was able to shut out all the bullshit in conversations that happened around our home. Now normally she should have gone through the same schooling process as we all did. But schools in India did not cater to children that were challenged in that way. So my parents made the decision to keep her at home (bad decision). She stayed at home and helped my mother with her sewing and any other jobs around the house that my mum needed her to do. She was a constant and much-loved companion for my mother right to the time of my mother's death, and no one knew my mother better than she did. In my eyes, Laurina was elegant, attractive, caring, kind, and talented in any which way—she could do anything and do it well.

Using her hands was her most precious talent. She made all our clothes and all the furnishings for the house, and she even made some money sewing dresses for the locals and anyone else that wanted a dress or any other material converted into something else. She sewed some amazing dresses and converted some of the most unattractive people into stunners. But the downside was that she was taken advantage of; most of the locals expected her to make them what they wanted and were always hesitant to pay what she truly deserved. Tight arses! As a child, I remember her always being at that sewing machine, feet moving very fast on the pedal that drove the wheel, which moved the needle along the clothing. If it was anything crafty, she would master the art and do it to perfection. She always looked immaculate, was very quiet, and loved a gossip with Collette; the two of them were very close.

Maggy was deceptive and fake, and she flitted around as if she was the most attractive person on this planet. She certainly was not, in my eyes. She was a bully and never practiced what she preached, and unfortunately, she influenced a lot of my young adult life which left me feeling very helpless and lonely most of the time. She was very successful, academically and professionally. She was a flirt, and whilst there is nothing wrong with that, it was always with someone's partner or husband. It did feel inappropriate, considering the values that were instilled in us as children. Her expectations of me were very high, but her standards were very low. She was never wrong and never apologised for any harm she caused. She just did not give me any reason to like her.

Maggy always wanted what was not hers. She wanted the boss she worked for, who was a married man, my sister's husband. She had a lot of talent; she had a beautiful voice and played the piano perfectly. She had so much going for her, but don't bother complimenting her on that, because she gave herself the gold stars. She was better than everyone else and was the centrepiece wherever she was. She needed to be noticed; she flaunted herself. She had absolutely no regard for anyone's well-being or their feelings, and if there was anything that had to be done, she could do it better. There is nothing nice I can say about her; she just was not a nice person. You can pick a lot of beautiful fruit from a tree, and there will be one rotten one—that was her. When I was younger, she did not have much of an impact on my life, but it was in my vulnerable adolescent years that she controlled and manipulated my life.

Phillis was the family favourite. We grew up very closely, as we were close in ages, but there was always that sexual energy about her that was very alien to me at that time. She always had her head stuck in a Mills and Boon book, and I guess what she read, she fantasised about. She was fascinated by the novel *Lady Chatterley's Lover*. There were not many attractive or eligible men around in the little village we grew up in, but she managed to find whatever was there to flirt with, whether it was a cousin or a next-door neighbour's son.

At one time, there was a confrontation between her and my parents, and there was a lot of screaming, crying, and verbal drama about her having relations with one of our distant cousins. They were about the same age, and that was the first time she was in the bad books with my parents. She had gone away on a secret weekend with him and had lied to my parents about where she was going. I think what my parents were most concerned about was that they had had sex and would bring disgrace on the family; they were trying to knock that out of her with a lot of questions and angry words. Affairs between cousins and family were very common, and sometimes there were babies from these relationships that disappeared and were never to be seen again so they could not bring disgrace to the families. Bad stuff was happening, but it was never talked about; it was gossiped and whispered about, because that was how the village handled local news. The authenticity of the stories was in doubt, but that did not stop the gossip.

Phillis eventually managed to marry the biggest loser in town. He was from one of the largest families in the village, and they were the creepiest family locally. I used to sit on the veranda wall and watch them walk past our gate and think, *Is there not one person in this large family that looks any better?* Nasty, I know, but what do you expect from a little girl? I disliked all of them. The family ran the local bakery, so most times, I would be at their front door purchasing bread for us and trying to avoid the creepiness of their appearance and feeling like my bread was tainted. The guy Phillis married never came anywhere near me at any time, but I was soon to learn that marrying Phillis was his ticket to having sex with the rest of the sisters who were willing to play his game. What a freak! What an absolute freak! He would, however, be very surprised when his sorry arse crossed my path.

In this part of my story, I want to say a few words about Garry, Phillis's husband. I had no idea what was going on within the family, as I had left home when I was much younger, to come to Australia. When my daughter was fourteen, I decided that I would go back to India, as there was a call for a family reunion (as if there ever was a union). I had no intention to take them up on this, but as I was married at the time, Edward was keen to visit India and decided that we should go. There was no way that I could persuade him that we did not need to. This was supposed to be my family, but I was not looking forward to going back home to dig up the dirt. Edward was persistent, so I thought I would use the opportunity to show Deva, my daughter who was fourteen at the time, my background and where I was born. I was hoping to also connect with my mother in the hope of repairing our broken relationship since I had left India for Australia.

I sensed a very uncomfortable closeness between Garry and Maggy. Lounging in a bed together and stealing an occasional kiss—it felt extremely creepy. This was not the family picture that I had expected, and when I confronted them, the explanation was that it was a normal display of affection within the family. Was I the abnormal one? I was the one being paranoid about how my family displayed and distributed affection.

I was so glad to leave and to come back to Australia. Before I left India, Phillis had a conversation with Edward about sponsoring her family's move to Australia. I was not in favour of it, as I would have rather brought Lenny, my younger brother, and his wife up; however, Lenny did not want to leave India. I did warm to the realisation that, considering Phillis had two young boys at the time, it was a good opportunity for them to have a better future than they would have had in India. It was more in the interest of her two boys that I started the sponsoring process. When they arrived in Australia, I was unhappily married at the time and processing my way out of the marriage, so it was not a good time for them to land on me. When I was in India, I knew I was going to leave Edward, but I did not want the family involved in trying to bring things together. We were struggling financially, but they landed on us with the expectation that we would support them. We returned from India with a big debt because my family presumed that, coming from Australia, we had just plucked money off our money tree, and they had decided to have a holiday on us as well. We had taken a loan to visit home, and that had to be repaid.

Edward loved the idea that they thought that we were wealthy, and what was meant to be some time to show my daughter where I was born and some of our history became a big family picnic all through India. Everywhere we travelled, we had to take the family around at our cost, and to make it financially possible, we hired a Datsun van and travelled all over with the family. Travelling in India was like taking your life in your hands. There were no rules on the road. Drivers used their horn; they had two—one on the steering wheel and a hooter as well, close to the driver's seat. It was a noisy experience. Road rules were a joke at that time, and everyone fought to get on the road and be on their way. Two-lane highways became five-lane highways, and with the trucks, cars, bullock carts, rickshaws, and all kinds of two-and four-wheelers, it was a traumatic experience. I just sat back and enjoyed it all, because it was pointless to be on edge like the rest of the family was. On the sides of the roads, there were trucks that had fallen down the winding roads, and they were still lying sideways, waiting for the not-so-efficient emergency services to come. The winding roads were a mass of vehicles, animals, and screaming, but to me, it was just an experience.

I want to mention a particular incident. On this trip back, I realised how much India had advanced electronically and financially, but they were still so backwards in so many other ways, like with castes and racial discrimination. As we had a driver, whom we hired with the Datsun to drive us around, I presumed that he would sit with us when we stopped to have a meal. He was an extremely nice man and very patient with all our travel needs, and he was a good driver. We landed at the first stop for the day; it was dinner time, so we went into a restaurant and sat down. Without thinking, I invited the driver to sit with us.

I noticed that he was not very comfortable with the request, but after a lot of persuasion, he sat down. We must have waited over half an hour for our meals; nothing was happening, and there were others being served who had arrived much later than us. I got up to ask at the counter why our order had not come through, and everyone I asked just ignored me or pretended that they could not understand me. I finally got a response from one of the waiters that they would not serve us because our driver was from a low caste and was sitting at our table; it was against their caste expectations. It had been a while since I had left India, and it was apparent how much I had forgotten about the absurd yet accepted practices. I had taken this as acceptable behaviour when I lived in the country, but being in Australia had changed the way I saw things.

I was not about to accept unfairness. I was so angry but thought it was pointless trying to change their response. Who was I to question their practices, especially that I was now Australian? But there is nothing wrong with a silent protest. I cancelled my order, and I got up to leave. I guess they did not expect that from a woman. They said they would serve us if the driver sat on the floor outside, and they would serve him a meal on the floor. There was no way I was having that. I was surprised that I was the only one, amongst all my family that were there, that was objecting to this behaviour. They suggested to me that I was making a drama out of a situation that should be accepted.

I guess I knew better then, and to ignore and accept such behaviour would only show my support for caste racism. Being a small business in a small village, every bit of trade was important. It was not every day that a large group would call in for a full meal. The potential loss of that income allowed them to change their minds. Most times, there would also be a big tip that came when settling the bill. This little business knew they would be stupid to let that go. Without any hesitation, we all sat down at the table, including our driver, and had a great meal. I realised that my decision would not change a country, but I could make a difference that was obviously in front of me —and that I did. Every day, every one of us gets a chance to make a difference in front of us; we can't change the world, but the little differences all add up in the end. We did not seem to have a problem at some of the little huts we stopped at for meals around the countryside, which made it clear that it was an attitude more than it was a caste issue; it varied, depending where we were. So our lovely driver became part of our family group and was involved in everything that we did.

I returned very tired, confused, yet happy to be back on Australian soil, with a quiet realisation that I was more Australian than I was Indian. If I did not look in the mirror, I would think I was Australian. Deva had started high school locally, and I was feeling very emotional sending her off to high school in a rush, as I had not had things well organised for her before I left. It was not the best time to have family arrive either, but there was no turning back.

We had to sign papers to take on the financial responsibility of them arriving in Australia, and I was happy to do so. The immigration system was much more focused at that time. The motive behind the policies on immigration were very clear and supportive of the country as well. We were able to sponsor family, but they were not able to claim social security. We had to sign a document that made us responsible for their financial well-being until they got on their feet. There were also procedures in place for them to be briefed by an Australian in India about the way of life in Australia and that the expectation was that we spoke good English. It was all fully justifiable. It should not be this government's responsibility to support them when they had not contributed to the country so far. Speaking good English at home and going to good schools made it easy to fit into the country. I knew we were not in a financial position to support them for too long, but they were well established financially; unlike I was, they were able to bring their money out of India. The rules had relaxed since I came. I was hoping that they would be understanding of our situation and get on their feet as soon as they were able to.

It seemed like they were never going to leave. They had it so good—four meals a day, with no effort on their part—and they loved the idea of staying with us, making no effort to find jobs or accommodation. The demands were straining my already limited time and financial capability. I had to work full days and also make sure that there was enough food at home so they could have their four meals a day.

At this stage, I was struggling in my relationship as well. Edward was drinking a lot. Since we had returned from India, he had suffered a liver disease as a result of his excessive drinking and, on medical recommendation, was supposed to stop drinking. It did not concern him a lot; in fact, he ignored the doctor's advice and continued to drink excessively. Every night, he would end up senseless and flop into bed, leaving me to arrange everything after a hard day's work. Garry would sit on his arse and do nothing; Phillis would run around after her eight-year-old son, trying to feed him his dinner. It was absolute chaos. I had resigned myself to putting up with this for a while until they were able to get on their feet, but I would make the decision to ask them to leave quicker than I thought.

One night, not too long after they had started staying with us, Edward had gone to bed after one of his drunken episodes, and I was at the kitchen sink, washing the dishes. It was after 10 p.m., and I noticed that Garry stayed around even though everyone else had gone to bed, including Phillis. He asked me to come and sit next to him. I refused, as I was in the middle of cleaning up the dishes, but he did not leave it at that. He walked over to me and stood behind me and rubbed his genitals against me. I was appalled, more so because I did not expect that from my sister's husband; I was angry that he used the opportunity of everyone being asleep before he decided to prey on me. He was a guest in my home, and he felt he was entitled to added benefits. He got the wrong sister. I elbowed him and told him never to try it again with me or he would be sorry. It amazed me how surprised he was at my reaction. Whilst he had had an easy ride with the rest of the family, he realised that he just did not know me at all.

I am no saint, but I was not an easy lay either. I struggled with the thought that he had tried this on all my other sisters, and I did not want my thoughts to go there. I disliked him to the degree that I just could not look at his ugly face any more. He had the audacity to live in my home, take advantage of my hospitality, and think he was entitled to a bit of 'red light' action. The fucking idiot! No one was going to treat me any less than I wanted to be treated. I realised that he had noticed that my marriage was at a breaking point, but that still did not give him the right to think that I would want his sorry arse.

I just could not sleep that night, as I was so angry. Everything was so wrong; I wanted it to change, but I did not know how. I just did not want them with me for another day. I needed to act quickly. The next day, I took Phillis for a walk and said to her that she had to find alternative accommodation and that I had had enough. The financial and physical burden was too much for me. I wanted so much to tell her the reason I was asking them to leave, but I felt that I had to spare her from hearing what I hoped she already knew. Even though I knew she should have been made aware of his behaviour, I loved my sister and did not want to hurt her feelings. But she knew the truth; she knew the type of person that he was and preferred to hide her head in the sand and pretend it was not happening. It was so typical of how my family dealt with things: just pretend, and it will go away. It was not that I did not have the capability to deal with shitheads like him, but he had no right to my home.

Phillis had a million excuses why they needed to stay with us, but I was not having it and asked her to leave the next day. I offered to spell out the real reason I wanted them to leave; she immediately knew where the conversation was going and refused to go there. She did not want to hear the truth and agreed to leave. They did not struggle too hard to get a rental property a few doors up the street from us, and it was obvious that they had the financial capability to settle themselves soon enough. It was also apparent that they had a lot of connections in Australia, which assisted in their easily settling in, so they had had absolutely no need to have a free ride on us.

I had attempted to talk with Edward about what was happening, as my daughter was also starting to feel very uncomfortable with Garry's advances. She was my daughter, and even though she was barely a teenager at the time, she was not having a bar of him. We had always had conversations about predators, and I had made her understand that even if this could be someone that was a respected person in society or even a family member, it was still not right. She did not like him at all, and I encouraged her not to go anywhere near him. The response from Edward was so disappointing. 'You are probably provoking that behaviour from him.' So I had to take the action into my hands. This was my family; these were the people that I grew up with. But their values were up their arses!

They found a flat not far from us and settled in, and the reality of being in a new country dawned on them. They had stayed with us for a few months, so they had not been able to come to grips with the reality of living in Australia. I had been prepared for them to stay for up to a year and longer, but with all that I was going through, I did not want him to deal with as well. Once they had settled in, I went over to make sure that Phillis and her two boys were all right and if there was anything I could lend them by way of utensils or linen. I kept an eye on her progress. I knew before long that they would be on their feet soon, as they were both qualified, and I also realised that they had access to enough money.

It took several attempts before Garry got the message that I was not free bait. I guess he thought that at some stage, I was going to succumb to his attempts. Even if I was on a deserted island, desperate for sexual pleasure, he would not be the one I would want that with. He had a smell about him that was as revolting as he was. There was one more time that he tried, and it was the last. They had been in Australia for a while and had purchased a home in the same suburb where we lived. By that time, I had finally bought a car for myself and decided to pay my sister a visit as usual.

At the end of the visit, I got into my car to return home, and he followed me and stood by the window of my car. I rolled the window down and heard him say, 'Are you not going to give me a kiss before you leave?' I always gave my sister a hug and a kiss before I left, and I avoided going anywhere near him, for good reasons. But he could not help himself; he stuck his ugly head into my car and tried to stick his tongue into my mouth. I grabbed him by the collar until he almost choked, and I said, 'If you ever try anything like that with me again, I will bash your head in, you bastard.' It never happened again.

I have never felt comfortable with anger as an emotion, and my way of dealing with it is always to convert the emotion into strength to handle the situation. There is always a sense of relief and empowerment that comes from that. He never ever tried that with me ever again. There will always be Garrys in this world, but what are we women saying about ourselves when we remain powerless?

I was hoping that sponsoring Phillis and her family's move to Australia would bring me closer to family. I wanted an extended family, and I tried very hard, in spite of all the pitfalls. I realised that I was very different from them. It was natural that I accepted my sister's values for what they were, so long as they did not have an impact on my life. It was harder for Phillis to accept me for who I was, for how I brought up my daughter, for how I dressed, and for the way I lived my life. I struggled with being myself and having to face their constant questions about all the things about me that were different. Yes, my family could treat me any way they liked, but because I was family, I just had to tolerate it. I was desperate to have family. I wanted to have a sister that I could turn to when I needed her, to love and cherish, and it would take me a long while before I realised that it would never happen. I had to be someone they wanted me to be before they could accept me. I had been working hard at my self-belief and self-esteem, and even though it would take a long time before I would be comfortable with myself, it made sense to work with the challenges of the self that were presented at the time. It was becoming very obvious to me that I would have to give up my immediate family, because it was in my interest to do so. They never did make me feel good about myself and never would.

Then one day I got a call from Phillis. She was in a regional motel room. She had just talked with a priest, who had given her the last rites, and apparently, her intention was to take some pills and take her life. As if! Obviously, she was not that serious about dying if she had called to discuss it with me. But at the time, all I could think of was how it got to this and if I would be able to live with the consequence if I ignored her call.

Numerous calls and lots of conversations finally got me to understand the depth of the situation and why she was where she was and the reason for her intentions. Whilst Garry was at work, she had gone to a drawer in the house to get his briefcase out so she could obtain some documents. She had opened the briefcase and was confronted with numerous explicitly sexual letters from Maggy to Garry, detailing their whole affair. It was reality. Why did that not surprise me? I wondered how it did not surprise her! How far down in the sand had she stuck her head? What planet was she on that she had not noticed what had been happening?

Garry and Maggy had been having an affair, and this had been very obvious to me when I had visited them in India. It had probably been going on a long time before that. It had still been happening when she visited and stayed with Phillis in Australia on the pretence of a holiday, and the affair had continued under Phillis's roof. How low could Maggy go? I was suddenly ashamed to be part of this family. Yes, have your affairs and explore your sexual fantasies, but not on family ground, not when people are going to get hurt. Whilst Phillis was at work, on the pretence of showing Maggy around Australia, Garry would take time off work, and I bet they did not leave the house! This was a stark awakening for Phillis. It all finally became real, and she had to face it rather than pretend it was not happening. But rather than face it head-on with him, she decided she would use it to gain attention. I was the sucker.

I swung into rescue mode. I would not have been able to live with myself if I had not made some effort, irrespective of the consequences, to try and turn her around. I made numerous phone calls to her and had hours of conversations with her. I finally talked her into returning home on the reassurance that I would always be there for her and would hold her hand through getting over this, which I was committed to doing. I had even fooled myself with the thought that this would be her reason to dump the bastard or make him finally accountable for his behaviour. She had had no intention of terminating her life; she had had no intention of terminating her relationship with him. She had had no intention of doing anything at all. It had just been a call for attention, and as that was not coming from him, she had turned to me.

I wondered if he would have cared if she did take her life. Had he missed her? Had he called to find out where she was? There were so many practical questions I wanted to ask her but did not get the chance to. Taking her life—would that leave an opening for him to carry on his affair with Maggy? To my absolute relief, she took the next train back home. I called a couple of days later to see how she was doing. I was not expecting the response I got, especially after my attempt at saving her life: 'It is probably better you do not stay in touch with me, as Garry thinks you are a bad influence.' Great. I deserved that. What was I expecting? Of course, they had got back together, and all was well in the world for her. I must have been on another planet; what seemed so wrong in my eyes was okay for her. I was starting to realise that in my desperation to hold on to family, my attempts were futile. I needed to let her go so she could live the life she wanted, irrespective of how it looked to me. This did not seem like family to me; the whole thing was just wrong.

Going back to my family, I was in the middle of Phillis and my brother, Lenny. I did not like my birth name, and consequently, I changed it when I was able to, because Prajna reflected who I was and came from the ancient language of India. I needed that to ground myself later in life, when I started to realise that my values did not fit the name I was given. I wanted to get as far away as I could from my British ancestry. Even though a name is just a name, I knew who I was since I was a very little girl. From as early as I could remember, I always was on a search for wisdom. I had a knowing that can only come from a soul connection, and I will always have that. I was a free spirit, and nothing that was human interested me. I looked for fun; I called things for what they looked like. I was not obsessed with how I looked. For most of my younger years, I was pretty much a tomboy. I have always and will always feel as young as my spirit.

I gravitated towards my younger brother a lot, and he was the perfect brother to me. I shared his interest for music, cricket, and dancing, and we always danced a lot together. We loved dancing with each other, and he had a style I warmed to. We just got each other on the dance floor. I have danced with a lot of boys and men, but no one fitted me so well on that dance floor like Lenny did. We knew each other's moves and got each other's grooves. We won a lot of dance competitions. I even hung out with his friends, and he would not have had it any other way. I fitted in well. What usually interested young girls did not interest me. I just got involved in all his activities, and he was happy for me to tag along. His friends had no option but to accept me. I was one of the boys. I had no need to look pretty or wear pretty clothes. I could hang out in yesterday's clothes, as his friends saw me as part of their little group. I did not have to try hard to look pretty like the rest of my sisters; I could hang out in my daggy clothes and was not judged when I was in their company. I could wear the same underwear for a couple of days, as no one was going to get into them.

Lenny was a kind, loving, and gentle person, and I never saw him angry at any time. Like me, he was not interested in studying, but that did not mean that we did not have a brain in our heads. It was geared differently, but because it was not all academic, we were the rejects of the family. So we stuck together. Lenny was pretty much a loner and struggled with family, studies, and making a man of himself in their eyes. He eventually ended up making a girl he had met pregnant. This would have brought disgrace on the family. What I respected him for, however, was that he made the decision to marry her, despite their disregard for her. Nothing was mentioned or acknowledged regarding the fact that she was carrying his baby. I was not at the wedding, but I received photographs of the event. It was very obvious to me that she had a belly in all the photographs. Besides, she was not wearing the traditional white dress, and that was a strong indication that she did not deserve to wear the virgin white. She was a 'spoilt' woman, which was the term that would have been used for her.

I was happy for him that he had married her, which said a lot about his values. I always wondered whether it was obligatory or if he really loved her. Was it to defy my parents? I wanted to believe that he loved her, because I wanted to believe that he was happy. I think Lenny accepted his situation, but he would have been much happier unattached and playing in a band, living his life freely and unrestricted by family. I was not sure whether to respect him for taking on his responsibility or to feel sad for him because he did not have the courage to chase his dreams—and he had dreams! But Lenny made it work. I always wondered what his life would have been like if he were here with me in Australia and if I had sponsored him and his family instead of Phillis's. Would I have finally had the family I so longed for?

Compared to the rest of the family who were pretty well off, not because of their own achievements but because they had a lot of investment from my parents, Lenny always struggled financially. He married Yvette and had three children with her, but he was always the outcast of the family. Lenny died too soon. It broke my heart when

I heard that, and I was convinced that he had died of a broken heart. He was my loving brother, and if there was any trace of a family in my life, he was that. Not only was he my brother, but he was my friend when I was young. He was my companion. He was precious. I will always think of him with love and sadness. I was not able to help him much or share his life a lot since moving to Australia, but the rare letters I got from him would bring tears to my eyes because I longed to hold him in my arms once more. Without him by my side, my family life would have been meaningless. I was helpless to help him at the time he needed me most, because I was struggling in my life. He was my salvation, my earth angel whilst I grew up in this dysfunctional family, struggling with my identity. .

There are two instances that I shared with Lenny that I will never forget. Amongst some Indian families, when someone is dying, the mourning starts even before the person is dead. Opposite our home was a little shack in which one of the village women lived. She was old; she was someone's elder. It was the night when she was preparing to take her last breath, and there was a lot of wailing and screaming coming from the shack. Sometimes, if there were not enough family members to wail, they would get hired criers. My brother and I had climbed on to the front wall of our house so we could see into the house to watch all the action. We were both in our early teens at the time. It did not seem that too many people cared about this poor old woman, but the wailing was ridiculously loud and so not genuine. That did not surprise me. Is it possible for no one to give a shit about you when you're alive, but people suddenly find those tears when you're dead?

But that night was not about this poor dying woman. I sat next to my brother, thinking I was also dying, and I was struggling with the words to tell Lenny that I would not be around for too long. I suddenly blurted it out. 'Lenny, I need to tell you that I am dying.' I saw the sorrow in his face when he asked what was wrong. 'I am bleeding and have been for the last couple of days, and I can't stop it.' 'Where from?' he asked. I could not even utter the word *vagina*, as we never mentioned those parts or talked about it openly amongst my family. Words like that were never mentioned. 'Down there.' As if it did not have a name. But he got the message.

So my brother and I sat there on that wall, and instead of being engrossed in the dying woman, we hugged each other and sobbed, as we thought I was dying. According to my little brother, if I was bleeding from down there and could not stop it, I was certainly dying. I did not tell my mother about it but kept washing my panties and wearing new clean ones; I did not know how long that would last before my nosy sisters would wonder if I was crapping my pants. Luckily, in the warm weather, clothes dried in an instant. Lenny made me promise that I would tell Mum in the morning, as he thought she might know a way that I could get well. 'I will not be able to live without you, so please, please tell Mum so she can do something.' I did and went through the humiliating process of being treated as if I was dying of some terminal illness. I was isolated from everyone and fed certain foods that were supposed to be good whilst a woman was menstruating. When I finally appeared in public, everyone in the village looked at me with this very strange look which yelled out 'You are a big girl now'.

The other incident that is clear in my mind was in the bedroom we shared as children. It was a large room, and my brother, Phillis, and I shared the floor at night, on mats which would be rolled up in the morning so the room could be used as a study and for other household purposes. It had a dressing room next to it. I was in the dressing room, looking for something to wear, when Lenny called out to me. 'I have got something to show you.' When I turned around, there was Lenny standing in front of me with a massive erection, looking very worried; he did not know what was happening to him or why every now and then his penis would get so enlarged it was almost unbearable. I did not know whether it was the size of his erection or the fact that I was seeing a man naked that panicked me, but I screamed at my brother, 'Don't you ever show that to me again!' His intention had not been to flash me; he was genuinely worried about what was happening to his body. My father had not had the conversation with him about the changes to expect in his body, and he was never going to. We were both very sexually ignorant and not aware of our bodies at all; we were never given that freedom to explore or understand. Nothing was explained to us at any time in our lives, and there was no access to any reading material, as that would have been considered inappropriate.

Neither of us had any idea about our bodies and how they functioned. There was absolutely no conversation about those parts; they were considered dirty. Sex education was non-existent. There was certainly no opportunity to even read books on sex education. Were our parents fearful that if we knew how it worked, we would want to go out and explore our sexuality? Was it better to leave us ignorant of the topic so it would make their lives easy? Was the expectation to just ignore those vital parts of our bodies and hope it will go away? I did not know what a penis looked like, and my brother would not have known what a woman's vagina looked like. How sad was that? So we took the lesson into our own hands and made a pact, like we had done with so many lessons self-learnt together. I showed him mine and allowed him to look at it very closely so he could understand what a woman looked like between the legs, and I looked at him naked so I could understand how a man's body looked. It was an innocent show-and-tell, but at least it gave us some idea of how different male and female bodies looked. If there was no opportunity to be taught, to discuss, or to learn, then we would find the best way available to us. This was it.

If there was anyone close enough to family for me, anyone with the values and kindness that should exist within a family, it was Lenny. There was never a time we fought; we just got each other, and in our own innocent way, we taught each other. I will always miss Lenny. Our lives drifted apart, but our connection with each other was there to his end. I often wonder what makes siblings so uncharacteristically different from each other. It was as if we both just did not belong to this family. My sisters seemed to have the values of my mother, and Lenny and I unconsciously took our values from Dad.

With Lenny's passing and my divorce from the family, Phillis sponsored Laurina to come up to Australia to live with them. I did not dwell on that too much because of the bad thoughts that would creep into my head. Would she become a victim of Garry's approaches? I had to make a conscious decision to let go. I needed to let go of this group of people who I was biologically connected to but just did not fit into and had no need for. I did not close the door on them; that door will always stay slightly ajar. But there will be no movement in and out of that door unless I am treated with respect, which has not happened. They do not feel like family to me any more. They are just people that have influenced my life.

My family will be people that have the same values as I have, that embrace and respect me for who I am, and I will give them no less. Just being born into a family does not necessarily make them family.

WHO I AM NOT

I am not my name, my family, my nationality, my colour, the clothes I wear, or the education I had. I am not what I look like or the jobs I have had; I am not the country I live in or this world I inhabit. I am nothing like what I look like externally.

My name does not define me. I am not my family; I am nothing like them. Hell, I do not even have their values. Being born in India gave me access to the spirituality of the country. I did not feel like I belonged there. If I had been allowed to immerse myself in the culture of India, if I had adopted one of their religions and dressed the way they did, I would have felt like I belonged, but my upbringing and schooling and the influences on my early years did not support that. I guess changing my name allowed me to identify with who I felt I was at the time., but my journey of self-discovery would start only when I left this village and my family.

Very early on, I had a sense of how I liked to look. It was some time before I started primary school, when I was getting dressed to go out shopping with my mother; she had allowed me to wear my favourite dress. I thought it was very special. It was an electric-blue dress with white spots; you could squeeze this dress in one hand, and it would fit and come out without a crease. It was pure silk, and I loved the feel of it. It was a dress that my father had bought me when he returned from one of his assignments. As it was my lucky day, I thought I would ask my mother if she could do my hair in a side parting with a bow in it, like she sometimes did. It was at that time I realised that I would not have a choice in how I looked or how I dressed, because I got a whack on the head with the brush that she was holding. She then proceeded to make a ridiculous middle parting in my hair and comb it flat on my head. I did not feel good, even in my favourite dress.

I don't remember much of my early years. There were a lot of photos of me as a child, and I liked how I looked when I was little. I was chubby, and I had a very cheerful appearance. Indians love fat babies but not fat adults. I only have those toddler photographs as documentation to identify my early years. I looked happy most of the time; that must have been before I discovered the family I was born into.

I hated school. It was an experience of frustrated Carmelite nuns that took out their frustration on little children by beating them for any reason they could dig up. Perhaps it was an alternative to getting over their sexual frustration. The village I lived in had the added advantage of having two of the best schools on the street: there was a school for boys, run by the priests, and one for girls, run by the nuns. Co-education was non-existent. The nuns that ran the girls' school wore brown habits, and their heads were covered with black veils. Most of them had joined the cloister very early in their lives, before they had even got a chance at sex. It was not hard to think that they were a frustrated bunch underneath the hotness of that suffocating material. There must have been a good reason they had their hands in their pockets most of the time! I have never been able to understand the idea of giving up sex for religion; religion just does not expect that of us. From the record of sexual abuse in religious establishments, that should be obvious. It is against human instinct. It is the vulnerable children that pay for their suppression. Religion always seems to make up the rules and tell us what to do, but it ignores their practices.

It was tough growing up, because most times, being the youngest, I was pretty much ignored. I had to find my own way, and most times, I was treated very similarly to Lenny. I could not relate to the girliness of my sisters and the attention they put on their looks. Very early on, I learnt that even though I always had Lenny's support, I needed to have my own back. I took care of myself. I had to have a false sense of toughness as my sword of protection. We lived within walking distance of school, so we would come home for lunch and return for the afternoon session. I was not liked by any of the nuns who also taught at the school. There were a lot of times that they would have loved to beat me or abuse me in some way. But with my father making a big contribution to the school and the local church, we were treated differently.

I am still trying to figure out this whole nun/priest role and their purpose in this life. There was one instance of many when a small group of us arrived earlier than the start of school, as we had a cooking lesson to attend and that was normally a class that took place before school started. Whilst we were waiting and preparing for our class to start, we heard noises coming from next door. The wall separating the two rooms only went up to a certain height, not completely to the roof; if there was anyone in the next room, they could not be seen, but their voices could be heard.

We decided to investigate. There were eight of us in the class, and some of us decided we would stand on each other's shoulders until we could see over the wall to check out what the voices were about. I was the one at the top, and I was dumbfounded when I got up there and took a look. There was a bald person standing absolutely naked, with their back facing me, and in front was a girl who was a classmate of my sister. I knew her well. She was without her clothes too. I presumed, because I saw a bald head, that the first person was a man; I only had a view of their back. I practically fell off the top of the human ladder when the man (I thought) turned around, and I saw that it was our female math teacher. This was a surprising sight for me, and I had no idea what they were up to—perhaps a science experiment! I could have stood up on that human ladder for a while longer; I wanted to see more, but the others kept asking to get to the top of the ladder. Afraid to make any noise and not wanting to attract any attention to what I had seen, I jumped off the top and discouraged the others from attempt another human ladder, telling them that I may have been seen. They pressured me to tell them what I had seen, but I was processing it myself and did not know how to put it in words for them. I decided that I would not tell them at the time but promised to tell them later.

I could not keep what I saw to myself and decided to tell one of my friends in the class about it. We both could not figure out why my sister's classmate and our maths teacher, who was a Carmelite nun, were standing and facing each other without their clothes on. I could not wait to take the story home and thought I would tell my mum about it. It was on my mind that whole school day, so when I got home after school, I approached the topic by asking my mum if nuns shave heads under their veils. I learnt from my mother that they do, as it is very hot and would not be good for their health if they had long hair under the thick veil. That confirmed what I saw. I should have left it at that, but I had to tell her the whole story. Wrong move! She slapped me across the face and said, 'Do not bring stories like that home, you liar! Nuns do not do such things.' Was she being naive? Or was it something she always knew about, but like most things dealt with in our family, it was not talked about or discussed? The priests, nuns, and anyone of the church could not do anything wrong in my parents' eyes.

Today when we hear all those stories of abuse in religious institutions, we call on those institutions to take responsibility for what happened to vulnerable children in their care. Have we ignored the fact that parents were also responsible and never held accountable for this? I do understand that they did the best they could with the ability and knowledge that they had at the time and that it was to protect themselves and what they believed in. But that is only an excuse and not a good reason to put their children in such a vulnerable position.

There was yet another time. The students from the girls' school were allowed on very rare occasions to visit the boys' school, and one of those occasions was to practice our parade for the Indian Independence Day. It was a day when everyone came together to celebrate India's freedom from the British rule, and all students were required to dress in uniform and march around the streets, waving the flag and singing the Indian national anthem. When the marching was over, all the children and whoever wanted to be part would gather at the boys' school grounds to celebrate with drinks and snacks put on by the schools and to be part of all the celebrations on that day, which included sporting activities.

I was on the boys' school grounds, and it overlooked the quarters where the priests lived. Whilst we were marching on the school grounds, my eyes wandered to the third storey of the school building, and there, right in front of me, was Father Christo sucking face with a woman. That was enough to shock me. I always saw things I would rather not have seen. Was everyone else seeing this, or was it just me? I shared this with my little brother, Lenny, as he was also in the parade. His reply to me was that it happened all the time. This particular priest thought it was his right to exploit vulnerable women. Lenny also asked me not to tell anyone, as no one would believe me.

I had to test it, of course, and as soon as I got home, I told my mum. I got the reputation for being the biggest liar in the family. So of course, I saw many more instances and kept it to myself, and no one ever knew because they did not really want to know. Strange things happened; there were incestuous relationships, abuse from priests and nuns, affairs between family members, unethical behaviour, and a lot more. But we did not talk about it. Not talking about it was another way of accepting that it never happened. I was never interested in the gossip of the village, but one thing I knew was that no one would ever try anything like that with me. I was a tough little girl because I just had to be, to protect myself. Hanging out with my brother and his friends was a good way to learn.

My early years and time at school were just that—time. School was an absolute blur to me. I just went through the paces and endured the abuse from my parents for not doing as well as they expected me to. I did not have many friends; I was the dag at school, just their youngest sister who had nothing to contribute. I barely scraped my way through high school, so I was never going to be the doctor, bank manager, teacher, or greater person that I should have been. I had to go into something ordinary, in keeping with my grades at school. I was criticised for being fat, for being useless at school, and for not taking interest in how I looked. I hated having to wear a bra; it had to be forced on me, and my sisters had a lot of laughs over me having to wear one. It was a very sad time for me, as I did not like becoming a woman. I just wanted to be that little girl holding her brother's hand and enjoying life, unnoticed and full of anticipation.

I did not like what my family looked like to me, because that was not how family appeared in my mind. Every child should be treated the same; no child should be expected to achieve the expectations of their parents. My soul cried out for that ideal family. It did not have to be functional, but it needed to be nurturing and caring, fair and not abusive, loving and not exploiting. I was going to try and be different when I had a family. I fantasised, in my play, about the perfect family and waited to leave this family so I could create my own. I hoped I would be very different and do things differently.

I thought family was a group of people with the same values. They accepted each other for who they were and nurtured each other to be the best they could; everyone was treated the same and given more love than status. Oh no, I just did not fit, and I was reminded of that every day. I felt very lonely within the family, and I was afraid that I would turn out to be like my sisters. I focused my attention on Lenny, and I am sure that if it was not for him, I would not have survived—or worse still, I could have turned out like the rest of the family. We were judgemental, discriminatory, racist, abusive, and on the ego train. Hanging out with my brother's friends gave me a different perspective of things; they were boys and did not get caught up in the gossip of the village. They kept me grounded. We just played cricket, walked a lot together, sang, played music, danced, and hung out and read comics.

One's early years are so precious. It is a very short period where, as parents, we are able to mould our children with love or turn them into clones of ourselves. Very early on, I had decided I was going to become who I wanted to be, do what I wanted, dress the way I wanted, and have the types of relationships I wanted. This was just a purgatory I would work through to get to my heaven.

My father was a gentle, caring man, and most of what he displayed that seemed brutal to me as a child was his way of playing his part within the family. Even as a child, I got glimpses of traits in him that I loved. I was very sick one time and had an extremely high temperature; my parents were not sure what it was, but I was delirious and in a bad way. I could not sleep, and my dad must have been very concerned about my health. I must have been around seven at the time, but I will not forget that night. He carried me against his shoulder and walked up and down with me until I fell into a deep sleep before he put me down. That was a tender moment, and those moments I will always hold close to my heart. There were not many moments like this, but those are the moments that a child remembers. It is not how much material things you give them ; it is how you treat them, the little things you do for them, the things that are important to them that you see as important too—these are the moments children take forward into their lives.

The boxes that I am put into just because people can relate them to me do not fit. Am I capable of confronting who I am not, shedding that skin to become who I really am? What does that journey look like?

SELF-DISCOVERY

You are not going to discover yourself standing at the end
of that cliff in fear; you need to find the courage to jump off
and trust that there will be wings to allow you to fly.

I have been blessed with a 'knowing'. I have not been a believer. All my knowledge comes from my intuition and just a knowing.

I had my first glimpse of joy when my parents decided to advance my education. I had to be sent away from home to one of the biggest towns in South India, where there was a convent that trained women to do secretarial work. There was no further education available in the village, and advanced education meant leaving home. It was a year's training that would qualify me to be able to get a job working in an office, using skills like shorthand, typing, bookkeeping, etc. It was training that, in my parents' opinion, would be best for me, as I did not have the brains to become what they would have liked me to be. Secretarial work was considered the last resort, something to direct your unacademic child to. It was the basic training they would provide for me so I could then support myself, and them as well, if that was possible. But to me, it looked like a totally different picture. I was not focusing on what they wanted me to achieve but on getting away from them, miles away, so I would be able to have some real fun discovering myself without the umbrella of my family.

Every child has potential. It may not look like what parents want it to look like; they may not turn out to be the academic person that the parents want them to be. It is the job of the parent and the education system to look deeper so the actual ability and the skills in that child are visible, embraced, and nurtured. Every child has the right to grow up and be whatever they want to be, without expectations. The education system teaches children to be academic but not to be good people. What is the point of being educated if you continue to stay ignorant?

The village that I grew up in was a beautiful coastal village, but the energy was stale and minds were narrow. It was filled with churchgoers who were try-hard Catholics but did not have a kind bone in their body. We went to church as a family. We owned a bench, like most others who wanted a place to sit when they were at service. The church provides nothing free, and of course, there was a donation required to be able to own the prime real estate of a wooden bench at the church. It belonged to you because a donation was paid regularly; no one else could sit on that bench. My mother would get very upset if anyone, especially an Indian, put their bottom on that bench. They would be asked to remove themselves. Now that is not kind! We would spend the hour or so in church praying our hearts out, but the moment we left church, it would be a horrible, judgemental conversation that would follow that service. The conversation would be about who wore what, what they looked like, and how inappropriate it was, and whatever gossip went around, everyone wanted a part of it. Most priests got up and talked, and it was absolutely boring. They would tell everyone what they were supposed to be like, as if the priests were the perfect example!

My train fare was booked, and I was packed to leave the next morning. I was given very minimal money, but that was the last thing on my mind. We had a favourite rickshaw-wallah that we would use to get us from the village to town, so we could get the sleeper coach to Madras. I was too excited, but very fearful too, as I had never left home on my own and here I was, left to fend for myself. I was put on the train and was met at the station in Madras by my sister Maggy. Maggy seemed to have taken it upon herself to look after my interests. She was now well established in a job and was going to pay my board and any other fees that were applicable, and the expectation was that I would dedicate myself to this opportunity. More than that, I would be obligated to her, and consequently, she would orchestrate my life. I was so frightened of this journey by train on my own, but there was not going to be any sympathy. Very early on, I learnt to conquer my fear.

I just could not get away from them. This establishment was also run by nuns, but this time they wore white, as if that made them different. Maggy stayed a night and was off the next morning, back to Calcutta, where she had to get back to work. That was the start of my freedom, and I used every opportunity to break every rule and displease my parents in every way possible. It was not intentional; it was like unintentional revenge on the restrictive parenting I had been through—all that controlling, all that abuse, all the suppression. I would be, in their face, a reminder of that, but that was not how they would see it. Parental controlling always has a detrimental effect; it is like a pressure cooker waiting to explode—that was me.

We were in a dormitory for four; there was four to a room, with a common bathroom, common place to eat, and communal outside space. We had studies each day but were free on the weekends, and each night, we were even allowed to go out, so long as we returned before dark. The curfew was 6 p.m. I stumbled through my secretarial course and did not put too much work into it. I got enough skill from my shorthand and typing, but I was totally disinterested in anything else. I was just happy to get some basic skills that interested me and that would get me a job so I could support myself and not have to rely on the little pocket money to survive from month to month.

There were numerous times that I would scale the walls late at night and return to my room and quietly slip into bed. There were times we would get permission to stay out overnight, so long as the nuns knew who we were staying with. I had made friends with a family who had three girls and lived a couple of streets away from the college, so I was able to sneak in there for a night or so. Their parents seemed very relaxed about parenting, and I already loved the freedom of being in a house that was a bit laid-back. We would go out dancing, and they all had boyfriends, who were allowed to come over to the house and even stay overnight. This was alien to me, as that was not something I would have been allowed to do. So their parenting and their life interested me a lot. I wanted to be one of their siblings. I think I hung around them so much they began to consider me part of their family. They included me in everything they did and always opened their home to me unconditionally.

One night, I decided to stay over at their house for the weekend. The girls had decided to go to a local hall where there was a band and dancing. Dancing was the social network of those times. This was how young people met partners, if that happened; however, the focus seemed to be more on enjoying life rather than picking up men. It was on that night that I met Clyde. We exchanged a few glances, and before long, he walked up and asked me for a dance. In my entire young life, until this day, I had never felt as attracted to a man as I did when he held me in his arms for the first dance. I felt an instant attraction to him and noticed that he was very handsome and had a naughtiness about him which was very similar to me. He had the most beautiful face and a very contagious laugh. I was sitting amongst my friends when he walked up and asked me to dance. We had every dance together that night, and Clyde was the first man I ever loved. We all remember our first love, that feeling in your gut you have never felt before. I was not sure about what love felt like, but what I was feeling was good; he had that effect on me. Clyde was not just that; he was such a big part of my life and a very big part of who I became. He was not totally into me, but he was totally interested in who I was.

I enjoyed the night, and as he lived locally, we soon started meeting most evenings. We did not have anywhere to go, so we would walk the dark corners of the streets, talking. We talked a lot, and that graduated into kissing. Those were the first passionate kisses I ever received and gave, and he was a perfect kisser. That first kiss—it needs to be special, tender yet inviting, long and sensual, and needs to feel like it is electricity going through your body. It is when you get a perfect kiss like that that you know the good kissers from the bad, the ones that think that having their tongue down your throat or slobbering all over your face is a turn-on. Yuck, like a dribbling dog! We were both perfect kissers. We would kiss for hours, which graduated to soft touching over my clothes, but nothing further than that. Everything with Clyde came naturally; he had a lot more sexual experience than I had, so there was a lot he taught me. He always took the lead, and thank goodness for that because I had virtually no life experience. He had come from very free-thinking parenting; I envied that about him, but that was what was most attractive about him and gave him the confidence I wanted to achieve.

The universe has a way of attracting the right people in life at the exact moment you need them. I loved being with Clyde, and even though sex was the last thing on my mind, I enjoyed being fondled by him, leaning against every tree we could come across, and kissing passionately. For the first time in my life, I started to feel sensations in my body that I had never felt before, and I was loving it. I had no idea that there was anything more. Clyde tried numerous times to take it further but soon realised that I was too afraid to actually go the distance. It was all just foreplay that left both of us hot and frustrated, but there was a deep feeling of passion. I think it was his experience and my ignorance that was the attraction. We talked about anything and everything, and I felt like I knew him from a previous life.

It was very special experiencing first love in those times. Rather than us being keener to jump into each other's pants, it was an innocent desire that never went the distance but allowed for feelings and sensual awareness, an allowing of the physical body to feel passion on a deeper level. It was a discovery of the sensual and intriguing physical needs of the human body. It always left so much more to get to know and not only allowed for that physical discovery but found time for the discovery of each other.

I was learning a lot from Clyde, and learning fast. At one point, he showed me a condom; I guess it was his way of asking for this friendship to go further, but it went over my head. I had absolutely no idea. We had conversations about how he felt so turned on when we were together that it hurt his testicles so much because there was no release; being unaware of how the male body worked, I was pleased to know how I made him feel but was totally unaware about how sexually frustrated he was. Clyde was very patient with me, and he was a guide on all levels. I guess he knew I was ignorant of all that stuff, and he understood why. He had sensed that my parenting was a lot more restrictive and, consequently, had not allowed for my experience in dating.

It was the holidays, and I had to return home. It was Christmas, and we were at the dinner table, having our Christmas dinner. I had the wishbone of the chicken; it was tradition that whoever got the wishbone would hold it with someone and pull it apart, and the one with the head of the bone had the chance to make a wish, in silence. I got the chance at the wish, and without hesitation, I wished that Clyde would walk through the door. At the time, it was for want of another wish; I had wished for so much in my life without any change, but my faith always allowed me to keep wishing. Hopefully, the universe would grant my wish if I deserved it at the time. I missed him very much, but I did not want to say anything to my family because I was certain what their reaction would be; that was not in my interest. I ached to see him again.

With all the intent of my heart, I wished that he could share that Christmas with us. I was not ready to tell my family about Clyde. I just could not find a way to break the news to them because I was not sure how it would be received. I was hoping the universe would make it happen, and it did. What a wish, what a surprise! No sooner had I made that wish than there was a knock on the door. Be careful what you wish for! It was as if the universe had been waiting to grant me this wish.

Clyde always did what he wanted to do; he was fearless and took a lot of risks. This did not change for the whole time that I knew him. He went for what he wanted, and I was very attracted to his humble confidence. He did not seem to fear anything or anyone. Clyde had travelled a great distance to my home town, which was a day by train. He had relatives who lived a few doors up the street from us; he used that as his excuse to drop by our home, but I knew that his intention was to spend more time with me and visit my home so he could learn more about me. I liked that feeling. I loved seeing him, and for whatever time he was there, I spent every single moment with him.

I had the painful task of introducing him to my parents, sisters, and brother. There was surprise on all their faces, but it seemed like they took it very well. There was a sense of surprise that I had the capacity to attract a man! They always allowed me to think that I was winning the battle—and then shot me in the head! That would come. Clyde told them that he had come to visit his relatives, and as he was there, he decided to call in, as he knew where I lived. The relatives he mentioned lived a couple of houses away from us but unfortunately were a family that my mother did not consider good, so we were not allowed to hang around them. But that was not my concern at that moment. I knew he had intentionally planned this, and I secretly hoped that it was because he missed me, as I missed him too. He had dinner with us and went back to his cousins next door. My parents did not discuss this any further with me. I should have been concerned, but those were things I did not worry too much about.

My family had a tradition on Boxing Day of packing up all the food that was left from the big Christmas cook-up and getting some toddy, which was a potent local processed liquor made from the sap of coconut or date palm trees. It was collected in clay pots that were hung on the trees. We would walk over to a remote beach an hour from home. There would be over thirty of us, all of them my mother's family—her brothers and sisters and their children—and my older sisters were allowed to bring along their boyfriends at the time. And there was my dad, always on his own, even though he enjoyed being around my mother's family. He always looked after them and treated them very well. We would picnic there for the whole day, drink toddy, eat a lot, and wet our feet in the beautiful ocean. Those that could swim would enjoy a swim before the meal. It was a very special beach hideaway and was surrounded by palm and coconut trees, and there were lots of rocks and secret places to discover. I loved this spot very much. It took me to another place; it was like a mini tropical holiday. The adults would relax, chat, drink, and eat the leftovers. It was their time to catch up with families that they had not seen for a long while, as my mother's family lived all over India. Their visits were long but very occasional. We would run around in the beautiful ocean all day. We did this each year on Boxing Day, and this year was no different.

Most of my mother's brothers would end up drunk on the toddy, and as children, we were allowed a few sips of the sour, sweet white liquid. We were only allowed a sip; the drink had a way of creeping up on you, and a few glasses were enough to allow my uncles to talk a lot of crap or fall into a deep sleep. My youngest uncle was truly funny, and we all loved him. He was the life of the party and was always the jolly adult that never took life too seriously. He would wear one of his wife's dresses and a funny hat and walk down the streets to our picnic spot. As we approached people on the streets (everyone knew him), he would have a laugh with them. He would sing all the way and was the loudest and most embarrassing family member, but I loved him. He and his wife were very different from the rest of my straight-faced uncles. They were my godparents, and I was fortunate enough to spend some of my school holidays with them. He was a railway worker and lived in a remote town, and it was refreshing to spend time there and do things that I would not have normally been allowed to do at home. It was a struggle to come back home after I had been with them on holidays.

Clyde came with us on the trip that year. I was so exstatic that he was there and that my family had accepted him enough to include him in this family picnic. Clyde and I sneaked off up the rocks when we were there, and that gave us some privacy to snatch a lot of intimate moments; it felt so erotic and so good to be able to get these intimate moments, even though my family was not too far away, unaware of what we were doing. He had a very special calmness and charisma about him; I loved being around him. At the time, I imagined being with him for the rest of my life. He had an appreciation for nature and immersed himself in it, as I did. He was a beautiful person; I was beginning to love being around him and loving him a lot.

My parents did not seem to show any dislike for the idea of us being together, so I presumed that everything was all right. But what I did not realise was that they were not going to allow this romance to get any further. They were starting to notice the closeness between the two of us. Knowing that he was related to the family they had little regard for did not sit well with them, and they had made a note of that. They made me believe that Clyde was accepted. Consequently, as he was leaving the next day, I asked my parents if he could stay one night with us before he left. He had been staying with his relatives a few doors from us, but we wanted to spend a bit more time together.

My parents were very clear that he had to make a field bed on the floor of the lounge; their bedroom ran off the lounge. I was expected to sleep with my sisters in one of the other bedrooms, which I normally did. However, that day was not normal. I guess my parents thought they would be able to keep a watch on us, as their room was adjacent to the lounge room. I always pushed the limits; I always did what was not expected of me. I had to go that step further. I loved the thrill of not being caught, and this time it was no different.

All were asleep at home. I got out of my bed and crept over to the field bed that Clyde was in, in the lounge room. It was as if he knew that was what I would do. He was lying there, awake, waiting for me. I know he was just as afraid as I was of being caught, and I hate to think what would have been the consequence. But we were like peas in a pod; I supported his madness, and he did mine. We had the best night together. I had on a very thin nightie, with nothing underneath. We still did not go all the way but were happy and almost thrilled that we could lie there in each other's arms, just being together and enjoying the heavy petting that was our limit for now.

I loved having his lips on mine. I responded to his touch; it was sensual and oh-so sexual. Sometime in the early hours of the morning, I crept back into my bed, and it was as if nothing had happened. We felt pleased that we had pulled it off.

The next morning, he left, much to my parents' relief. I felt a deep sense of sadness. My heart went with him, and the only thought keeping me going was that I would return soon and would continue to keep in touch with him.

I returned after the holidays, and we continued to see each other and develop a deep sense of love that was almost suffocating for me. I wanted him more than anything in the world. I loved him as I had never loved anything or anyone in my life. I had thought I was incapable of wanting to be with a guy, but this was telling me something different. I was growing up and getting to know my physical body and what it was capable of. I was realising that I could feel physically attracted to a man. Before this, I had not given boys a lot of sexual attention. After all, I was one of them; I could not feel this way about a guy. However, my focus was more on him and having a good time rather than on completing my secretarial course with high marks, so obviously, the results were not going to be great. At the end of the year I did not get a good report. That did not concern me, even though it was a major concern for my parents. What the heck were they going to do with me? I was not the brightest at school and did not do much with the investment in my secretarial training.

One of the girls who was a bit senior to me was doing very well in her studies and had already got herself a job locally and was earning a bit of money. She talked me into starting work before I got my certificate. She had done that and was working whilst she was continuing to get her secretarial certificate. I decided to give it a go. Companies were employing secretaries, so long as they were in the process of getting a certificate. She was working for a family business run by two brothers, and since she was offered another job, she asked me if I would like to work for them and then recommended me. I thought it was a great opportunity for me to earn some extra money to subsidise the pocket money I was receiving. I did not tell my parents, as they would not have consented to me working before I finished my studies. So studies were out the door, and I started working in this business in town, doing secretarial work for the two brothers.

It was the era of miniskirts, the sixties, and a great time for a young girl to experience anything in life she wanted to. It was the best decade ever. If I had to choose a decade to go back to, it would be the sixties. It was a carefree time. Sex was a choice, but most young adults had more interests in life; the focus was on feelings rather than physical gratification. The clothes were amazing, full of colour, and everyone dressed perfectly, no activewear in sight. It was a time that you could date a few men at the same time, and the focus was on having a lot of fun, a lot of foreplay. But there was a sense, in some of us at least, that there was a distance that you could go. It was a time when I felt so safe in my world.

I loved the clothes and rocked the miniskirts because I could, and if I could have worn it any shorter, I would have. I had developed my unique sense of dress, and it attracted a lot of attention because it was nonconventional and screamed different. If there was a dress code, I challenged that. I was a distraction at work because of the way I dressed; although I thought nothing of it, it attracted a lot of attention, and I liked it. But it also attracted negative attention. One of the brothers (they were both married, with family) approached me and asked if I would like to have some photographs taken. I did not feel very comfortable with that, so I refused. But he did not give up. He tried another plan. He asked me if I wanted to come over to his house. He was having a family gathering, and he wanted me to meet his wife and family; it was important for the business that I did so.

I agreed. That was a bad move; never put yourself in a vulnerable position. Most times, it is the people you trust the most that do not deserve your trust. He was the guy I worked for, and I had no reason to doubt him. He said he would pick me up from the hostel and return me when it was all finished. I got dressed in my best dress, and he got his driver to pick me up. But things were not as I had expected. When I got to the house, he took me over to a secluded part. It was a large family home; it seemed like there was no one in that area of the house. I started to feel uncomfortable because I had thought I was going to meet his family and arrive at a party. It was looking nothing like that, but I was now too far in to turn back. I could have; I could have run out and taken a taxi back. But I was intrigued and wanted to find out what he had planned.

He sat me down at a coffee table and offered me a drink and ignored when I said that I did not want a drink. Even though I refused, he poured me a gin and tonic and asked me to drink it so he could get me another one. I did; this was my chance to have a drink, as there would be no opportunity for that once I got back to the dormitory. I had another one, as you do when you are young. There was not a responsible bone in my body. My vision was getting a bit blurred, and I was starting to feel the effects of the alcohol when he put some magazines in front of me and turned the pages. All I could see were pages and pages of naked women. I now knew why I was there and what he expected of me.

He started taking photographs of me, with my clothes on, and he was saying words to me that were meant to be complimentary so it would encourage me to go along with how he wanted the evening to go. I was drunk by this stage but still able to stay on my feet. He removed most of my clothing and gently exposed more of my body. I felt helpless under his control; by this time, I had consumed a lot of alcohol and was not in control. I remember getting stripped down to my panties. Each time he pulled down my panties, I pulled it up. I faintly remember standing there in the bright light of the lamp with the camera clicking. I had my breasts displayed. I had a vague notion of having my panties on, but I could not be sure because we were having a tug of war, him taking it down and me pulling it up.

I have to admit that being out of control and in this vulnerable situation actually was a bit of a turn-on and was something of a fantasy I wanted to experience. I had absolutely no feeling of fear. I think there was a very brief moment that I felt that I was actually enjoying it—standing naked in front of a camera, in front of the man I worked for, absolutely out of my senses, feeling aroused. It was not a good place to be, but it was an experience. I sensed there was nothing more he wanted from me. I guess it could have gone any way, but I had not thought that far. I now know it was my restricted upbringing that led me to places I should not have been, but it gave me the experiences that I needed. To fully experience life, I needed to take the risk.

I was barely sober when he asked me to get dressed and then put me in the car. His driver dropped me off, without any care of whether I could walk safely or not. I walked, unnoticed by anyone. It was late evening, and I just ripped off all my clothes. Smelling of cigarettes and alcohol, I crawled into bed and cried myself to sleep. Astrid, one of the girls that I shared the room with, repeatedly asked me whether I was all right. She knew where I had gone because we confided in each other. She did not get any sense out of me and gave up. The next day, I told her what had happened, and she was very upset for me, even though it did not seem to bother me any more. That was yesterday; today was another day. I still had the task of going to work and facing these bastards because I wanted to keep the job. I needed the money. I just could not believe what I had allowed to happen, but like everything else, I had to face it head-on.

I can empathise with women that find themselves in similar situations, because sometimes we expect people to do the right thing by us. But we make bad decisions based on our expectations of others. I could have walked out; I could have screamed. I could have kicked him in the balls and ran out the door. Could have, could have. But I chose not to. That does not excuse his behaviour, but nevertheless, I had played a part in it. Do I then have a right to come up fifty years later and trace down the person to hold him accountable? I had the power; I did not know how to access it. I did not want to be in that situation, yet I got some joy from it. It could have been worse. The best solution for me at the time was to put it behind me, call it an experience, and move on.

I returned to the office. Karmal, the guy I worked for who took the pictures, showed them to me. His brother was present in the room at the time. I had no idea where those photographs were heading. I just did not want to ask. I wanted to shut it out of my mind and be able to keep the job. However, I noticed that they started to favour me a lot, and I got a lot more recognition at work. I did not see anything ugly in the pictures that he had taken of me; they actually looked very professional. I just could not get it out of my head that I had allowed myself to be manipulated, and it was not getting pleasant coming to work every day. I had to leave because every day that I was in there was a reminder of my mistake—a mistake I was so glad to have come out of scarred but not damaged.

I walked away from my job. I had to go back to the basic pocket money my parents were providing for me. However, in the meantime, my parents had become aware that I was not leading the life they were paying for me to live, that I was not getting the education they expected me to get, and to make things worse, that I was still seeing Clyde. They had talked to the nuns that ran the college I was in, and the nuns told my mother that I was working as well as studying. They thought that I had told her, as I should have. That was not a good thing for my future.

I had no hesitation in sharing my exploitation with Clyde. There was nothing I could not tell him; Clyde was so tolerant and non-judgemental and always encouraged me to do anything I wanted. He told me to take it as an experience, although we both knew I had put myself on dangerous ground. I think we were both happy that it did not turn out to be any worse. I even had his support if I wanted to hold them accountable. Like a lot of things I had experienced so far, I did not allow it to control my life.

I had to leave the job, so I was back to being dependent on my parents' money to survive for the rest of my time at the boarding school. But that did not last for very long. My parents had already worked out a plan, and Maggy was at the forefront of it. She was working in East India at the time, and we were all returning home for the holidays. I was not looking forward to going home because there would be too many questions thrown at me and I would not be able to give the answers that they wanted to hear. But the pressure was on me to go. My parents were still supporting my education, so I had to show a bit of gratitude and go home. It was the most uncomfortable homecoming, as my parents had learnt that I had not been as successful as they had expected me to be with my studies. However, nothing was said about my Stint at the office, because I had saved some of the money and gave it to my mother when I arrived. It was sort of like my peace offering so my stay at home would be pleasant—in other words, a big, fat bribe—and it worked.

It was the day before my holiday ended, and I thought that I was returning to Clyde, to some of the subjects I had not done so well at, and perhaps to another shot at finding a job. I would feel those butterflies in my stomach at the thought of meeting and catching up on my romance with Clyde. He was constantly on my mind., He was my first love. I was learning a lot about who I was, my feelings, and the niceness of having someone that loved me. I could see myself settling down and nesting with this guy, and I was not looking any further. For the first time in my life, I was experiencing someone that truly cared about me and wanted to be around me. Of course, my mind was totally focused on that.

I was called for a chat with my mother and Maggy. They had decided, irrespective of my feelings and my intentions, that they would pack me off to live with Maggy. There was no consultation or conversation about this with me, but that was not unusual. I just was not able to contradict my parents; the decisions were always made, and there was no choice. I was just expected to accept their decision. There was no discussion. The train ticket was already arranged, and I would be leaving the next day with Maggy. I would be staying with her in the boarding house that she was in, and she would be in charge of finding me a job as well.

My heart sank. I was so disappointed and felt so low, as there was no way I could even contact Clyde to let him know. My whole life was falling apart; I was so young and had a whole life ahead of me, but that day, I felt like it was the end of the world. It was their devious little plan to pack me off so my wicked sister could keep an eye on me, and consequently, I would not be able to continue my relationship with Clyde. I wanted to die; life was not going to be the same. I had no control. It was as if my destiny was their right, and they were going to dictate my existence. I was virtually helpless to challenge them. They gave me no reason for this drastic decision, so all I could think was that it was their way to put a stop to how I was conducting my life and to give my life some supervision. My freedom had been short-lived.

So off I went, and I arrived in this shithole of the world. They say that we die many times in our lives; this was one of them. This was a life sentence that I would never forget. I was sharing a room with Maggy. It was a two-bedroom, two-bathroom house, and the couple that owned the house used the other bedroom, which was next door to our bedroom. Compared to the South of India, this town in East India was a crowded, dirty, dusty city, but it was where people came to get jobs. It had a lot to offer if you wanted to work. This couple was the most hideous couple I had ever come across. Maggy, being the pretentious person that she was, had gained their respect, and not only did they think she was great, she thought she was too.

Accommodation in this busy city was hard to come by, so most single people stayed in boarding houses or shared accommodation and paid a rent for the room, which was most times very basic. Some boarding houses offered food, but that came at an additional cost. That was the arrangement that we had with this couple. We paid them a fortune for our keep, which included food and board, dinner on a daily basis, and other meals on weekends when we were around. We had to always give them notice if we expected extra meals. I ate larger quantities of food, and she would watch what I ate. There was no chance of extras; dare I take an extra potato or have a second helping, she would make a comment that would almost choke me. The conversations were uninteresting, and even though the food was very basic, that was the highlight of my time with Mr and Mrs Smith. Everything at the table was polite, although in my head, I was hoping that Mrs Smith would choke on something and that would be the end of her. Mr Smith was very submissive, and when they went to bed, she would lie there and, for our ears, call out, 'Lover, your hands feel good.' She would put in words, what she would have liked him to do to her. 'Don't touch me there. Touch me here. Oh, lover, you are such a naughty boy.' There were some try-hard sounds that would accompany her words. She thought she was fooling me into thinking that she was having great sex with lover, but lover gave it away. I heard him snoring when his head had barely touched the pillow, because he could not possibly bear the thought of doing what she said he should do with her. I could only feel sorry for him. He was nice man. Pity, his life was sentenced to her.

She disliked me for my boldness and for the way I dressed. My little shorts and miniskirts made her feel so inadequate because she could not look the same. It was a hot summer day, and I was wearing a tiny pair of white shorts and a tee shirt. I was running around, doing my chores around the house, when she came up to me and said, 'Stop flaunting yourself in those shorts. Have some respect and stop wearing clothes that are so revealing.' I was very surprised at her comment, but I was quick to react. 'You wish you could wear clothes like this, but you would have to shave your hairy legs first to be able to.' That shut her up but gave her an excuse to dislike me even more. Did that worry me? No, because there would be so many more reasons for me to upset her, and that was the start. She realised that I was very different from Maggy. I was not going to be tolerant of her putting me down. I was very sharp with my words and very aggressive in my behaviour if I was challenged in any way. It was how I had learnt to cope with confronting people, and even though it was not nice, it was the only way I knew.

I was already a very angry young person. My life was a rollercoaster from one controlled situation to another, and there was no other way I knew to regain control over my own life except to translate this into bad behaviour. I just went from one bad situation to another, and it was intentional. If there was anything that I could do to make Maggy unhappy, I wanted to try just that.

Mrs Smith used to run these 'water parties', as I called them. Every month, she would invite everyone she knew to attend a party at her house. No alcohol was allowed, but there was plenty of water. It would start around 8 p.m., so most of those that attended had dinner before arriving. There was lots of good music, and everyone that came had to dance. The chairs in the lounge room were rearranged so there was room for dancing. She spent money to keep up with the latest music at the time, and she and her husband both loved dancing. In those days, music was played on stereos and was on cassettes. The music of the sixties was made for dancing, and there were so many good dancers at the time; you were never short of a partner.

I loved dancing too, and that also allowed me to meet some hunky guys, as I was ready to take on the world of dating. I realised there was no hope for me to ever get in touch with Clyde or let him know what had happened. He probably thought that I had deserted him, so why would he want to be in contact with me? I had to move on with my life and have different experiences, but he was never far from my mind. I was so angry at the loss of him that I took a pin and scratched his name into my forearm. I felt no pain as the blood from the scratched skin formed his name. I would never forget him now. It was sore for days, but that did not concern me; I wanted to remember him for as long as I could.

At one of Mrs Smith's parties, Dayne came along. There was nothing impressive about him. He was much older than me. Even though I could not see anything interesting about him, I noticed that there was a very sexual vibe about him. He had an ugliness that was attractive, something like Mick Jagger. I was never someone to be attracted to looks; it had to be the energy of a person that would draw me to them. He had an energy about him, I noticed, that attracted women, and I liked the way he approached me. He had a way with words and a lot—a lot—of charm. His words turned me on, as well as the way he held me when we danced, our bodies against each other, like they were two bodies in one, so close I could feel every part of his body, as he did mine. It had absolutely no meaning; I had no feelings for the guy. I was totally not in his league, but sexually, it felt good at the time. Most of all, I liked it because

I knew very well that that would make Maggy's blood boil. I just loved getting her angry. That was my mission, my way of getting back at her.

Dayne was not hesitant to kiss and fondle me on that floor. It was as if no one else was there except the two of us, and I loved the way he made me feel, physically—just physically. He continued to come to all those water parties and even started to visit me in Mrs Smith's home. We would sit on her couch, holding hands and talking dirty. Mostly he would talk dirty to me, as I had no idea of dirty talk at that stage in my life, but I was a fast learner. There was not much we could do sexually, as my time with him was always supervised. I could not go out with him; he had to visit me at home. But we used to sit there on the couch, and there would be a lot going on verbally, enough to turn us both on. He was quite vulgar and open with his conversations about sex, and rather than it offending me, I thought it was quite funny. I laughed a lot when I was with him; I liked that about my time with Dayne.

I took advantage of every moment of experience that came my way, because I always had this feeling that it would not last for very long. This one did not either. I may not have had the opportunities to learn life skills, but that was not an excuse for me not to use experience as my teacher. I had to rely on learning from those that came into my life. I did not have access to any literature or advice on such topics, so I had to plod my way along that process. I had to let the men that came into my life let me know how I felt within my body. Most times, the grownups in my life would tell me what to do rather than be empathetic about my needs as a young adult. There was no positive advice or guidance; all they knew was control.

Maggy became very jealous of the attention I was getting from Dayne. The limelight had to always be on her, and if that wasn't happening, she was not happy. I was getting all the attention now; I was much younger than her and fresh to life, and that was the energy I was giving out. She hated the fact that the energy had shifted from her and was being directed to me. She had to stop that. She had a way of working up a devious plan. She had manipulated my life so far and enabled me to lose my first love. She would not be happy unless she had total control of my life, as hers was spiralling out of control. She was not getting the same attention that she was used to, as that attention was now directed at me.

It was just another water party on Saturday night, except this night, I noticed that a new guy I had not seen before had turned up. He was covered in tattoos and looked like a rocker gone wrong. His hair was vaselined into a rock-star puff on the top of his head, and either his tee shirt was too small or his muscles were so big they popped out of the sleeves. He was definitely pushing some weights. It seemed like Maggy knew him through some of her contacts. She was determined to make a desperate attempt to distract me from Dayne and decided to introduce me to Edward in the hope that he would sway my attention. Dayne apparently had a bad reputation with women, and it was not appropriate that I should be in his company; however, I did not think so. Maggy called me aside in the middle of my dance with Dayne to introduce me to Edward. She also made it very clear to me that Dayne was not the sort of person that I should be associating with; I think she would rather it was her. She was very verbal about me not dancing with him if he turned up, and she wanted me to pay more attention to Edward. I could not understand why it was any of her business. I just ignored her.

Dayne turned up that night as well, and I focused my attention on him. He was starting to make me feel like I was the only one that mattered, and I was going to enjoy my night. Sometime during the night, I noticed he was not around, and I was surprised that he left without letting me know. Edward was a bodybuilder, and his looks were threatening. His arms were covered in tattoos; I was not used to seeing a man that looked like a newspaper. He came across as gentle, but there was something about him I just did not like, even at first sight. He had a couple of dances with me. He just could not dance. What do you do with a man that can't dance? Edward was trying very hard to make some sort of connection with me, but I just did not like him. I did not like the way he looked and dragged his feet on that floor.

I learnt later that Edward had taken Dayne aside that night. He said that he was interested in dating me and that if Dayne tried to see me or stay that night, he would be beaten up; therefore, it was in his interest to leave. Dayne was a skinny athletic-looking guy, but he would not have stood a chance in a fight with Edward. So he left. I realised later on that Edward had a reputation for being violent. That was what his upbringing was like, with the society and people he associated with. If you did not like someone, you beat the shit out of them. I understood then why I never saw Dayne ever again. Maggy did not give me a reason to like her at all.

When you are in sync with the universe, things always happen. Everything I needed to know, I got to know. I had a great surprise one day when Clyde, out of nowhere, walked into the boarding house that I was in. It felt no different seeing him again. He called in with his dad. I took an instant liking to his dad. It was the first time that I met his dad, and I could see that he liked me. He was charming and had a very contagious smile. They were so much like each other, and there was a closeness between them that was really precious. I did not even think to ask Clyde how he had found out where I was; that was the last thing on my mind. I was so glad to see him. It was so unexpected, as I thought I would never see him again. But I got the biggest surprise of my life when I asked Clyde why I had not heard from him.

It was not what I had expected to hear; I did not think that Maggy would stoop any lower. He told me that she had written to him and said that I was not interested in him any more and that he should not try to contact me. He was told that I was already seeing someone and that he should stay clear. I hated her from that day on. She was killing every experience that I wanted out of life. With my whole heart, I had wanted Clyde as part of my life, and she had deprived me of that. I just did not have any way to control it. I confronted her about the reason for her intervention; her response was that Clyde was not from a good family background and I should not be associating with someone like that. It was what my parents wanted too.

I could never understand how someone's family background was like a backpack that you had to carry even if you had turned your life around and become your own person. But there was my family again, criticising another family when we were not at all perfect ourselves. Nothing was going to make this better; my whole life had turned around. She had made it her duty to call him aside and say that he needed to get on with his life and move on, as there was no hope of a relationship with me. My family would not allow that, and consequently, I never saw or heard from Clyde. My meeting with him that night was very brief and sad, especially sad, because we both knew that it was not possible to make it work. My family was totally against it. We were in two different cities, a couple of days away on the train. If there had been hope and support, we would have made the distance work. If I had had the choice, I would never have left. But there was no hope because we were defeated right from the very start. We would, however, connect again; the universe had strange ways of allowing me to close unfinished business. We had a life contract to fulfil, and that was going to happen, irrespective of the hurdles.

I started to drink a lot and went to parties where any type of behaviour was tolerated. I was in a miserable job and barely knew what I was doing there, but it earned me enough money, most of which I had to give towards my board and other expenses. But I found men that were wealthy enough to take me out, pay for me, and give me a good time. I always managed to keep them interested enough to stay around so I could enjoy good times. Most of the men I hung out with were Indians; they were wealthy doctors or businessmen, and they liked hanging out with girls that were happy to accompany them to nightclubs and dinners, especially since most single Indian women were not seen in places like that. Most of those men had memberships to some of the hottest clubs in Calcutta and exclusive nightclubs, so that was a boost to my fun. There was also no threat of a committed relationship with any of them because in the end, they always married their own kind. I liked that aspect because it made it uncomplicated. I was not planning to immerse myself in any intimate relationships; I had not got over my separation with Clyde. This was just another way that I got on with life and found the fun that was in front of me. I needed to express the pain I was holding on to.

At the same time, Maggy was trying to force Edward on me, and he was calling in at the boarding house to see me more often than I wanted. He was keen on a permanent relationship, but I did not like him at all and wanted to let him know. Maggy invited him around often and organised outings with her boyfriend to make up a foursome, hoping that at some stage I would warm up to the guy. Edward had told his parents that he was seeing me, and things seemed to be moving too fast. I still had no interest in doing the girlfriend thing. Edward now called in unannounced and uninvited, and was becoming an interruption to my plans. He walked into the boarding house on one such visit, when I was on my own. Maggy was a few doors up the street, getting her hair done; I knew where the place was. Edward had brought me a present—it was my very own mug, which his mother had sent me. I had mentioned to him that Mrs Smith got cranky at me because I had used one of the other cups, as mine was dirty. Apparently, it was not something I was allowed to do. We each had our own mugs, and they must have had invisible names on them as if they belonged to someone. .

His gesture was good and very thoughtful, and I was so appreciative of it; I was going to treasure that mug. I told him I had another appointment, and as I had not expected him that day, I would not be able to spend time with him. It was as if he went from 0 to 100; his whole demeanour changed. He grabbed the mug from my hands and threw it on the concrete floor, and it smashed into a lot of tiny pieces. That behaviour was very unexpected. It frightened me so much, as I had not seen anger expressed in this way, and I ran, ran as fast as I could to the hairdresser's, where my sister was. She was surprised to see me there because she had told Edward that I would be alone at home and that he was good to visit. So when I turned up to tell her that he scared me with his violent outrage and that I did not want to be around him, her response was very predictable. 'What did you do to get that reaction?' The bitch—she was supposed to protect me, but she threw me to the wolf. I knew then that I was facing a battle to keep him out of my life.

That was my sign; I should have run miles away. But where was I supposed to run? That behaviour did not feel right, and I was not comfortable with it. I wanted to put an end to the relationship. It never happened because the more I tried to stay away from him, the more he seemed to come around. He was always encouraged to visit. I had a discussion with Edward about his behaviour the next time he dropped by, and I was very clear that I did not want him around. But he was not prepared to give up easily and decided he would do things a lot differently. So he started the whole courtship thing—taking me out to dinner, buying me little gifts and organising date nights, going to the movies, and doing all the things in his attempt to make me feel special. He had Maggy's approval, and it was as if I had no control over him being around. Then I started to see an absolute change in his behaviour. It was as if he had decided to put on the charm, as any other effort he was making was not winning me over. I had no option but to tolerate having him around; I took advantage of the material lifestyle he brought. My life was already full of excitement at the time, even if it was not the right sort of excitement, and he just fitted like the rest of them did.

It was very common to date a few boys at the same time. This was what was so great about the sixties; it was not sleeping around, just dating, which very rarely happens these days. Even though there was a lot of premarital sex that was happening, I just did not let that happen. I knew the distance that I would go with any one of them. I had a very limited understanding of sex, even at that time. I had just begun to understand that there was no way I would get to intercourse, because that meant babies, and I just did not want that in my life, more so because that would bring disgrace on my parents. I did not quite know what that meant in real terms, but I knew where to draw the line; my only reason for that was that there was no way that I was going to mess my life up with a pregnancy. At the time, my freedom was very important to me. It was very common practice to focus on the foreplay, lots and lots of foreplay, but you never went the distance! I had no need or desire for children.

I gave in to Edward coming around, but I was not seeing him exclusively. If he wanted to hang around, he could do that. I was dating everyone and anyone I felt like at the same time. He lived an hour away from me; it was not easy for him to get a bus to where I was, so that allowed me some time to explore my horizons. As long as I could do what I wanted to do when I could, a bit of him in my life was bearable. I could see that Edward was starting to fall in love with me, and I could not see why; we were so different.

Maggy finally managed to find herself a boyfriend. He eventually became her husband. I did not like him, but I tolerated him because he always treated me well. I think I had a bit of empathy for him for what he had to put up with, being her partner. She never treated him well but always kept him around whilst she flirted with anyone else that was game enough. On the positive side, it took her focus off me when he was around. He must have felt very inferior to her, because he hung around in spite of how she treated him.

Hanging out at nightclubs with my Indian friends became very regular for me. I was an adult now, and Maggy was starting to lose some of her control over me. On one of my nights out at a local nightclub, I met Rashti. He was introduced to me by an Indian girlfriend I knew, and he showed a lot of interest in me. I decided I would hang out with him for a while. Maggy was exhausting all her resources to keep a tab on me. I always walked out, never telling her where I was going or what I was doing, or even lying to her about where I was going. That frustrated her very much.

I started to like hanging out with Rashti and meeting him in private, and we would drive off in his car. He was from a very wealthy Indian family. I knew that there was no way that this would become a forever thing, but that was okay for me. I always arranged to meet him a distance from home, and I would walk there to meet up with him so I was not seen. We would drive out for miles and sit in the car and make out. We never went all the way, but each time I went out, we explored new things in the sexual realm. I was learning a lot more about my body. I liked that and was not going to stop now; I was going to take it as far as I could, keeping my boundaries in check. It was hands-on learning, literally, and I was totally enjoying it. It felt good because it was not something I was encouraged to do.

There was one such night I was out with Rashti. He had one hand on the wheel of the car, and he put his left hand up my short skirt whilst he was driving. It felt good. We had driven out for miles and were on a deserted road. It felt good to have his hands on my bare skin. He grabbed my panties at the crutch and pulled it off my legs, and I liked that too. I wanted more. I had not yet felt a man's hands between my legs; his fingers penetrated me, and it went deeper and deeper. The sensation was so stimulating; I liked how I was reacting to that. It was a totally new sensation. Was this how real sex felt like? I was feeling sensations I had not felt before. I had not even heard of the word *orgasm* and would not have had any idea how that felt. I am sure I had a few that night. It was an evening I could not get off my mind for a long time. This was my first lesson in sexual foreplay.

By the time I got home, Maggy was not there, so I was happy about that. The first thing I did when I got home was to jump in the shower, as I smelt. I could feel a wetness in my underwear, and it was a very strange feeling I had not experienced before. As I took my panties off, I saw that it was covered in blood, and as ridiculous as it was, I thought I had got my period. I washed my panties and got to bed. When I woke up the next day and discovered that I did not have my period, I was worried. My sexual ignorance at that moment did not allow me to understand that this was my virginity I had lost. I had lost my virginity to a man, in a car, and it was to someone who I was never ever going to be with. Do I regret it? Shit no, I may not have got another chance at an experience like that. I learnt that a woman did not need to have intercourse to actually lose her virginity. I learnt that I could have multiple orgasms without actual sexual penetration. Another lesson in sex learnt the practical way. It was a good experience, and I was happy it was with someone who knew what he was doing rather than a guy who stumbled around the whole experience.

I soon learnt, during other visits with Rashti, that he was seeing the friend that introduced him to me. She was Indian, and she was most likely to have his parents' approval. We needed to stop seeing each other this way. I was not sure how to feel about the whole experience; however, I had no choice but to end it. I was starting to recognise the temporary nature of situations and life. Everything in life is temporary; there is no permanency. I pushed aside the hurt. What right had I to feel hurt? This was what I had chosen, because of the nature of the relationship. After all, I knew it was never going to be a forever thing. But I was just beginning to enjoy my time with him; now I had to find a new escape.

Maggy had been having conversations with my parents about my behaviour, and she knew that she could not directly control me. She tried all the indirect ways that she knew, and it did not work; so she had to find a devious way to do it. I would soon spiral out of their control, and they could see it would not be too long before they would not have any control at all. I guess in their small minds, they were thinking that I would get pregnant by some dickhead and that they would have to face the shame. I did not expect them to credit me with any common sense. Hell, they did not credit me with any sense at all. I had no lessons on life taught to me, but life would allow me to learn all the lessons that I needed, even if that was the hard way. Life is a great teacher on any subject, if we would only allow it to teach us.

I had been seeing Edward off and on, but we had got to first base, which was a few kisses. It was totally revolting. He was a terrible kisser. There was nothing sensual about his lips touching mine; instead it was an instant tongue thrust down my throat. So I tried to avoid his kisses. He took me over to visit his parents. He had three sisters and one brother, and they lived in a one-room shack that was pretty much in the slums. It was not because they were poor, which somehow would have been a better reason for their housing. Instead, his father, despite having a job, was an alcoholic and spent all his money on gambling and drinking, and the family had to survive on the bare necessities. All the money he earned was spent on drinking and gambling, with a very minimum amount given to run the house. He was an abusive and very controlling man. He was arrogant, rude, and very self-opinionated.

Edward was helping the family with the income he was getting from working in a factory. His mother was pathetically submissive. She was so scared to contradict his father, in case he got violent with her. Consequently, he was violent to his two sons and very controlling of his daughters, and she subjected all her children to this verbal abuse. He had a very big influence on Edward's life. Edward was not allowed to drink like his dad did; his focus was expected to be on building his physical body, and alcohol would not serve that purpose, although it would have an impact on his life in his later years. I felt an instant dislike for his father when we first were introduced. The feeling was mutual; he did not take a shine to me either.

Edward was starting to spend a lot of money on me, taking me out to movies and dinners and buying me a lot of gifts. I was beginning to feel that he wanted the whole relationship thing with me and wanted to make it exclusive. I was not ready to commit to that. It was uncomfortable being around his family because I knew that they did not like his relationship with me. They saw him spending a lot more time and money with me. I was not their choice for Edward. My feelings were starting to shift. I was starting to sympathise with Edward as I got to understand more about his family situation, which caused his behaviours, and without me realising it, he grew on me.

It was sympathy, but I now wanted to spend a lot more time with him because I could see that my influence in his life was positive for him. I had not witnessed any more anger or violence when we were together, and I was beginning to enjoy being around him. I was a product of dysfunctional parenting, and who better to relate to him than me? I suddenly started to relax around Edward spending a lot more time around my space. I noticed a young man struggling with a controlling father who was abusive towards his mother, whom he loved, and his siblings; it was as if he was crying out for some love and kindness. It suddenly felt all right for me to settle down and become exclusive with him. He aroused the compassion in me.

Sympathy is negative. Empathy is positive. One allows for wallowing; the other supports change. I decided to take on this relationship because I felt sorry for him, but there was no way I was going to save him from himself or save myself from him. I had no understanding of what it was like to empathise; that would come later on in my life. Sympathy has no power at all, but empathy has enormous power. If I had a sense of the difference at the time, I would have been able to walk away, in both our interests.

I was desperate for someone to care for me; he was desperate for someone to care for him. The two negatives attracted each other. Once he realised that he had me pretty much on his side, it was easy for Edward to be nice. I experienced a different side of him which I was starting to like, and I was happy to be around him and see more of him. I did not date any other men and saw more of Edward, and we did a lot of fun things together; for a moment, I relaxed into a relationship with him.

We had not been exclusive for very long, and in that time, I visited his home a lot more too. The first few visits were tolerable, but I never felt comfortable any time I was there. I would watch his father come home to the family absolutely drunk; he would become abusive, and they would all tread softly around him. I noticed his controlling and demanding ways around Edward but did not realise what a damaging effect this would have.

Edward knew that his dad did not like me, but it did not seem to bother him at all. I noticed, however, that they had a lot of conflicts. When I would go around to his home, his dad would take him out for the whole day and return late at night, unconcerned that I was left in that depressing place with his mother and sisters. I did not enjoy being around his family, especially his mother. The house only had two rooms, and it was cluttered; there was no extra room to swing a cat. It was not so much the space that bothered me as it was the energy of the home. Edward started to hang out a lot with the friends he had locally and started to go out a lot more. He figured that being with his family would be enough for me. I had no desire to walk around the streets of that town, so I was virtually a prisoner in his home. We never did much together when I was at his place because there was never much to do around there. It was not pleasant walking around the streets. It was dusty and full of rubble, and there was nothing interesting to see or do.

I decided to spend as less time as possible with his family, as I hated being around their home. Edward felt safe leaving me with his family, as that was his way of having some control over where I was, but I was not going to be controlled. I had worked out how to get to the local bus so I could travel back to town, which was an hour from the village he lived in. It gave me the incentive, especially when I was pissed off with him not being around, to be able to hop on the bus and go back home. He always followed when he could; we would go out, and all would be back to normal—if you could call that normal.

His family had a bit of Scottish background. It was hardly visible and was so far back it would have been washed out by now in a few showers, but they never failed to bring this up at any chance they got. I was already starting to resent the racist conversations and behaviours. The conversations about their white skin and their put-down of women who were dark-skinned surprised me a lot. Had they not noticed the colour of my skin? Most of his family were light in complexion, but it was not something I had immediately noticed.

Edward now started to confide in me a lot, and in one of our conversations, he mentioned to me that his dad, in a drunken screaming session with him, had said to him, 'Of all the women you could have had, why did you pick this black girl?' It upset him because Edward's feelings were already invested in me. However, it did not surprise me at all. It had been heading that way for some time. I expected nothing better from his father. I can't say that I was ever in love with Edward or that I even loved him. I did not choose him; he was chosen for me. But suddenly I chose to be with him.

Edward and I were now dating regularly. We were exclusive, and I resigned myself to being his girlfriend. Those early years felt good, as most relationships do in the early stages, but it was very much a love/hate relationship for me. There was something about Edward I knew I was yet to discover, and I always felt guarded about getting too close to him. He did not excite me as much as the other men I had dated; they partied hard, drank a lot, and lived dangerously, and I wanted a part of that. But some part of me wanted someone that would love me for who I was, and I thought Edward was that person. I wanted to believe that he was that person; I wanted to hang around him enough to find out, but my gut feeling was telling me different.

I loved my life now. I was able to buy things for myself; I was able to spend money on myself and fool Maggy into thinking that Edward was exclusive in my life. Edward and I were becoming an item, and I think Maggy was happy because her understanding was that she could now relax; I was committed to Edward, which meant I would be less of a headache to her because it would mellow my life. Edward was only my next escape, and I immersed myself in a life with him, which was becoming interesting.

We did a lot together, and I started to learn a lot about his interests. I have always believed that everyone is a good person; it is just their behaviours that are bad, and we can all change our behaviour. I started to see the nice side of Edward, and he spent less time with his family and more around me and my environment, which was a good thing because his family was not a good influence on him.

Cinemas in India were a big thing. Going on a date usually involved dinner and a movie. The theatre usually showed Bollywood films or classical Indian films. Films were a big recreational thing for Indians, and occasionally, the cinemas would show an English film. The foreign movies were heavily edited so the sexual content was limited. It was not what the Indian audience wanted to ee. . The risk was that the cinema could be burnt down. If you went to the movies and sat in the normal seats, there would not be a chance to get up close and personal with your date, because that was ridiculed, so some cinemas in India had what they called box seats. You had to pay a higher price for those seats, but they were booths for two and were completely enclosed so couples that wanted to do more than watch movies had the privacy to do so. It was somewhat of a third-world gold class, without the gold! There was only room for two. If you wanted to take a girl to the movies and had intentions of making out, these were the tickets that you would get. When you walked out of the boxes at the end of the movies, the 'I know what you did' looks you would get were embarrassing but were a small price to pay for the enjoyment and privacy.

Edward had bought two tickets to take me to the box seats at the movies. It was for a Sunday evening, and I was excited to go to the boxed seats, as I had not been before. Maggy, being a try-hard Catholic, decided that it would not be right for me to go to the movies, as I had not been to church that day, and she expected that I would go for the evening service, which coincided with the time of the movie. I just could not understand the whole church thing. It was as though going to church on a Sunday would wipe the slate of sin clean. It had no meaning for me at all, but I was expected to do as I was told. She decided that, as she had been to the morning service, she would purchase the tickets off Edward and go to the movies instead. She was always there to ruin a good time for me, and I felt powerless to stand up for myself; it seemed futile to resist. I knew that the motive behind her actions was that she did not think that it felt right for Edward and me to go to a private place like that, where anything could happen. She justified that she was entitled to. There were a lot of times that we did go to the box seats, except those times we did not tell her anything about it. If there is a will, there is always a way.

Then one day, without much warning, my parents turned up in Calcutta. I had no idea that they were coming. I expected that it was just a visit, as they lived a little over a day's travel by train. By this time, Maggy and I had moved out of the boarding house into a place of our own. It was nice enough, considering the other dumps around the town. There was a lot more room, and to my astonishment, it had a massive terrace. Most of the housing was cluster living; the buildings were a few floors high and had terraces on the top, so children and adults had a common place to play and relax in the sun. There was not a chance of having lawns or gardens, except for the wealthy. We were fortunate to have been able to rent the third floor, and this rental gave us exclusive rights to the terrace.

I loved getting out on that terrace. A lot of the locals would get up on their terraces and fly kites. The sky used to be a blanket of beautiful kites, dancing in the wind, and even the little children were experts in flying them. Kite-flying in India was an actual sport. The kites were handmade from tissue paper, and it had to have a precision about it so the finished product had the right balance to get itself up into the air and, once it catches the wind, fly, fly, fly. The professional kite flyers would have manja at the end of their string, which was a mixture of broken glass glued to the rope closest to the kite. The idea of this was that when the kites were up in the air, one kite flyer would try and cut the other's kite; having manga on the string closest to the kite enabled them to do it with a bit of art. It was actually a recognised sport, and big money was paid at festivals to the last kite flying when the rest had been cut. There was an art in getting those kites up and not only holding them up in the air but keeping them flying unrestricted by anything against the sky. . I loved standing on the terrace and watching the mass of coloured kites dancing in the bright-blue sky, the children yelling in Bengali to each other from one terrace to the other.

This created my love for flying kites, which I continued to do for a long time into my adult life. It was also my excuse to get away from the house and breathe. I felt the freedom of those kites; I felt their vulnerability. I was one of those kites, flying without any fear until I was cut down. Our apartment was close to town. It was a dirty city, polluted, and the only attraction was the nightlife in the town. It was a depressing city to live in, with no open spaces. I now looked forward to Edward's visits, as they were another reason not to be around Maggy. I would fantasise about moving out and happily living together in a world alien to what was my world, and in those dreams,

I actually saw happy times. Obviously, I must have been very miserable to be having such fantasies!

My parents did not stay for very long, but it must have been important for them to visit. Maggy had insisted on inviting Edward and his parents over for lunch at our place that day so they could meet my parents. I was so detached from the whole thing and had no idea why this visit was planned. They had been chatting about this without my knowledge. The reason for inviting Edward's parents was to ask about his intentions, and between the two sets of parents, it was decided that an engagement would be arranged.

Edward's family was planning to move go away to Australia because their eldest daughter had moved there with her family, and she was going to bring the whole family up to Australia. Edward was the first family member that she would sponsor. His eldest sister wanted very much for him to arrive in Australia and find an Australian girl which she hoped he would marry. My parents were concerned that if they did not force this match between Edward and me, he would move to Australia and I would never hear from him again. I was approaching my twenties, and they were concerned that I should be married before I brought them any disgrace. Australia was focusing on families in their immigration policy; any immediate member of a family that was in Australia was given priority to enter the country, with the condition that they would be the financial responsibility of the family that sponsored them until they got jobs and got on their feet. Edward was going to take advantage of this immigration loophole.

I was in a comfortable job in a tobacco company and was moving up well in the organisation. It did not concern me much that Edward was moving to Australia, because he had discussed this with me and had said that if he ever went, it would not be too long before he would send for me. I believed that he would. If he left, yes, I would miss him for a while—maybe for a long while—but there would be a next big distraction that would come into my life; I would soon forget him. Hell! I had no intention of leaving India; I did not want to go to a strange country I knew nothing about. The pressure was coming more from my parents than his, as I already knew that his family did not want me in their lives. They were hoping that once he was with them in Australia, they could convince him to forget about me, as there would be lots of women that would be more suited for him. However, the deal was sealed, and my parents went back to their home.

Rather than take this very seriously, I treated it as an adventure. One very ordinary day, we went to mass at the local Catholic church, and in front of the priest, we blessed rings and exchanged them. I did not have any feelings about what had just happened. It felt ordinary. We celebrated with his family over lunch at our place. It did not at all seem binding in any way to me; it was just something that happened that I had absolutely no control over. It was yet another experience. He would soon leave for Australia, and my life would get back to normal. The ring would not mean a thing, except that he had bought me the most beautiful ring; it was a large alexandrite embedded in twenty-four-carat gold, and the stone touched my skin when it was on my finger. It changed colours depending on my mood, and it fascinated me. It was a very special ring; I hate to say it, but I loved the ring more than I loved Edward.

The day finally arrived, and Edward was on a plane, leaving for Australia. I felt sad for a while after he left. I did not expect that I would ever hear from him once he left for Australia. It was not a time of Internet or mobile phones. Hell, he probably did not even have access to a landline. The only possible way was to write, and Edward was not a writer. After a while of waiting for some contact, I gave up and got on with my life, spiralling out of control again. I went straight back into the fun life I had had before Edward came along, and even though it had absolutely no meaning, I was going out a lot, drinking a lot, and finding fun wherever I could.

It was not too long after that I got the news that my dad had died. I did not hear anything more about how and when, but Maggy tried to get plane tickets for me and her to go down for the funeral. We had to go back to that village, and I did not like the idea of that. I was still very angry with my dad and had not come to terms with the time that he beat my sister Laurina, who was so vulnerable, and all the beatings I had received from him throughout my childhood. I had distanced myself from him since leaving home. I hoped I did not have to go to his funeral. This was the first time that I faced the death of someone within my family, and I could not shed a tear. To cry would have only felt fake; the tears were not there. I was not sure whether it was because I just did not care or because it had not yet sunk in.

We did not have to rush to India for his funeral. It was the monsoon time in South India, and planes were grounded, with the flooding of the heavy rains. As soon as the rains were over, we would take the train down in time for the seventh day remembrance of his death. . Christians honoured the dead not only with the funeral service but with the seventh-and thirtieth-day remembrances as well. Maggy arranged for a black dress to be tailored for me for this occasion. I felt like I had lost something, something I did not have. When I arrived home, there was a lot of crying and a lot of stories told and retold about how he died.

I am not able to relate to funerals; the whole thing is so dramatised, and I have always wondered if the dead really care about this depressing and sad saga. I have witnessed Hindu burial services, and they always seemed like a celebration of life. Because Hindus believe in rebirth, they celebrate death. There would be a lot of colour and bright flowers, and the dead were carried in open coffins, with a lot of singing and drumming. They propped their dead up so they were seated, and in some cases, they would stick matchsticks in their eyes to keep them open. Now as scary as it looked, that made sense to me. Rejoice, as the dead have gone to a better life. At the end of it all, the dead were burnt, and everyone in the grand parade would witness it. No fancy services or coffins or fake words about the dead or making funeral parlours rich.

When I used to travel with my father to some of the remote villages he had to visit whilst working for the British, there was one time that the place we stayed in was very close to a burial site. We could see it from the house, and it seemed that it was all part of life and existed with everything else that was living. We would see the bodies jump up from the burning pyres as the fire hit their nervous systems, and that was something I could not get out of my mind as a child. My father had a way of discreetly allowing us to witness life as it was.

Is there a need for expensive coffins, pretentious services, and all that drama of remembrance ceremonies? If you have shared good times with the people you love, that is remembrance enough to keep them close to your heart, where they should be, instead of in graveyards. The spirits of the dead have left their bodies and have probably gone to that place of ecstasy and are ready to start a new life in a new body. I can understand grieving and can empathise that everyone grieves and has to grieve in the best way they know. It is our attachment that does not allow us to let go, but let go we must so we can release them from life to move on to what is next. I see empty and deserted graveyards. Do the dead need a plot of ground to call theirs? To hold their bones when the spirit has flown? Why do we always feel the need to say only good things about the dead when in their entire lives, we may not have let them hear those words? Why do we need to be at funerals when we did not share their lives?

My dad had a habit of going to see anyone that was sick. He did a lot of good work within the community and was at the forefront of organising a lot of events for adults and children throughout the year. He had been walking over to see an old female friend of the family who lived on her own, and was very close to her place when he started to feel unwell. He was in the process of having a heart attack and managed to grab a cycle rickshaw that was close enough and jumped into it and asked to be taken back home. Everyone in the village knew my dad. Everyone that truly knew him had the greatest respect for him. He was truly a good man who did the best he could in the best way he knew for everyone equally. News had already reached my mum that Dad was unwell and was coming home, so she prepared the bed and was ready to welcome him home and put him to bed for a rest. He arrived dead, and I can only imagine how that felt for her.

My mother died with him. Even though she lived for much longer, she was never quite the same after his death. He was everything to her; he did everything for her and was always there for her. Who did she have now? They were a team, I know that, and she had been so dependent on him that she was going to find it hard. In those days, men and women had their roles, and those roles supported each other. It had nothing to do with equality; that was how it was, and it seemed to work very well for them. I did not know much about love at that time, but what my parents had between the two of them was a great deal of respect for each other. Nonetheless, it was a better way to love; it was an acceptance of what was.

As soon as I got home, my instinct forced me to rush into his room. The bed was there, as well as the desk that he used to work on—nothing had changed. I hung on to the curtain and sobbed my heart out because I realised then that I had not made my peace with my dad, and this was it. I had lost my chance. I wanted to say to him that as much as I respected him, I was not at peace with his beatings. I wondered what his reply would have been! Would he have had an explanation, and would it have been acceptable for me? There were so many conversations I wanted to have with my father which would have been so inappropriate when I was a child. I did not know what it was to be close to my father, but I heard those words he very rarely said, the words that had a big impact on me and would guide my life. For that, I am grateful, because I am more my father's daughter than I am my mother's, even though I was not very close to him. I may not have made him proud, as I was not academic like the rest of my sisters and my brother, but he knew now that his words were education enough for me. It moulded me into a better person, and I am grateful for his influence.

Both of my parents have now passed away, but I am more connected to them in death than I ever was in life. I have come to the realisation that if we do not make peace with the ones we want, there is a chance to catch their spirit and hold it in your heart forever. That's what I did. I have both of them in my heart. In spirit, we always revert to the good souls that we are. My parents played their role, and for that, I am grateful. If they had not been my parents, I would not be who I am today; I would not have the challenge to be. But I think they both get me now as they never did in life, and that is good enough for me.

It was weird being back. I arrived in time for the rembrance day seven days after his death, and the village felt as weird to me as it did the day I left. There was a brief service at the local church and more prayers at the grave. Then the whole family returned to our home. I am sure that everyone that was there wanted to be there and had the highest respect for my dad; that was the only reason that they were there, and he deserved every bit of that respect for the man that he was. There was no one there for just a free feed. We were all expected to line up—my mum and my youngest brother and my sisters. The people who attended this lunch then walked up to each of us and said how sorry they were for our loss. I was not convinced, but watching my whole family sob their eyes out touched me more than all those words I could barely hear. I cried too. I cried because I had not had the courage to say what I wanted to say to my father. I wanted to say thank you for being the father that he was. What I most wanted to say to him was that I did not forgive him for the beatings that we had received, especially the day he laid the cane on Laurina. That was what I cried for, and I cried because everyone else was crying. I just could not feel the loss of my father, and I was not sure whether it was because I was not close to him or because I was angry with him.

I looked around at the people in the house, and I felt like an alien in a human world. I could not relate to this village and its people. I was already starting to discover that I was very different; this was the place of my birth, but I did not belong. I wanted the day to come when I would get away, and even though where I would return to was not a good option, it looked pretty good at the time. I wanted to go away and not spend another day there. It reminded me so much of what I had left behind, and even though my life was no less challenging, it was better than being back there.

Getting on with my life did not last long. Soon a letter arrived with a sponsorship from Edward for a visa that required me, on my arrival in Australia, to marry him within three months. My mother was so elated that he had sent for me. He had been in Australia for a year now and had suddenly decided that it was time he sent for me. If I had a choice at the time, I would not have gone, but my mother would not have it any other way. I was going to Australia because the nice man had sent for me. It was also her opportunity to get rid of me so she would not have my life on her conscience; my behaviour was out of control, and they were losing control of me.

I had got used to my life now and was starting to find myself amid the chaos. Was I going to be able to move from my comfort zone into a new world with no friends and only Edward and his family to depend on? Was I expected to feel comfortable with discomfort? It did not take me too long to dwell on it, because I soon saw this as my next escape, my chance to again get away from this controlled lifestyle and have a new life. I started to fantasise about having a great life with Edward. We would have our own home; we would be the most loving couple and have beautiful children. I had it all sorted in my mind. This would be my next escape, and this time from family. I was going to create my own family.

I had saved a lot of money, which paid for my plane ticket to Australia. I had to leave the rest of my money behind, as the Indian government would not allow emigrants to take more than $20 out of the country, but any savings could be spent when, at some stage, I returned to India. I was not going to let this become a setback. I was going to make the best of a bad situation like I knew how. This was going to be my escape from a family I could not understand, a bunch of people I belonged to biologically but did not relate to in any way. This may have been my tribe, but it was not my family; I would have to create my own. The universe had given me my ticket to the next phase of my life, and I was going to take it.

Without the suffocation of my family, this was my first chance at discovering myself. How well would I take on the journey?

ORANGES AND SUNSHINE

The country of birth or the country of growth?

Thank God! I did not see it at the time, but this was my big break. Even though it would come to me with a lot of heartache and more abuse, I was going to take the risk to find myself. I did not anticipate the rollercoaster ride I had got on. I boarded that plane on my own, with no idea of what I was going to do when I got to the other side. I had never been on a plane before this. I had travelled on bullock carts, rickshaws, cycle rickshaws, steam engines, and cars, but never a plane. However, there is a first time for everything.

The flight was a direct flight to Melbourne. On the plane, I happened to be sitting next to another Indian woman, except she was returning to Australia, as that was her home now, after visiting her family in India. I was so happy to have someone to talk to, but I soon realised that she had a stopover in Hong Kong before she had to catch another flight to Melbourne. I allowed her to talk me into changing flights. I am not sure what story she gave the airline, but I soon got off in Hong Kong with her and explored Hong Kong for a day. She had obviously done this many times, and the next day, we boarded our flight to Melbourne—except for one thing.

I had changed my flight, but my baggage had been on that direct flight to Melbourne. So I arrived in Melbourne and only realised it when my baggage did not appear at the carousel. Pam (that was her name) took me to the Cathay Pacific airlines office, where we were told that the baggage had arrived earlier and that they had stored it, on the realisation that I was arriving on a different flight. The baggage holding area also informed me that the suitcase had arrived damaged, so to keep it together, they had to strap it together. Pam's boyfriend had arrived and was waiting at the airport to drive her home. He was Australian, and it was the first time I had set my eyes on an Australian. It was not what I had expected. In my weird mind, I thought that he would be a stunning man, just because he was Australian, it was not what I expected him to look like. He appeared cranky because he had to wait while I messed around with my luggage, and his looks disappointed me. He decided he was going to drive Pam to her place and return to pick me up, as we had realised that there was no one at the airport to meet me.

I could not believe that Edward had not even cared enough to come to the airport to pick me up. I had his sister's address, with the understanding that he was living with her. Pam's boyfriend knew where it was and drove off with her, as she could not wait to get home. I grabbed my suitcase, which had busted only because it was a cheap Indian one and the workmanship was not all that good. Then there were the escalators. Stairs that moved? I had never seen steps move. What the heck? I stood there and stared at it for a while and just jumped on with my suitcase—not a good idea. It was the one coming down, and I wanted to go up. Oh, the joy of ignorance! With my back towards the landing place, I fell to the ground, and my suitcase burst open again. So there I was, in total shame, pushing it all back into the suitcase, with most of the stuff trying to escape. What an arrival!

Till today, I am petrified of escalators and always take a deep breath before I get on one. Encounters like that must escape into some place in your psyche, never to be forgotten. I got to the outside of the airport and collapsed, not sure what to do if Pam's boyfriend did not turn up for me. I had no way of calling anyone and had reduced my expense account of $20 by a $7 airport tax—yet another thing I was not aware of when I had changed flights with Pam at Hong Kong. I reflect on this now. This woman was my earth angel; they are always there at your desperate moments. I was too unaware at the time to recognise that. I would have been in all sorts of bother if I had not met her on that flight.

Michael did come back for me. He had dropped Pam off at her home, and I was relieved to see him. He threw my suitcase in the booth, and I wondered what he thought of this destitute Indian woman coming to this country. She could not even afford a decent suitcase! I got into the front seat. He had started driving when he observed that I was not wearing a seat belt. I had no idea that this was a driving requirement in Australia. I had not seen or used one, and the first one I encountered of these strapping devices was on the plane. I had to ask the air hostess to put it on for me, but she seemed unsurprised to be asked that. I could understand the seat belts in planes, but cars? I was sure she had taken a lot of Indians on that plane and was used to our ignorance!

I come from a country of chaos on the roads and not a seat belt in sight, so pardon me for not knowing the relevance of it. Michael said to me, 'Put your seat belt on.' I refused, because in that already petrified mind of mine, I was thinking, *What the hell will he do to me once I am strapped in?* He asked me once more, and I said I would not. Then came the words 'Put the fucking thing on, or you will pay the fine, not me'. He was blunt, very Australian, and did not have any understanding about my naivety and the fact that in India, there was no such thing as seat belts. So there was my first encounter with an Australian male.

He got me to the address that I had provided him, which was in S Kilda East; dropped me off; and drove away. It was a block of flats, and this was where Edward's sister stayed. The staircase was dark, and she lived on the first floor. I dragged my suitcase up the stairs and knocked on the door. There was no answer. Of course, she had not known that I was arriving, and they were at work. At the time, it did not strike me that I had changed my flight and that the airline had advised them that I was arriving on the earlier flight that I had booked. I had had enough by then. I sat down on the floor and cried my heart out. What if this was not the place that they lived in? Had they moved? I cried and cried until I could not cry any more. What had I done? The intensity of the whole situation was so overwhelming.

They turned up after work. It was late in the evening. It was cold because it was nearing the winter, and I was not used to the cold. I did not even have a warm jacket in my bag. A jacket or coat was not a clothing accessory in India because we did not have the climate that required. it. If there was a winter at all, it was very mild, and most times, a light cardigan would suffice. Edward's sister was very cold towards me, and her words were 'Not another person that is going to come and dump themselves on us'. There are no words to describe how I felt. Not only was I in a strange country, but I was not welcome.

She allowed me in. It was an older-style two-bedroom flat, but it still felt like heaven to me. She showed me around. I had a shower and got into bed, and as soon as my head hit that pillow, I cried and sobbed. It seemed a long time since I had had a good cry, and I had been holding a lot in that I just needed to release. This time it was uncontrollable; I just could not stop myself. I had so much tears; it was as if I had stacked them someplace temporarily, and this was the moment to let it all out. What was I doing here? Here I was, on a three-month visa, which was a visa issued by the Australian government to those that came with the intention of marrying in Australia. What if Edward never showed up? My crying was too annoying for Janice (Edward's sister). She walked into the room and asked me to stop crying, as it was not allowing them, her husband and her, to sleep. They had work the next day, and they needed their sleep. I just could not control myself, and these were tears I had not cried in a long time. I needed to let it out.

She then started to tell me some stories which I just did not need to hear at that time. Apparently, it was a mistake that I had come, because Edward was already seeing another woman. In fact, he was probably out with her this night. He was boarding with a couple, in a bungalow at the back of their home, and had fitted very well into the Australian way of life, drinking with his mates, and I was really going to be an interference in his great life in Australia. She said she would call him the next day and was hoping that he would take me to stay with him, because they had no intention of letting me stay with them.

They left for work the next day, and I was left in this little flat on my own. At this stage, I felt very confused and wondered how seeing Edward would make me feel, and I was already questioning whether I should be there or not. Edward walked in sometime in the afternoon. It seemed he was happy to see me, but it soon became obvious that he was more interested in getting into my pants than actually seeing me. Realising that I could not stay with his sister, Edward arranged for me to stay with him. The couple, Jen and Brian, had a daughter and lived in a house in Brighton.

Edward rented the bungalow outside the house. We had access to the kitchen and the bathroom in the main house, which was shared. It was actually a converted garage; it had no heating and was one big room, in which there was a bed and all of Edward's things scattered around. If this was Australia, I was already very disappointed with how my life was going to look like here. Had I left India for this?

Edward did not have a job. He had no money and was in debt, as he had purchased a few useless items, like an expensive guitar and expensive clothes and shoes; he had not saved any money for my arrival. He had guaranteed to support my stay in Australia until I got on my feet, but he just did not have the funds to do it. I regretted not being able to bring any of my money out. Most of what he had purchased was on hire purchase, so he had a debt he was paying off and not much cash flow. I had expected that, having been in Australia for over a year and sending for me, he would have had some stability and a home to bring me to. I was very surprised because he was so broke he even took the very little money that I had on me.

Did I travel all that way to live in this garage? I felt so let down and really sad that this was going to be my home. I would sit in this garage, which was my home, on my own for numerous nights, whilst Edward would go out. He always said that it was with the boys and that was the reason that he couldn't take me along. He did not fool me, because I knew that there would be women there. Rather than feeling jealous, I felt abandoned. Was he ashamed to introduce me to his new-found friends? I was in a new country; there was so much to see and do, and all I was doing was staring at the walls in this garage. I had no idea how to get myself around, and that feeling was indescribable. It was a feeling of total loneliness. I realised the position we were in, and I was so angry that he had sponsored me on grounds of marriage in a country that was strange to me, where I had no family or friends and now no money at all. I was dependent on him, and that was scary.

I asked to use the phone in the house and called my mum. I had to pay for the phone call, but it was important that I called. I had enough money left in India to pay for my passage back. When my mother answered the phone, I was in tears, and I asked if they could pay for my airfare so I could return to India, as I was not happy in this country and nothing was what I thought it would be. The response was 'You made your choice, and you need to get on with your new life'. I never saw that money or had access to it. That left me very broken. I was on my own, in a country I did not know, with a man that did not love me and whom I did not like. I had no friends or family and not much money. I felt sorry for myself for a while, but I just could not afford the time to feel sorry; I had to get on with my life. I had been told that I had not given my arrival in Australia enough time, and I needed to make it work.

Edward did have a job, but he never seemed to go to work; most times, he got kicked off of some workplaces for not turning up. I knew I had to get work, or we would not survive. I started to look for work; every morning, I would get out and hunt for work. Jobs used to be advertised by employment agencies; I had to get to one, and they would send me off to interviews. I had a lot of secretarial experience in India and had worked through the ranks to become the personal secretary to an executive at the tobacco company before I left; I had arrived with a lot of references, but it seemed that there was no hope of me ever getting a job because I did not have Australian experience. How the hell could I get any experience if I was not given the opportunity to do so? I felt very much on my own, with no support from family and friends and absolutely no idea of any community or organisational support to place me or advise me on how I could settle into this alien country.

I had never used an electric typewriter, as all typewriters in India were manual. 'Have you used an electric typewriter?' was what they would ask me at every interview, and because I had to say no, that would be the criterion by which they would decide not to give me a chance. Things were starting to get so desperate for me financially. I realised it was close to winter; I would be struggling with the cold. In the seventies, the winter was severe, especially for me, having come from the warmth of India. My feet and toes used to get frozen in my cheap Indian shoes; I could barely feel them. The roads used to be iced, and I wore warm borrowed clothes, as I did not own any. I noticed how appropriately everyone else was dressed, and I knew I had to find a way to purchase some clothes, as I needed to look presentable at the job interviews I was hoping to attend.

I managed to get a few dollars from Edward, which I am sure he had borrowed from the couple that we were staying with. Thank God for opportunity shops! Jen, the woman that we paid rent to, told me about a local opportunity shop which sold second-hand clothes, and she suggested I get something there, as it was more affordable than going to the boutiques in Brighton. It was within walking distance of where I lived, so off I went. I had worn second-hand clothes in India and had always dressed very well, but that was not something to dwell on. I could not believe what I was able to purchase with the little money that I had. Thank the universe for opportunity shops. I just did not have the finances to go into a boutique and purchase something off the rack. I bought an orange minidress from the op shop. It had an A-line cut, with long sleeves and white cuffs on the sleeves and collar, and I loved how it looked on me. It was warm but felt scratchy; however, it was special. I was even able to buy a pair of boots and a couple of other warm clothes that would have to take me through my interviews and the winter until I was able to get a job. I barely spent anything near five dollars for all that stuff.

I soon realised that to get a job, I was going to have to lie at the next interview. In the meantime, I needed to take any job to be able to get some money, as Edward was in a lot of debt and I had no resources to turn to. I went for an interview for a stenographer's position. It was clear during the interview that I was not going to get the job for the very same reason—I had no fucking Australian experience. I was sick of hearing this dumb statement all the time. How in hell is a migrant to the country able to get the experience if she is not given the opportunity? I picked up the courage to ask for any job that was available, as I told them that I was new in Australia and needed the money to get me through until I got the job I wanted.

The guy that was interviewing me told me that the only job that he could offer me at that stage was a tea lady's position. He almost expected me to say no, but he was very surprised when I said that I would be happy to accept that. In the seventies, corporate staff had it good, because tea, coffee, and even soft drinks were served to their desks by tea ladies. That was the term used for them. They had a trolley loaded with not only drinks and a hot urn but also cakes and biscuits, and they would go around the office, sometimes around two floors, with a laden trolley, serving it up to the staff. Sometimes staff would walk up to the trolley, as it gave them the chance to get away from their desks and have a chat around the trolley. But whoever did not come up to the trolley had their drink served up to their workstation. I had never done anything like this before, but it was going to be my means of survival.

It was humiliating because in India, this job would have been frowned on. It was a job that only the uneducated people would do. I had to soon clear my mind of those thoughts, because I realised that a job is a job and that all that mattered was that it paid the bills and put food on the table. The only disappointment I had was my belief that I was capable of doing more than that. But this was only going to be my stepping stone, and I would rather do that than nothing at all. I had no other access to money, and I was not good at depending on people. It was nothing more than my bread and butter. I arrived each day, loaded up that trolley, and walked around that corporate floor. There was not much attention for this tea lady but a thank you as I placed their drinks on their desks. I did this twice a day, and most of the day went into washing the dishes and loading up the trolley for the next shift. The trolley went around twice a day.

This was only going to be an interval for me. It was a job, I needed the money, and I had to stick it out for a while. I didn't expect that I would do this forever. Most times, when you have the drive to do what you need to, the opportunities always turn up, with the knowledge and information to support it. Not soon after, I learnt that I could contact an employment agency and sit for a test with them to obtain a certificate that would indicate my speed in shorthand and typing; that would let me get another foot in the employment door.

I contacted Centrecom. In the seventies, most executives dictated their correspondence to their secretaries. This would be taken in a short script, shorthand, and then typed out as a manuscript or letter on an electric typewriter. The paper was in triplicate, with a carbon paper between each page, as that was the only way to keep copies. It was in triplicate and consequently did not allow much room for mistakes. The original went to whom it was addressed to, one copy was put into a running file in the office that was responsible for the correspondence, and the other one was archived in an enormous file graveyard. Accuracy was a key selection criterion. I went into the office of the agency prepared to sit for my test. Of course, the question came up again. 'Can you use an electric typewriter?' This was when I lied. I said I had and asked for some time to familiarise myself with the typewriter, which they were very pleased to let me have.

I practiced for fifteen minutes, and I got the hang of it, realising that the only difference was the return key. It was on the keyboard instead of being a roller that was pushed manually across the typewriter. I got an excellent certificate of over 100 words a minute in shorthand and 60 words a minute in typing, and a beautiful document to prove it. I had the certificate now, and there would be no stopping me. Besides, my fingers moved so fast on those keys because it seemed like the Rolls-Royce of typewriters compared to the hard keys of the dinosaur manual models that I was used to.

I got my first job. It was in the dairy industry, and I did not know what to expect. Edward was very happy that I had landed a job, because that meant that there would be money coming in, whether he worked or not. I was happy to be employed; it made me feel worthwhile, and I knew this was my road to financial recovery. I had to look after myself, and my father's words rang in my ears. 'Never depend on a man to support you.' 'Get your own financial independence.' I looked as smart as I could with the limited clothes that I had, and I got to work very early to familiarise myself with what I was absolutely not ready for.

There were a lot of desks and chairs scattered all over this floor. The place was dead quiet. I had got in really early, before anyone else had. I had travelled on a bus for what seemed like a lifetime to get here, and I was not going to be late on my first day. I decided to check out the layout, the floor, the kitchen, and I suddenly found myself in front of a large door. Not thinking, I pushed the door. It opened, and I saw a large meeting table with chairs around it. On the table were two naked bodies. There was a man's body standing at the edge of the table, over a woman's. She was lying on the table, and I did not get a good look at her. Too much information for that time of the morning. I could not believe what I was seeing. They were having a fuck on the board table! Of course, to them, it may have been the fantasy to tick off the list. I had no idea who they were, but the guy turned around, looked me in the eye, and asked, 'What do you want?' He was old. I got a good look at his face. I would see him later that day; he was one of the executives that sat in one of the offices on the same floor that I would work on. I thought I had one on him, but he did not seem to care.

Well, I certainly did not want a threesome! I slammed the door and rushed back to one of the desks and sat myself down in a daze, waiting for the day to start. It started at the crack of 8.30 a.m. The whole place was full of people—men, women, and tea ladies. I was so glad I was at one of those desks. I was escorted around by a short cranky-looking gentleman who appeared to be a staff manager for the typing pool that I was supposed to be working from. All we did all day was type pages of stuff that were brought to this pool, and we had to churn out typed pages of these terribly written notes. Occasionally, those of us that could take shorthand were summoned by some cranky old executive to take notes or letters and type them out for their signatures. It was monotonous, but it paid well at the time; I was going to persevere with this.

I kept to myself. I looked nothing like any of those glamorous executive women who could strut around the workplace, getting away with doing nothing but flashing as much of themselves as they could. They all looked so lovely in their designer clothes and fashionable hairstyles; it made me feel so insignificant in my old clothes and very plain looks. I had to just work because that was all I had to offer. They seemed confident, knew who they were, knew what they were doing, belonged to the right circles, and flirted with some of the executives. I was a loner and stayed away from it all. They stayed away from me. I worked and came home to Edward, who was most times not there but was always ready to take money off me for whatever he needed. I was happy to let him have it, hoping that would change the way he treated me.

I was not going to live in this pathetic bungalow for very long either; I was putting away some money to be in a position to gather the bond and month's rent to get into a flat, hopefully, so I could have my privacy, and in the hope that when Edward and I would start living together, things would be different. Whenever I had the opportunity to chat with anyone, I tried to get as much information as possible that would assist me in gaining stability. Even at this early stage in my life, I realised that I was going to be responsible for what I wanted in my life, and I had to make the moves if I wanted that. What I did not have was the understanding that it did not matter what I did; Edward was never going to change unless he wanted to, but I thought making a home that was comfortable and having a place to call our own would make him feel more grounded and settled. How naive was I at the time?

I was getting a decent wage now. My first pay cheque was $54, and it was a weekly wage paid to me in cash. It was the actual dollars put into an envelope and handed to me on payday once a week, and at that time, it felt like a lot, especially because you could get a whole month's groceries for $10. I saved the deposit and paid down for a furnished one-bedroom flat in St Kilda. It was cosy but always lonely. I worked, and Edward spent most of his time getting to work if he was able to after a night of drinking with friends. I just accepted that this was the way it was and went on with my work and home routine. I could not even cook, but I tried. There were a lot of disasters, but we did not starve; I am thankful for that. I focused more on establishing myself in Australia, as I knew I would feel more grounded once that happened. I had to find my own place.

It did not take too long for us to move into a one-bedroom flat. It was fully furnished, which was a good thing, as we did not have the money to purchase any furniture. It was getting close to three months, and my visa was about to expire. With no money, we had to make the decision to get married in a registry office or return to India. I felt so sad that I could not have the opportunity to have the whole white wedding, with the whole day being all about me, but I soon got over that, as things were too real for me to dwell on fantasies. It was the most depressing occasion. I had an evening dress that my sister had made for me before I left India, and it barely fitted me properly now. I had started to put on a bit of weight from all the good food I had been eating since getting here, and it was the last time I would fit into this dress. It was Indian silk in beautiful shades of pinks and greys. It was figure-hugging, but I was slowly losing the figure I had when it was made for me. It would get me through, so we went to the registry office; our marriage was witnessed by the one good friend Edward had. Terrance, Edward's friend, invited a couple of other guys that he knew to join us for lunch. I cooked an Indian meal that we shared, and that was it. It was April, nearly before my visa had expired, and the reality of it all had set in.

I was now a permanent resident of Australia, and as soon as I was able to, I was going to become a citizen of this country. For the first time since arriving, I was starting to feel like I had my feet on the ground. I was married, but that meant nothing to me. I had no option but to let that happen, or else return to India. Would that have been such a bad thing—going back? Definitely! If I had only had the money for my passage, I would have given all this up to return. At least, that was how I had felt at the time because I had begun to sense that things were not going to be as great as I had fantasised. From the little one-bedroom flat, I would walk up the road and get the tram to St Kilda Road to work, and I would do the same thing after to get back home. But I was happy just to be able to have the job and have a place to call home in Australia. In three months, I had achieved this, but that sense of achievement was tainted with sadness because I would have liked to feel happy about my relationship with Edward.

The universe has strange ways of making things happen. One day, like all my lucky days had come in one, I was walking home from the bus, which was a short walk to the flat, when someone came behind me on the road and lifted me into the air. I just could not believe my eyes—it was Clyde. The last time I had seen him was in India, with no idea of whether we would see each other again, but the hope to do so had been there. The joy on his face and the happiness in my heart was the only way I could describe the emotions at the time. He was already in Australia, had a job at a gas company, and was married, with a couple of young children, but we were so happy to see each other. I had had no idea that he had made the decision to immigrate to Australia as well. The absolute joy I felt was impossible to put into words. I walked him over to my flat, and we sat down and stared at each other in amazement. How could this have happened? But it was meant to happen. We had found each other. We had a chance to talk and tell each other what happened; there was a lot of love in the room, and we were both truly ecstatic. Apparently, he had got a glimpse of me walking down the street in St Kilda but was not sure if it was me, as it had been a while since we had seen each other. He had decided to follow me a few times to make sure it was me, and once he had worked that out, he decided he was going to surprise me—and that he did! The power of love! I walked home at the same time every day, so that was not so hard to figure out. Where else would I go? I did not have much of a life then. We were very glad to have found each other.

In my moment of ecstasy on meeting Clyde on the street, the thought that we were both married was at the back of my mind, I had a feeling that I was pregnant by then. But the energy between us had not shifted, and it was nice sitting there on my couch at home, talking with him about the past and where both of us were at this stage. I hoped what was on my mind was on his. Whilst he watched me making him a coffee and walked up to me, I thought, *This is how it should feel. This is how it should be—him and me.* I felt a deep sense of sadness at that moment that we had met when we were both in committed relationships. Were we not meant for each other? We were perfect for each other.

I disliked Maggy every time that thought came into my head, because I blamed her for manipulating my relationship with Clyde, resulting in us not being together. Edward had got a job working night shift at a factory; I was hoping to have some time with Clyde before he had to go home to his family, but that was short-lived. Edward walked in the door and was very surprised to see that I had a visitor. How could I have a friend? He soon realised who it was. I had mentioned Clyde very briefly to Edward in a conversation about my past, but he had not expected that Clyde would turn up in my life again. I felt his discomfort at the thought of Clyde being around, as he could see the atmosphere in the room had changed. He had not witnessed the happiness that he saw on my face at that moment in the entire time I had been with him, and it must have made him feel threatened, even though I had no intention of crossing that line.

Edward was polite to him, but it was uncomfortable enough for Clyde to understand that it was time to go. The next day, Edward discussed with me that it should not happen again and that it was not appropriate for me to be seeing Clyde, especially when he was not around. Obviously, I was not allowed to feel moments of joy in this very boring existence with him. I did not give it much thought; to me, it only meant that I would not be inviting him home any more. There were a lot more places to meet, and I would pick up on this later.

It was sad, because once again, I had to let Clyde know that it would not be right for me to stay in touch with him, as we were both married. Even being friends would not be seen as appropriate by both our partners. At this stage, Clyde did not want to mention to his wife that he had caught up with me, as he knew that she would find that very difficult to accept as well because she was aware of our past too. So we parted again, and I was not to be in contact with him—at least for now. I surprised myself sometimes. I actually felt that it would not be appropriate for me to be seeing Clyde, knowing how I felt about him and being unhappy in my marriage to Edward. I just had no intention of crossing the line now that I was married. My loyalty to Edward surprised me. I felt it was the right thing to do, but my heart wanted to run away with Clyde and forget this life I barely had with Edward.

Life went on, and before long, it was confirmed that I was pregnant. I intentionally had not used any protection against pregnancy, as I had decided that I would have a child early in this relationship. I was hoping to have something that would motivate me to either stay or leave the marriage. But when I realised that I could be pregnant, I felt sad that I was bringing a child into a very unhappy situation. I spent a lot of lonely times thinking about how I would manage without any support, without any love, without any knowledge of being an adult, let alone a mother. I drank and smoked a lot during my pregnancy, as you did in the seventies, and my focus was more on my relationship with Edward. I hated myself, as I just could not love my belly and the beautiful person in there that would be my saviour.

I was too broken, too sad because Edward was never around. He would be out most nights, drinking with family and friends, and I would be at home alone. His family was no support to me. Edward had started to become complacent and comfortable in the marriage now. We were having a child, and that was my department; he was free to get around and be with the boys. He carried on with his bachelor life without any responsibility for our future.

But my baby stayed strong, in spite of the numerous ways I abused my body. I would have done things a lot differently had the environment been different, but I just did not know any better, especially how to pull myself out of the deep state of sadness I was in. Then one day, the thought came to me. I would have this child, and it would be my saviour. The baby would be my purpose for living, and every bit of energy I had in me would be dedicated to the growth of this child. This would become my life. It was then that I realised that I would leave Edward at some stage, and I had to focus on making myself mentally strong for it. I had nothing else, but I had strength to pull me through.

I had a purpose to live now. There were many times that I would have liked to disappear and take my life. God knows I had abused my body enough. But someone was looking after me, and I think it was the soul of my unborn child, my earth angel, that allowed me to refocus. I had to do it for her. I wanted to change for her. I got my life on track and started to take care of my health better so I could have a healthy baby.

There were no scans done in those days, just basic tests to make sure that the pregnancy was going smoothly. There was no way to find out the sex of the baby. I was hoping that it would be a boy, because the pressure from the family was to have a grandson, as most of the grandchildren on Edward's side were girls. I focused on having a boy and started to buy and fill a little cupboard with blue things and clothes that were more appropriate for a boy. I went through my pregnancy hardly even focusing on it. I had just moved into a new department within the corporate organisation that I was with, and I had a new boss. I had to break the news to my boss that I was pregnant, but he was very supportive. At that time, there was no availability for maternity leave, so I would have to give up the job once I had the baby. I knew we would not survive on the very little wage that Edward brought in (and it was occasionally).

I worked through my pregnancy until seven and a half months. I did not discuss my pregnancy with anyone at work. I had to work as much into my pregnancy as I could to accumulate enough money to subsidise my time away from work. I struggled as I tried not to make my pregnancy obvious. I had not been in this job too long, and I did not want the rest of the staff to start gossiping about my pregnancy. I had managed to keep my personal life separate from work, and I was not going to change that any time. I was already socially at a disadvantage at work and did not want to be the object of their cruel gossip.

I was worried, as I did not know the basics of being a mother and what impact a child would have on my life, but I just knew I had to have a baby. That was enough. The staff at work kept observing that I was putting on weight, as I tried to hide my pregnancy under oversized clothes. I carried very small, and most of my weight was the baby. If they knew, they never asked me anything about my changing body, and I was glad that I did not have to discuss this with them.

I did not, at any time during my pregnancy, get any support from Edward. In fact, he was totally disconnected from the whole process and left me to manage my morning sickness, my cramps, and all the changes in my body, without any opportunity for me to even discuss it with him or share the whole process of pregnancy. There were times I would be ready to cross the road to get to work and would then be paralysed by cramps and would not be able to move my legs. All I could do was burst into tears, because it was not only painful but embarrassing. I worked until I could not work any more, and at seven and a half months, I had to leave work, unsure about whether I would be allowed to return, let alone how I was going to survive financially.

My water broke very early one morning. Edward drove me over to his mother's place, as he had to get to work that day, and she and his younger sister accompanied me to the hospital. He actually managed to stick with the job he was in, which was the motor industry; he had made a few friends there, so work had become interesting for him. My labour was long and painful, and I was so exhausted. The hospital staff decided to induce me, and it was as if I had been put on a production line. I could hear other women in the birth cubicles, and the maternity nurses were moving from one cubicle to the other, checking the process of the various births. There was no sense of nurture or compassion from the nurses, and all I could hear was them yelling at me to push. I vaguely remember Edward coming sometime during my labour process, but he did not stay around too long. Men were not encouraged to be present at births at the time, but I do not think he wanted to be anyway.

I gave birth on my own, and even in that painful labour, I felt the knife cutting my birth canal to allow the baby to come through. My heart sank when they told me I had a baby girl. I glanced at the clock; it was minutes into the next day. I felt not my disappointment, but the disappointment from the pressure that was put on me to have a boy. I just could not bond with my little girl. I was given an anaesthetic before the birth, but it did not put me out completely; I could hear the conversation between the nurses, saying that the doctor had cut me brutally instead of allowing the birth tear to happen normally and that he had a reputation for doing that.

Almost unexpectedly, I got a feeling of complete joy. I felt as if I had conquered the world. I had done something extraordinary, yes; I had delivered a gorgeous baby. I had not seen my baby yet, as I was left in the delivery room, with my legs pressed together until the doctor arrived the next day to put stitches where I had been cut by the doctor who assisted with the delivery. It was a painful process. I could feel the needle as the doctor put the stitches in, but I had an injection to numb the area so it did not hurt as much. However, after a long and hard labour, I was ready to conquer the world and all the pain in it.

I was in a bed. For the first time, I got to see my beautiful baby girl, but I just did not know what to do with her. She was so tiny, with a mass of black hair. The nurse put her on my breasts, but the process she used to familiarise my baby with my breast and allow feeding was so painful and brutal. The nurse kept squeezing my nipples, forcing my little baby's face on to my breasts, and the process was so distressing; I hated the whole experience. Breastfeeding was something I did not look forward to, even though I loved holding her in my arms, so tiny and precious. Was I capable of taking care of her? Was she getting enough milk? I had no idea. I felt humiliated, exposed, and degraded by the whole hospital system, and I asked to go home.

I was in the hospital for three days, and they sent me home on the condition that a nurse would visit me to make sure all was going well. I did not want any friggin' nurse coming anywhere near me and the baby. I would fumble my way through all this as I had always done in the past. I had already started to get a hatred for the whole hospital system. I had felt like I was on a production line; there had been no compassion or empathy for a woman having her first baby. I had no support or any advice on how to be a mother, but I would rely on my strength, which I was slowly but gradually building on. I had always had the inner strength; I just did not know I had it. I would continue to build on this strength—more so mentally—at this stage. Strength on one level alone is not good enough. It has to all work together. Not only would I have to be physically and mentally strong, but I would also have to work on my emotional and spiritual strength to become holistically strong.

Before I left the hospital, a social worker came into the room and asked me whether I wanted to have the baby adopted. I just could not understand the stupidity of the conversation and was not sure what fucking reason they had for asking me that question. Perhaps they thought I was a single parent, as Edward was not present for most of the birth, or they thought that, with my having been in the country for such a short while, I did not have the financial capability to support the baby. I had no idea about the sensibility of the question, but I left it to her ignorance. It was very obvious that they had already made judgements and assumptions because of my background.

Before I checked out of the hospital, as part of my discharge medication, they handed me some contraception pills and asked me to take it as soon as I got home. I had no knowledge of the impact that this would have on my breast milk, so here again they had judged me. The hospital staff thought that I would rush home and commence the process of having another baby. After all, Indians mass-produce babies, don't they? That was the last thing on my mind. They had the task of making the experience of a first birth and the connection between mother and baby a good one, but they had stuffed the whole process up. I just could not wait to get out of there. It was the most humiliating mass-production experience I had encountered, and I was glad it all ended. Why in hell would I want to have another child, with the hospital system like it was and a father I was never sure of? I had already made the decision that this would be my only child. In a better situation, I would have probably loved to have three.

This was all I wanted. This was my little girl, and in loving her, I would save myself. That was enough for me. I would work out the whole mothering process. I would make mistakes, but mistakes are what we learn from. I would be the best mother I could be, even if I was to do it on my own. I was a mother now. To me, it felt like purchasing a doll and taking it home, as I had no idea what my world would turn into.

How dare hospitals expect donations from the public? How dare they ask for organs to be donated for research when they have very little respect for human beings? I realise that others may have had positive experiences within the medical system, and there are good stories; however, I did not experience those, and I can only talk from my experience. It is just a business like any other business. If it was not, then every human being would have the right to medical care with kindness, without judgement, without discrimination, and on a means-based cost system—that would be humanity at its best.

It had been barely three days since I got home when Edward wanted to have sex again. I was still hurting from the natural birth, and I could not bear to have him near me in that way. I was struggling with the whole feeding thing, and the process used at the hospital to introduce my baby to my breasts had scarred me. I just could not enjoy that intimacy. I did not feel sexy at all, and there was no way I wanted a bar of Edward. It made him very annoyed now that he was not the centre of attention. Besides, I had no idea that taking the birth control pills would dry up the milk in my breasts. No one at the hospital had given me any advice on this. I learnt this later; again, the hospital system had failed me. I struggled for a couple of weeks. My little angel was losing weight and was always crying because she was hungry. I had to work it out for myself—a mother's intuition. I soon learnt that breastfeeding was a bad idea; try something different if what you are doing is not working. I decided to put her on the bottle and, with some advice from the local maternity unit, managed to get a bottle routine going. My little girl thrived.

I was still a child. My adolescence had slipped past me. Now I was a mother, and I did not know how to be one. However, like a weed, I kept getting dug out but had the strength to keep growing. Here was life, giving me the opportunity to create my own parenting style, to love my daughter like I had never been loved, to protect her, and to accept her for who she is, whatever challenges it should bring me. I trusted the eyes in the skies to look after and guide me. In fact, whenever I could not decide or was troubled, I would look up to the sky. I would see the eyes looking down on me, and I would feel like all was going to be well in my world.

The sky, the clouds, the sun, the moon, and the stars had become my guides and my reassurance in my sad and dark moments; they always reminded me of my connection to the universe and gave me a sense of trust and love like I would never know. I have always had trust in universal guidance and in abundance rather than madly creating wealth. I would always be looked after if I stopped worrying and just enjoyed the moment I was so blessed to have. I was away from my family and in my own control. Yes, I had a hard journey in front of me, but I was going to focus on what I had going for me. —my little girl. I would turn my attention to her and her life. She was my family. This was her country; she was born here. I would work on making her life here the best that I could, and she would make mine better.

I was going to focus on being a mother, not a wife. I had tried over the last year, and being a wife was making me very unhappy. That was not how I had dreamed it to be. I now had to create my own new dreams, and I would survive this marriage until such time I was ready to leave.

I could already see that my journey was becoming challenging, but it was the journey I needed to take to give birth to the person that I wanted to become. Challenges can be a struggle or an opportunity for growth.

EARTH ANGELS

They always come into your life when you need them most.
They might appear as our saviours, or they may appear as a challenge.
Nevertheless, they are our angels on earth.

T here was a tremendous shift in me. This was my little girl, and I was going to
love her with all the love I never got but felt for her. I would hug her very close when I
fed her, even though she was bottle-fed, and the bond between her and me was slowly
building because it was just the two of us. Edward was very proud of his little girl,
but it was more like an achievement. In all fairness, he just did not know how to be a
father or how to love when he was not shown any love in his life. But I do not say this
as an excuse; everyone has a chance to change and become a better person. . I did
love seeing our little baby in his arms, and it touched me when one day he came home
with a blow-up lion for her. He did love his little baby, but he was not ready to be a
father. He had love in his heart, as we all do, but he did not know how to translate
that into acts of love. I had hoped that seeing our little baby grow up would allow
him to graduate from being just a dad to being a father and a parent. Being a dad is
the easiest thing; it is just a physical act. Working to be a good father and, most of all,
a good parent takes a lot of work. The men that achieve that make a massive impact
on their children's lives.

The pressure was on me to get back to work, but in those days, there was no way
that a woman could have a baby and return to work a few months after. Childcare
centres did not take children that were still in nappies. But every day Edward put
the pressure on me to go back to work, as we would struggle financially if I did not.
I just did not want to leave my little girl and go to work. She was getting under my
skin; she was becoming a part of me, and I wanted to be with her always. I did not
want the pressure of our financial difficulty to affect our marriage, and I thought of
my next plan.

It had been a couple of months since I had Deva. Like an angel, she brought joy to
my life, and I saw glory in her tears, her laughter, and her dreams. I would just watch
her, whether she was asleep or awake. I loved being home with her, but going back to
work was not far from my mind. I wondered how hard it would be to return to work

once a woman has had a baby. The workforce was not as open to young mothers, but I was also conscious that not returning to work was not an option.

The universe took charge again. I got a call from my boss, Mr Casper. He had news for me that the legislation had changed and that it was possible for me to return to work in the next month. If I returned within three months, I could have my job back. This was a big relief. It was the first few steps to bringing in maternity leave allowances, and even though I would not be compensated for my time away, I was happy to have a job to return to. I realised that this meant that I had to find alternative care for Deva. We had no choice but to ask Edward's mum if she would look after her for us so I could return to work. She reluctantly agreed. I was able to return to work, but my heart was not in it any more. Mr Casper was extremely considerate and supportive of me being a mother, so that made it easier for me to keep working. He was open to negotiating the best working plan so it would balance with my family life, and that was far advanced for where organisations were at the time. I was very fortunate.

It felt very awkward, as no one in the workplace was aware l that I was away having a baby. I kept it very low-key, and I accepted that it would eventually be known to the staff, as they put pressure on Mr Casper to tell them why I was away from work. The research organisation that I worked for had now taken up location in a bigger building and was renting premises off a major dairy organisation. I just wanted to go to work and get home so I could play family. Deva was being dropped off at Edward's mother's place, where she was also looking after his sister's daughter. The two girls were close in age, and I was glad that Deva had company, as they played together well. I often had Nina visit with her parents over at my place, and the two girls played well together. I felt better that she was in the care of family; it was easier for me to return to work, and we had agreed to pay Edward's mother for the care.

Edward's whole family had now immigrated to Australia; they had settled into the country and were renting not too far away from us at the time. The care did not last for very long. It lasted only a few months. At the end of one day, when I went over to pick up Deva, the mood was very different. Edward's mum looked very grumpy and decided to break the news to me very bluntly: Deva was too much work, and she could not handle it any more. She just did not feel that she could handle the both of them together and asked us to make other arrangements. I felt so deflated; it came without any warning. I was now left with the job of finding a crèche. That broke my heart. For the first time, I noticed that Edward too was so disappointed in his mother because we had to look for an alternative place for Deva's care. He was upset that she had decided she would look after her daughter's child, Nina, and that we were abandoned. His mother had always favoured her daughters and was less connected to her sons, and that was very obvious. I think this was the first time that Edward had to acknowledge that. It did not surprise me that he was annoyed at her decision, because that had an impact on both of us, especially me, as it had not been long since I had returned to work. But that was her decision, and we had to work with it.

We had to desperately look for a place for Deva to be cared for, and there were not many good childcare centres around. I decided to take a day off work and make it my task to find one as soon as possible. After numerous attempts, I finally found one in Glen Iris; it was a long way from where we were, but it was the only one that would accept children that were in nappies. Deva was only eight months at the time, and I had already started training her to feed herself and hold her bottle. I would put her in a potty chair and give her the bottle. My heart broke, because whilst she sat there drinking her milk and going to the toilet at the same time, I could get ready first. I would clean her up and get her dressed after I had showered and got ready for work myself. I realised that if I paused to contemplate what I was doing, I would only feel like a cruel mother. I just had to do what I needed to let her fit into the life I needed to live; it was an enormous guilt that I carried with me every day that I went to work.

She was the sweetest, easiest gift of a child, and whatever we tried, it was as if she understood what I was going through and wanted to make things easy for me. Edward would get ready and get himself out of the house even before we were up, as his job started early and finished early. We had since moved from our small furnished flat into a two-bedroom place in St Kilda East, as we needed a bit of extra space because of the baby. Edward had bought himself a car, so he was able to drive himself to work. There was more money now that the two of us were working.

I had to get Deva and myself from East St Kilda to Glen Iris and then get myself from there to St Kilda Road, where I worked. The only way that we made this possible was by getting a taxi to pick the two of us up. I would drop her off at the centre in Glen Iris and then take a tram to St Kilda Road. The arrangement was that Edward would pick her up, as he had the car and finished work before I did.

With the both of us working now and being on top of all our debts (we had a loan on the car and rent to pay as well, and we were managing all our other bills), I spent every spare dollar I had on my little girl. I had a lovely playroom and bedroom set up for her, and she had the prettiest clothes and shoes. She came first before my needs. I had no regrets because she would play in her room for hours and was so self-sufficient. It was a blessing when I had to not only work a whole day but get home and get all the domestic stuff done on my own. She was the perfect child. My next move was to get my licence so I would be able to drive us around and not have to rely so much on taxis and public transport. But we did not have the means to own another car.

The first day that I dropped her off, I cried all the way to work on the tram. There would be many days that I would cry when I dropped her off. The older lady that managed the centre was a very lovely woman and always welcomed Deva with open arms, but there was not much development for children in those days. It was just basic care; the children were fed and changed, and they sat in their cots for most of the day with toys to play with. Deva was the most beautiful baby in my eyes, and I just could not wait to get to her after work and have her in my arms and around me at home. She was a real pleasure.

I carried so much guilt as a mother because every time I dropped her off, I felt that that was not the deal. Isn't a mother supposed to be at home, caring for her little angel? I was not working because I wanted a career or because I wanted many luxuries; I was working so we could survive financially. If the situation did not depend on me working, I would have liked to be at home to share those very precious moments in my child's growing up and to savour every moment and each first in her life. But I had no choice, and I compensated in other ways—some of it positive and some of it not so.

I used to bring her little surprises, most times a choc bar. She probably did not need it, but it satisfied my guilt and I wanted to see that smile on her face, not only at seeing me but also at the surprise I had for her. Mrs Miners caught me at the door one day and asked me to stop bringing Deva chocolates, as she said it would put pressure on the other mothers. 'Bribery is not the way to satisfy your conscience,' she said. I had not looked at it that way, but I gratefully accepted her advice; I never took Deva chocolates ever again. I replaced it with fun things that I would promise to do together when she got home, and Deva soon forgot about the treats. There were some days that I would drop her off and she would cry when I left. I guess every mother knows that feeling: you want to walk back and grab her in your arms and say, 'Let's go off and spend the day together.' But I had to earn a living. Without my job, we would not survive, because Edward was not very reliable financially. He just did not stay in jobs very long. I could not trust that he would work without interruptions, so I did not have the luxury of being a stay-at-home mum.

There were times I would get a call from the crèche saying that Deva was the last child there. When I had expected her to be picked up by Edward, he just did not turn up for her. The thought of her having feelings of abandonment made me anxious. I would jump on the next tram. It was frustrating slow Every stop was so painful, until I reached the centre and had her in my arms. Edward knew nothing about responsibilities and was not in the least aware of how other people felt; everything was centred on him. He just did not know how to support a partner and a beautiful little girl. I used to be happy with every moment he spent with her, because I knew it made her very happy. She loved her dad, and she was not going to judge him. Edward was not a bad person; he just could not handle the responsibility of being a father.

My little girl was growing up, and nothing made me happier than to hold her little hand and walk down the street. We were inseparable. I wanted to spend every spare moment that I had with her, and all my time out of work was devoted to her. I had no friends anyway; most of the people around me at the time were Edward's family and his friends. I had nothing in common with them and did not like any of them. I watched the things Deva liked to watch on television. At times, she would sit on the bench top in the kitchen, helping with my cooking in her gorgeous way. When she was a toddler, she held on to my legs when I would cook. There was never a moment I did not want her around. I went to all the children's movies, I played games with her, I sang her to sleep, and I would have rather slept in her bed with her than in bed with Edward. I was blessed; she was the most easy-going little girl and was so easy to be around. I tried very hard to be a good mother. I had no guidance or anyone to ask for advice, as none of Edward's family was capable of giving any sensible advice.

Edward was not a person to worry about being financially sensible; it was all about servicing his needs and spending money on enjoying life, entertaining, and going out with friends. Whilst all that is harmless if you are a single man, he now had responsibilities and needed to get his priorities right. He was quite happy buying updated furniture, a stereo, or unnecessary material things, and whilst we managed to live well, we were not able to save any money. I did not want to rent for long, and with me having Deva as a responsibility, owning a home was on my agenda. I did not care what it was, as long as it was ours. But it was virtually impossible to save the money for the deposit. I set financial goals and tried to save the money, but Edward always found a way to spend it. It seemed the only way to achieve this was to go further into debt.

I had Deva christened—not because I wanted to, but because that was the expected thing to do. I was not religious, but I had my beliefs. I did not need religion for that. I had a conscience, and that was my god. But there was pressure from Edward's family to have her christened, as they were Catholics. Consequently, being christened, Deva inherited godparents. Diedree was a friend of Edward's, and her husband, by default, got the job of godfather. Other than being friends, they did not have any capacity to supervise the spiritual growth of my child, which I knew was the role of godparents. They loved her, and she got on well with their three children; that was good enough for me to have them in my life.

I never looked forward to their visits, which is a terrible shame. Instead of having a good time together, it was always a big drunken session and involved lots of cooking and cleaning, which I did. It would leave me feeling very exhausted because my mostly tidy home would always end up looking like a bomb had hit it. Edward loved cooking; even if he was not that good a cook, he thought he was. I was not a good cook but had to learn to be one very fast. We had moved again, as the distance had become hard to battle; this time it was to a slightly bigger unit in Glen Iris, so I was able to walk Deva to the crèche. She was growing up into a gorgeous little girl and loved dressing up and looking pretty every day. Those toddler years skipped by so fast into her schooling years.

The first day I walked Deva to school, I had the realisation that my little girl was growing up. It would have been nice if we were there as a family, but yet again I was the only one there. It was her first day of school, she was looking gorgeous in her uniform, and it was just the two of us. I was starting to get the reputation of being a single parent. I am sure she was frightened about going to big school, but she was being such a brave little girl. I felt like the pathetic parent. There were dads and mums there sharing the experience of their child's first day at school, and I had to manage it all alone. I did not go to work on her first day; I walked myself home and cried and cried until I could not cry any more and it was time to pick her up. I missed my little girl, and I kept hoping that she would be all right in that strange world. I am sure she had a lot of challenges in those early years of schooling, but she never once whinged about her school day to me. She was a little girl with a big, big soul.

Deva made friends, and if she was having a difficult time at school, I was totally unaware of it myself because she never complained. I was struggling with the pressure of being a full-time working parent and then coming home to a drunken husband who followed me around the house, verbally abusing me. He was always very apologetic the next day, and the excuse was that he had no recollection of it. It would be that I was late coming home or that the food was not up to his standard or that we did not have enough money for what he wanted—it would be just about anything, but it would make him aggressive. I was actually becoming very frightened to come home; my only motivation was coming home to my little girl. I started to get concerned that Deva was taking in all the conflict at home, and I was concerned about the effect this would have on her. There were not many signs to indicate that, but children absorb and view things a lot differently; I wondered what was registering in her mind as a result of all the verbal drama.

Deva did very well at school and soon had a little batch of friends that she talked about with me. I always planned my weekends and made sure we went to gardens, had picnics, had a treat to eat, and walked around the shops; whatever we did, we enjoyed and had a lot of fun together. She went to after-school care, as Edward and I were both unable to pick her up after school. The lady that cared for her after school was older and very capable, and Deva was starting to get more confident and accepting of what her environment was like. The lady would pick up a small group of children from the school and look after them in her home until parents were able to pick their kids up. . I was grateful for that, as it allowed me to manage my work hours as well. It seemed that I was unconsciously planning my life so I was self-sufficient, and it was virtually making Edward extinct.

Edward was very happy to come home after his day at work and sit down to drink and drink until he could not any more and have his dinner before he flopped into bed. Pretty sad! I understood that his issue was not so much the drinking as it was the underlying issues that he just did not acknowledge and refused to seek help for, so nagging him over his drinking was not the way to go. Encouraging him to seek help was the better option. But he had to want to do that. He just could not and did not accept that there were underlying issues, as most men did in those days. They grew up being so emotionally suppressed and unable to express their true feelings, and it was a 'man up' situation that men, even in these days, have to deal with to have functional relationships. Issues do not just disappear; they get packed into the body's backpack, which is carried by the individual and can eventually become a big burden as it gets filled with more issues that are caused by the already existing issues. They need to be unpacked and dealt with.

Women are not an exception. Not all women have the support and integrity of a group of friends, or even one friend, with whom they can confidently discuss their feelings and what is actually going on in their lives. Just being able to talk about things helps; sometimes it may be rewarded by other experiences and advice that could be useful. As women, we need to reach out to the right people, and if we do not have those people in our lives, we need to be humble enough to realise that talking to a therapist—a good one—can also be helpful. There is a lot of help out there, but we need to start with the first step. I had no one that I could rely on to give me the sensible advice that I needed. I reached out to my spirit, and with supportive yoga and meditation groups and numerous self-development courses and resources, I found the strength to move forward.

Women need to empower other women rather than bring each other down. We need to support not only the women in our lives but the men too. However, we have to know that we can't carry their baggage for them. We need to know when to go and how long to stay and if it is good to stay forever. Relationships with anyone should be positive; otherwise, rather than trying to change the person, we need to just walk away in all respect for them. Take a good look at who you are surrounded by, whether it is family or friends, and do yourself a favour: Be honest with yourself. If anyone in that group does not embrace and accept you for who you are, do they really need to be in your inner circle? Empower or be empowered. Uplift rather than drag down. Talk about real things and feelings amid the bullshit. We need to be more honest with ourselves and with others. It allows us to be more authentic and allows them to choose whether they want to be part of our lives or not. Everyone has a choice.

I did not give up on my plans and thoughts of purchasing a home because I did not want to be moving with Deva from one flat to another; I wanted some stability for her so she could continue at the same primary school. So I started looking for something that would come up for sale close enough to the school. I was on my own in this exercise, as Edward was not at all interested in owning a home. He was not prepared for the financial commitment that would come with that, but I was just not going to accept that.

After all, I trusted that I had my earth angels. The journey might be tough, but the help would be there when I needed it.

WHOSE LIFE IS IT?

You can dig the soil; you can plant the seed. But without
the hard work, there will be no growth.

The abuse was just verbal at this stage, but I was starting to recognise the devastation it was causing my emotional and mental state. I had a licence, but it was worthless because Edward would not let me drive. Yet he would drive both Deva, who was just a little girl at the time, and me when he was drunk. I used to sit in the car with my heart in my mouth, wondering when the crash was coming. I always pictured him coming out of it alive. It was this indirect control that was creeping in.

The verbal abuse happened daily. He did not like anything I wore; he criticised everything I did. I could not have friends or go out on my own at any time. He could do whatever he liked, but I had to be the dedicated wife and mother. There was a time when Deva was around two years old, I asked him to stay at home and look after her, as I had no more sick leaves to get time away from work. He was keener on having the day off than looking after her. When I got back home that day, I noticed a mark on her upper arm that did not look good, and I confronted him about it. She had not been behaving the way he wanted her to, so he hit her on the arm, hard enough to leave a visible mark. No, that was never going to happen to her! There was not going to be any beating in my home! I had seen enough of it in my young years to never want to see it around me ever again.

I did not realise the power I had in me as a mother, but I screamed the words 'If you lay a hand on her ever again, you will be so sorry'! It must have been by the look of a madwoman on my face that he realised that I was dead serious, because he never did that ever again. I did not know what I would have done, but I was very serious that he could never ever do that to her again.

Whilst I can empathise with women that are in abusive situations, they are adult enough to understand that you never put your children through that; they do not deserve that. Consequently, I have no sympathy for those that not only allow themselves to go through abuse but subject their children to it as well. There is no excuse for that. Subjecting yourself to an abuser is your choice, but no one has the right to put a child through the abuse as well. That is unforgiveable. If there was ever a time that my anger for all the beatings that I had received as a child surfaced, this was the time. I had had enough, and there was not going to be a repeat of it.

I wanted to get out before it got to the next stage of physical abuse, because I knew that would come. So when Deva was seven years old, I decided that would be the time to walk out on him so the abuse would not reflect on her growing up. At this stage, the abuse was mental, emotional, and spiritual, and whilst I was strong emotionally and spiritually, I knew I did not have the mental strength, after all I had been through, to make sensible decisions in the interest of Deva at this stage. I had a lot of conversations with Edward about it. I always had to pick the right moments to have these conversations. But it would be good for a couple of days, and then he'd revert back to the same behaviour, as is the pattern of an abuser. I could not change him. God knows I thought I could at that stage, but I soon realised that the change had to come from me. Abuse is very discreet. It is so discreet, and sometimes it is not noticeable until the robbing of the soul has commenced. Now I may have put up with a lot of the verbal abuse, but my soul was strong and very aware; that would never happen to me. I would be out of there as soon as I was in a position to leave.

I had to first get a flat and move Deva and myself into it. I had already told him that I was planning to leave, and his words were 'Piss off. Who needs you anyway? You will never leave me.' So I always presumed that he would not care whether I left or stayed. I begged him to consider getting help for his drinking or whatever else was troubling him, but there was such minimal help in those days, especially for men. Things would not get better. According to him, he was not the one that needed the help. 'Do you think I am insane?' were his words. According to him, I was the one that needed to fix my brain. I probably did, but I was not sure where to turn and was too ashamed to tell anybody what I was going through. His family were the only ones that knew, but they did not seem too concerned. His mother and siblings had lived with abuse all their lives, so to them, it was an accepted part of life. I had no option but to rely on my inner strength rather than get professional help. I could not afford that, and I had always relied on that inner strength. 'You can do this' were the words I always used to encourage myself. I mapped out how this would all work out.

I started looking for a flat and found one which was close enough, so I would be able to walk her to school and arrange for her to go to after-school care. I was always honest in my conversations with Deva, and even when she was a little baby, I talked to her as if she understood me. I had decided to take her along with me to see a flat and had a chat with her at the time about moving out. I had the conversation with her, but she was so little that not much was absorbed. In those conversations, I was very careful not to put her dad down in any way but rather discussed things positively and made sure that I explained it at her level. I knew this was my only option, but had I considered how this was going to influence her? Whilst we walked over to look at the place, I talked to her about how this would happen and said that she would still be seeing her dad and that it was just that I was so unhappy with him and needed to stay in a different place. It seemed that she was taking it all in, until her responses stopped.

Deva had always been a very talkative little girl, and she questioned everything; we were always able to have good conversations. When she was in doubt of anything, she always asked. I always found the answer that she would be able to relate to. That silence! I turned around, and when I looked at her, she was in tears. My heart cracked once again, and I hugged her so close to me. I did not know whether it was her I was consoling or myself. What right did I have to decide for my little girl? I guess it did not matter who he was; he was her dad, and she loved him. I had to rethink the process.

It was at that time that I decided I would go back and stay with Edward until such time Deva was ready, as I knew one day she would want to leave him as well. What right did I have to take a child away from her dad? I wish I had had some sensible person there at the time to give me a good kick up the backside and say, 'Yes, you do. You do need to take your little girl and yourself away from him, irrespective of her sadness and her tears.' I was giving myself advice, and that was not always a good thing. I could see that she loved him very much and made so much of the attention she got from him. I do know also that he loved her, but on his terms. I grabbed her beautiful little hands, and we walked back. I would never consider leaving for a short term. I longed for someone to put things into perspective for me, but there was no one. I had to get used to making decisions for myself. Right or wrong, I was not sure, but they had to be made.

I decided that it would not be wasted time. I would use the time to work on my mental strength and empower myself, so when the day came, after he had run out of every chance that I give him, I would have the capability to walk away and never look back. It was going to be a long and hard journey. Even though it was Deva making the decision for me to stay, it was divine intervention telling me that I was not ready to leave. I needed a bit more time to prepare myself, and that I did. I was so glad I did not leave at the time. I was so mentally and emotionally vulnerable, and without any support around me, I may have gone back to this dysfunctional situation. Well, things have not changed too much even today. Women in abusive situations are given monetary help, accommodation, and advice, but we still fail them in support services. Services need to make sure that every woman in an abusive situation has her support system: the right people to call that are around her, that are in her inner circle, and that she can rely on when the first few days away get truly hard. My inner strength—that was my support network, and that was what I had to rely on. I did not have any other choice.

All the things that I was not allowed to do because he needed to stay in control, I had to gradually allow into my life. I loved Australian rules, but I was not allowed to watch the games. My few attempts to watch a game on television when I was on my own would be short-lived as he returned. 'You do not need to be watching that,' he would say as he turned it off or switched to a channel that he usually watched. I tried an alternative approach to my passion for the game. I decided that I would lie; I would say I was going to visit a friend of mine for the day. Carlton was playing Hawthorn, and I sneaked off with a friend from work and her partner to watch the game. I fell in love with the whole atmosphere. The thrill of being at the MCG, the vibrant crowds, the action, the screaming, the game, the smell of the Aussie pie, the game colours, the flags—I loved all of it. Hawthorn won that year, and that was going to be my team, the team that I would support forever—so I thought at the time. I had not realised that by the time I got home from the game, it would be so late. I intentionally told him that I had been to a game with them. I wanted him to know that he was losing control. I was prepared for the anger, a lot of screaming and abuse; he made it very clear that he did not like me going to the football game, as it was not the scene or the place for a woman. How ridiculous could he be! Even though he said that this would never happen again, I knew it would. I would become a football fan and go to as many games as I wanted to. I may not have been able to do it during my life with him, but my time would come.

I had got my licence but had never driven because he would not allow me the experience to drive, even when he was in the car. I always knew to pick my time and the words to use when I wanted things to happen. I talked Edward into purchasing a car for me ; I started to assert myself. I started to do numerous courses in self-esteem and self-love. Any course or group session that contributed to my self-growth, I found the time to attend. I was far advanced in my yoga and meditation practices, and it gave me strength of body and clarity of mind. I started to understand that Edward was not a bad man; he just was not a good father or partner because he did not have any role models in his growing-up years, which resulted in his bad behaviour. I was not able to nurture him through that; I was barely keeping my head above water. It was not my role to change him; he needed to want that change, and he needed to want us in his life to make those changes.

There were times of deep lows when I did not have the ability to think. I hated waking up to face my day, but I got up and did. I would curl into a ball on the floor and just not want to get up. I would cry all the tears that I possibly could; I had nowhere to turn. I just had to get on with my life, and I had no time to dwell on feeling sad. I was off my head most times. I had thoughts of ending it all many times, but my inner strength was what took me through all those dark, dark times. Not for a moment had I thought of seeking medical help. I did not want to be prescribed Valium or some ridiculous drug that was the most popular mood suppressant. It would only be temporary help and would make me reliant on it to move forward, but that was not how I saw my life. I realised that I was not feeling sound in mind and in emotion, but I knew I had the inner strength and needed to have my wits about me to be able to access that strength. Being off my face on some drug was not going to help.

Empowerment is a powerful tool every woman should have in her box of tools (not leaving out the sex toys, which have equal importance in that box). I could not avoid what was happening, but I certainly had the power to walk away. I needed to take responsibility for my own well-being; no one was going to be able to do it for me. They could help me to the extreme, but I would have to be prepared to do a lot of the work. With virtually no knowledge of any external support, I had to rely on my inner support system and the strength of mind and spirit that I was building in myself.

I worked really hard and threw myself into work so I did not have to feel when I got home. I was working hard on strengthening myself physically, emotionally, mentally, and spiritually. I still had a lot of work to do on my physical appearance. I hated the way I looked; each time I looked in the mirror, I saw a physical self that this new woman I was becoming did not relate to. I did not have much money to buy myself any clothes off the rack; none of my clothes were attractive. I had put on a lot of weight and did not want to look at myself. I was aware that I also needed to find some time to get into physical exercise as well.

It was New Year's Eve. Edward's group of friends had a tradition of attending a massive ball organised by a club that we belonged to. It was a club with mostly Anglo-Indians on their membership, but it was open to anyone that wanted to join. We always attended the New Year's dance. I did not have the money to buy a new dress off the rack for the occasion. I decided that I would buy some material. It was a lot of effort, as I was not much good with needlework. I used to make all my little girl's clothes, so I decided that I would make myself a dress. I bought the material; it was white with embossed black dots on it. I made an evening dress, and it was to the ankle and very basic. It was the best I could do, as Edward wanted to go to this dance. Most of his friends were going, and their partners were going to be there. I was ashamed to go, as I knew they would all be dressed up in clothes bought off the rack. I was in my awful home-made dress. I knew what the reaction would be.

I walked into the hall. All the women looked glamorous, dressed in their formal evening dresses. I felt like the ugly duckling. To add to my already deflated feelings, one of Edward's friends, Bruce, turned to me and said, 'Don't mind me asking, but where the hell did you get that dress from?' I wanted the ground to open so I could sink as low as I was feeling, just disappear and not have to be in that situation ever again. But like everything I had taken on the cheek, this was one of them, and it could wait its time. I had to work on not letting words control me as well. I had so much self-improvemet to do; it would take me a lifetime. Words are powerless, and only I can give them power. But I was not yet at that advanced stage of self-love. It hurt, but I would hurt as long as I gave it power to hurt me.

I started running around Albert Park Lake during my lunchtimes, as we had showers at work. I started to see my body change, and I reduced from a bloated 14/16 to a 10/12. Soon I would get myself down to a size 8. Without any permission from Edward, I started going into dress shops and buying myself beautiful clothes. I was earning enough to do that. I needed to get it into my head that I deserved it. I deserved to be able to buy what I wanted for myself and not be controlled by my restricted thinking. I have always loved good clothes that reflect my personality, and I did not want to restrict myself any more. I wanted to gradually recover all my personality that I had lost in allowing my marriage to turn me into a person I hated. I started with getting the body I wanted, which would accommodate the dress sense that I loved.

Yes, there was never anything that I could wear that he would like, and I had to hear all the negative comments. But these were only his words, and these were starting to bounce off me. They had no power.

I opened a separate bank account for myself so Edward would not feel he had a right to raid our joint account for his drinking and gambling. I got myself a credit card and maxed it and paid it off slowly. I was starting to get an attractive wardrobe, and now I had to work on getting myself a car. It was very obvious that Edward had started to notice the changes I was making, and it was frustrating him. He was losing his egocentric power; I was getting empowered with each day. I may have been in front him, he may have been able to see me, but what he was seeing was an empowered woman; his inability to upset me with his words and actions was frustrating him. I was slowly regaining my sense of self, and he was not in that picture.

The argument for getting me a car was that it would allow me to stop relying on him to drive me and Deva to places. He saw it as freedom; we would not have to be on his agenda. I got myself a little second-hand Honda. It was one of the best things that I had ever done. It was my first step to independence. I was hardly a good driver, as I was not given the confidence to drive. To this day, I am always a cautious driver. That fear for driving must have gone into my DNA because of the many times he criticised my driving. The times that he sat next to me whilst I drove, I had to hear a lot of negative comments from him, which impacted my nerves when I was on the road. I just did not have that confidence that I see in most people. However, it did not stop me from getting on those roads. I would have liked to be more of an adventurous driver, but for now I was happy just to be able to get myself to the places I needed to go.

I was so excited to have the freedom now to drive myself anywhere I wanted. I could drive my little girl wherever we wanted. We went to the zoo, the movies, the department stores, parks, markets, anywhere and everywhere. It felt so good. I had the licence but absolutely no experience or road sense. Getting on the road was the only way to give myself the experience now, and no sooner had I got my car than I was on the road and developed the confidence I needed. I could never be one of those people that do road trips on their own or love driving. I drive to get myself to where I need to go rather than to places I want to go.

It was raining, and the conditions on the road were pretty bad. It had been only six months since I had started driving around. Edward's sister and her partner were at our place, and she suggested that we go to Chadstone and have a game of bowls. I liked the idea; more experience at driving could not be a bad thing. I was not sure how I would drive in the rain, but the only way to do it was to get the experience. Edward was very against us going out; he said that we would crash in weather like that, and he was very clear that he did not want me to go. Normally, this would be the time when I would succumb to his negative words, and I probably would have decided not to go out that night. But things were very different now. I ignored all that blabber and went anyway. Every day, I felt more and more empowered to stand my ground and stand up to him. I was beginning to understand that words do not make me who he says I am; all that negative talk belonged to him, and I was not going to carry it. I was going to ignore it. The consequence was a lot of verbal abuse, but that did not have an effect on me any more. I did not feel the need to react to any of that stuff. We had a great game of ten-pin bowls. There was Brenda, Deva, and me, and my little girl was in her glory, going out with the two of us.

That was not enough for Brenda. She wanted to be driven to McDonald's so that we could get some food. I had cooked dinner for us, and I said to her that perhaps we should go home and eat. But she insisted on me driving there. It was only a few metres away, so I decided I would do it. Because it was a wet night, as I got into the parking bay of McDonald's and was about to put the car in park, my shoes slipped off the brake and fell on the accelerator. Fortunately, the car hit the concrete slab at the end of each parking bay, which broke the impact before it flew up in the air, hit the brick wall, and dropped to the ground. The front of the car was totally damaged. I will never forget the faces of the people with half a hamburger in their mouths, their eyes popping out when they saw those headlights coming for them and coffee flying from their hands as they thought that the car was going to come through the glass window and land in the shop. It is funny now but was not at the time. I was so distressed that this had happened and angry that I had allowed myself to be talked into going to McDonalds. I was so worried that the engine had been totally damaged.

We were all OK, just a bit shaken. I was not so much worried about the car as I was about what I had to face when I got back home and had to tell Edward about this. It was distressing to see my car being driven off in a tow truck. I burst into tears. Had I lost my car? There was also the damage it had done to the wall of McDonald's, which had to be included in my insurance claim. Would it be a write-off? What would I tell Edward? I went into McDonald's to finalise what was needed, and my mind was everywhere but in my head. I heard the manager say to me, 'Please order everything that you three want to eat, on us,' as if that was foremost on my mind. I could not believe it, but Brenda sat down to put in her order. I did not allow her that, because I was very angry with her and upset to see my car in the state it was. I ordered a taxi instead, and then we were on our way home. I was counting the cost of the damage, and I had a bad feeling all the way home.

I kept turning the words over in my head, wondering how I was going to explain all this to Edward when I got home. Brenda was his youngest and favourite little sister; she asked me to leave it to her, and she would talk to him about it and take the blame for the decision. It softened the blow, but he had a bit of leverage now. He had told me this was going to happen, and it happened because I did not listen to him. I was astounded when the insurance company covered the damage to the car; it was repaired and returned. I was back to having a car. . I was not going to allow the fear of my first accident to stop me from jumping into my car. There had been numerous times in my life so far that I had felt fear—fear on various levels—but to sit in fear is very disabling. It is the little lessons in courage that prepare us for the bigger jumps, and I had jumped off a lot of cliffs so far. No doubt there was going to be a lot more. The courage was there; I needed to tap into that more.

As I started to work on my independence, it also did a lot for my self-esteem. But the most important thing I needed to work on was leaving Edward. I do not know where this thought came from. I was in a deeply unhappy situation, and being home, which should have been my safe haven, did not feel right. I was sitting on the bed one day, deep in thought, wishing I had someone I trusted to talk to. It was a day when I was at home on leave, and my thoughts wandered to Clyde. I guess I just wanted to talk to someone, and there was no one else I could turn to. Again, it must have been divine intervention, because I knew the place where he worked. A few days earlier, I was visiting my sister and overheard a conversation she was having with a group of her friends. I heard his name being mentioned by one of the girls there who knew him. She mentioned the place where he worked, and that was enough for me to encourage the thought of getting in touch with him again. I was so sure that if I was able to get in touch with him, he would get some sense into my head.

I was nervous and excited as I dialled the number. I asked for him when the girl at the switchboard answered, and like a miracle, he answered the phone. It was as if no time had passed. We chatted for a while, and I felt the butterflies in my stomach. He was as happy to hear from me. Somewhere in that conversation, he said, 'Perhaps we should meet at some time and start an affair!' But that was Clyde. He always said things as a joke, but it became reality at some stage. It went over my head because that was not the reason I was calling; it was my desperation to talk to someone that cared about me, and I knew he did. I was still conscious that we were both married, and even though my situation was dysfunctional, at this stage I had no intention of starting anything with Clyde that crossed the line.

We started talking for hours on the phone. The conversations were getting regular, and most times it was when I was at work. I did not in my wildest dreams think of taking it any further than having someone to talk to. We were just able to talk about anything and everything without judgement. I just loved the conversations that we had; we were on the same wavelength, and I was always able to take something away from our talks. I liked how he had no sympathy but a lot of empathy for my situation. Clyde always had a way of taking charge of things. In one of those conversations, he suggested that we meet in the city after work. Somehow this seemed to be the right thing to do. It would not only allow us to meet in private but also give us some time to talk freely, as I did not want to be seen with him and risk the news getting back to Edward. I had to play this very carefully.

I had to come up with some story for Edward. Clyde said that he would book a room in a city motel, as we both worked a short distance from the city. He took charge of that. The intention was to have a bit of uninterrupted private time together, and I wanted that so much. Next thing, I had the name of the motel, took time off work, and said to Edward that I was going to work late that evening. I had no expectations but to be able to have uninterrupted one-on-one time with Clyde. I just wanted to see him again. The Rubik's cube of life was clicking; the universe was in motion and bringing us together again. Had we some unfinished business? Was he the earth angel that always seemed to be there when I needed him most?

It was a nice motel on Collins Street. I met him there, and as I walked in, it just felt right; nothing else mattered. I had known Clyde for most of my young adult life, and even though we had got close enough, we had never seen each other naked, because there just had not been an opportunity. However, things were different now. I was going to leave my marriage, and somehow, at this stage, it just felt right. I was so scared of what could happen. My mind was so far away from the consequence that awaited me when this was over.

I entered the room, and I walked over to the window to catch the view of the city. It was an amazing view, and I felt all my senses being aroused. It felt naughty and nice at the same time. I felt no guilt about being alone with him, because there was nothing left for me in my marriage—physically, emotionally, or mentally. This felt nice; it felt like there was nowhere else I needed to be. I stood at the window, looking at the view, because I was not sure where to start. I knew the conversation would start. We had no problem with being honest about what was going on in our lives. He walked up and put his arms around my waist whilst he stood behind me. Feeling his body against mine was comforting and erotic at the same time. It was the best feeling in the world. I felt so safe and so wanted. I just wanted more, but I was still not sure what I wanted. I did not think that we would take this to where it went, but there was no stopping us now.

Clyde was the best kisser, and I could kiss him for hours. It was the sweetest coming together that had been waiting to happen for a long time. I will not say that we had sex, but we made love so many times. I know a lot of men who have said to me, 'I do not have sex, but I make love.' If they have to say that, obviously they have no idea about the difference. Sex is just a physical act; it is animalistic and can be done any which way, so long as it is with consent. Making love is when you are not only there physically but emotionally, mentally, and spiritually, and you are so much in the moment that it becomes a very different experience. It is not just the baring of the body but the baring of the soul as well. We would get up sometime in the middle of it all, walk into the shower, walk out, and start all over again. I just did not want that night to end.

It felt like the most natural thing. He owed me this; I owed myself this. We had unfinished business, and this was life offering us the opportunity to do it. Life is never judgemental. There was nothing more I needed, but if it had to be more, I would take it. At some point in the night, it was time for both of us to leave. We had a bottle of champagne between us and a lot of cigarettes, and then we had yet another shower. I left to return home, and he left after me. We talked, we laughed, we were in the right place, and it was the right time.

He told me that he had plans to leave his marriage. Mine was a disaster from which I was not sure how long it would take me to walk away. I returned home very late at night. I had no feeling of guilt. It was the first time that I had sex outside my marriage, but for good reasons, it felt empowering. I was capable of being loved and loved perfectly. Edward sensed that something had changed, even though he had no indication of what it was; in his mind, I would always be his possession. I was not being intimate with him. It was too late to expect anything to change for us. There is an aura about an empowered woman, and it is actually scary to weak men. I did not want him in my life any more; he had taught me to not need him in my life. This thing between Clyde and me was what loving should feel like. It was as if I was on some drug and could not stop taking it. I was stuck on Clyde, yet I had no expectations of him.

I was not going to turn that tap off. This was going to be my distraction from my marriage and my means of walking out. Being with Clyde—even though I knew it would not be permanent—gave me the courage to work on my separation from Edward, and I was well on my way to doing that. I almost felt empowered that Edward did not know what was going on, and it became easier to continue living a false life with him. There was joy outside of it, and I was experiencing that.

I saw Clyde at least once a month. We would book a motel somewhere, we would take the day off work, and I would meet him. We would spend all day together. It could have been a hole in the ground, but at that time, it would be heaven as long as Clyde was there. In my dark moments, I would just keep thinking of it until I saw him again. We talked a lot over the phone too. It was so nice to have someone to talk to about my feelings, my dreams, my day, myself, what was going on in my life, what I was thinking, and what my plans were. No one had cared until Clyde came along, and I had no other expectations of him.

I had conversations with Edward and said that I was not happy and would leave the marriage if things did not change. He did not take me seriously, as he thought that it was only words. He thought I would never have the capability to leave him and survive on my own. In both our families, there was never an instance of divorce, so Edward just did not see that as something that would happen to us. We would just continue in our dysfunctional relationship; no one would see it that way, but it would always look good on the outside because we were together. I needed divine intervention to trigger the move. I was stalling. The universe gives me numerous opportunities to make a change; if I take too long, it usually kicks my arse into gear.

This was one such instance. I had gone to meet Edward at Deva's godmother's place. He had the day off and had taken her to visit her godparents. It was close to Christmas; I wanted to do some shopping, specifically to get Deva's present, and did not want her with me while I was doing that. I was going to meet them there after shopping, and we would all drive home together.

When I got there, Edward was absolutely drunk. He could barely stand; his words were slurred. He insisted that he would drive us home. I would not allow that, and I said I would not go home with him unless I drove the car. He got angry at my refusal to allow him to drive us. I looked at my little girl, sitting on the floor, playing. There was no way I was going to allow him to drive us in that state, not ever again, as I had risked our lives in the past. I asked him to stay there for the night, and I would get a taxi so I could take Deva home. I had been shopping for a special gift for Deva, and with the work pressure and the busyness of the season, I was exhausted and needed to get home. Edward would not allow me to take the car home or do the sensible thing and get a taxi, and he insisted that he drive us back.

I called for a cab and walked down the stairs to wait for it with Deva. He came behind me. I could see he was angry, drunk, and unsteady, and he asked me once more to wait and he would drive us home. And then it happened. I said no and continued to walk down the stairs. He walked up and slapped me across the face for being a 'difficult bitch', as he put it. It hurt on so many levels. I was in a public place. It was so unexpected, but it should not have been a surprise that it got this far. I stumbled; it was so fortunate that I did not fall down those stairs. I know he was always trying very hard to avoid that. In that instant, both he and I knew that we had stayed too long together and that it had only been a matter of time before this happened. I ran down the stairs with my daughter in my arms and jumped into the taxi. I was so happy to get home. I secured the inside lock on the door so he could not come home. I thought it would console Deva if I gave her the Christmas present I had bought her. It was a huge doll, one she had wanted, and that took her mind off the terrible night. It took her mind off, but I am sure it had a massive impact on her well-being. I was always trying very hard to compensate for Edward not being around and not being a good father. This night was no different.

Deva loved her dolls. There was always a new doll that would be introduced into the toy world, and if she wanted it, even if it meant depriving myself of my needs, I would get it for her. To see the joy on her face was my joy too. She had Cabbage Patch Kids, Barbies, crying dolls, and dolls that would wet the bed, and she loved them all. From the time she was a toddler, she would spend hours in her room, arranging and rearranging her dolls and playing and talking to them, and sometimes I would hide behind the door and watch her for hours. These were intimate moments that would always be stamped into my brain. There was a child all on her own in intense play, loving her space.

Edward came home the next day, barely sober. He was so apologetic, with promises that things would be different, and he begged me to give him a chance to show me that. Now even in my broken state, I knew this was never going to happen. He had been given numerous opportunities, and he just could not see how much he had broken me, broken me into tiny little pieces that even I did not know how to fit together. He had killed my dreams of what a marriage should be and any hopes of a family life. I could not be with this man, no matter what he said.

This time, I gave him some alternatives. I wanted him to give up his drinking and gambling and to see a professional so he could talk about what was troubling him and consequently causing his negative behaviour. His response was very predictable: he did not need help, and I was the one that needed help. But I knew that, and I was getting all the help that I needed. I was becoming what I wanted to be, getting closer to excavating who I truly was, and was not that the reason I was moving away from him every day, in every way? I was empowering myself, and I was not going to put up with his behaviour.

That sealed the deal for me. I told him I was leaving, and I did not know whether he was relieved that he would not have to change in any way or whether he thought I did not mean what I was saying. He had said to me on numerous occasions that I would never leave him and that if I did, he would never miss me. Things started to move very fast towards our separation, more because I had already made up my mind, even though there was a slight glimmer of hope that he would ask me to stay because he wanted to change so things would work out for us. It was not going to happen. He could not see that there needed to be change; after all, in his eyes, I was the one that needed to change. I was the one that needed to be tolerant of his behaviour. Tolerance! Be who you want in your space; I do not have to tolerate your bad behaviour in my space!

We had to sell the house as well. We had a mortgage on it. We had moved from the lovely single-fronted house we had inner city, which was the first home we had bought. When we bought our first home, we had absolutely no money saved for a deposit, but I gave it a try. We looked at a single-fronted house in the inner city, as it was close to the primary school that Deva was in at the time. It was an old house. It had holes in the walls, the ceiling was exposed, and it had a lot more damage than our unexperienced eyes could see. But I had just got Deva into the local Catholic school, and I could walk there to drop her off, as I did not have a car at the time. It was central to transport to get me to my workplace, so this was it. I was not looking at the broken down state of the house; rather, I was seeing an opportunity to get myself into the housing market and to not have to rely on renting and moving all the time.

Edward just had no interest in home ownership. I had to make the decision and find a way to make it work. The house was on the market for $28,000. It was a three-bedroom single-fronted house with a little courtyard in the front and a big enough backyard and a shed. There was no toilet inside the house; the dunny was outside. But it was all we could afford, and even of that I was not sure. I borrowed the deposit from a financial institution and went to the bank to organise a mortgage. The bank was not aware that we had borrowed the deposit. There was no question about our ability to pay, as I was earning a good wage and so was Edward. In less than a month, the deal was all signed up, and we were finally able to move out of the flat into our home. I naively thought that that would change Edward and make him closer to us. I just wanted to try everything before I gave up on him.

Now isn't that very common practice? Somewhere in our insane minds, we picture things better in faint hope. In my case, if we had our own home, Edward would feel a lot happier, and that would make him want to be a better person. Consequently, things would be all happy family! I was no different. I made all these lame changes in the hope that Edward would change. I desperately wanted to keep my marriage and somehow make it work.

We moved into the house and realised we had a mighty mortgage, but the house was falling apart. The buyer had tricked us into buying a weatherboard that was on hardly any stumps, and that was the reason that the walls were cracking. Fortunately for us, banks in those days had a conscience; they never lent you money unless they were sure that it was affordable and secure financially, and they stood by their loans. Our bank, on the inspection of the property for finance, told us that it had requested the vendor to fix the stumps and the walls and to paint the whole home before it got involved in the sale. The vendor dishonestly patched up the house; when we got there for the final inspection, all looked good under that paintwork, until we moved in and the cracks started to appear again.

I contacted the bank and informed them of the state of the house, and they immediately got in touch with the vendor. We had already moved into the house. It had only been less than six months, but a miracle happened: the vendor had decided that he would fix it all up. We were not involved in any of the discussions and talks between the vendor's and bank's solicitors, but obviously, there must have been some legal bearing on the vendor; he agreed to put us up in a flat until the stumps that held up the house was repaired., painted, and totally fixed before we could move back in again. How lucky had we been? That would never happen today, with so much dishonesty between banks and their clients. The universe was on my side again.

We had to move again, but this time it was into a brand-new three-bedroom unit in Caulfield. We would live in this unit until the house was fixed, which would take three months. This was at the vendor's expense, so we did not even have to pay any rent for the time we were there. I could not believe my luck. I loved the spaciousness and newness of this unit and quite easily would have loved to live there instead of the house, but that was not the deal. We were soon back again, but this time the house was stable. I had no time to get to love the house, even though it was my first home. I wanted to live there forever. It was a lovely little house; it had a nice feel about it and was close to everything. It was a vibrant inner-city suburb, and there was a great lifestyle here of shops, cafes, greengrocers and supermarkets, and pubs, of course.

But things soon went from bad to worse here. We were close to the local pub, so Edward was never at home now because it was possible for him to walk over to the pub, stay as long as he could, get so drunk, and barely walk himself home. I felt so gutted that it still was not working. His family was renting a house a few doors up the road from us. I tried his mother for support. I was already beginning to see things spiralling down, and it was exhausting. As a last attempt to save our marriage and this home which I loved, I reached out to his family for help. Instead of supporting me, his mother suggested that it would be good if I got drunk with him rather than opposed his drinking, because in her weird thinking, this would supposedly make him feel supported. We were on different planets; I just could not get her trend of thinking. I soon realised that it was the reason she ended up in the state she was with Edward's father.

Edward and I just existed together; there was no intimacy or togetherness in our marriage, and we were just functioning. Our focus was on the mundane running of the home and keeping awkward distances. We distracted ourselves with a few renovations to the house to make it a comfortable home; we were getting ahead financially and had built up a lot of collateral in this home. It was starting to look like a very trendy inner-city house, and I just loved being in my home. Deva would have her cousins come up, as they were walking distance from us as well, and Edward's brother would bring them over; it was nice having company for Deva. It would have been a great investment and a great place to live and for Deva to grow up in, but it was not too long before we sold it again. The value of the house had tripled, but so had the unhappiness within our home. If the walls of this house could talk, it would have had a lot of sad stories to tell. I was a very sad person, and it was having Deva in my life that kept me focused and functioning.

I hated the person that I had become. I felt so pathetic and like a useless mother for having my beautiful daughter exposed to such a situation. I was trying a lot of band-aid solutions in the hope that something would click for Edward and that he would be happy enough to make us a family and spend more time with me and Deva and less on self-abusive behaviour, which was having a negative effect on us. I just could not understand that with all we had put together as a family, nothing seemed to fit; I was starting to feel tired and so depressed with my life. It was the loneliest I had ever felt, and instead of things getting better, they were actually getting worse. Nothing was going to make the situation better unless I made the changes, and that was a very scary prospect for me at the time.

I was treading softly around Edward. When he got home, he would say a lot of hurtful things, use abusive language, and throw food around the place if it was not to his satisfaction, and every time he went out, I would curl into a ball and sit in a corner, wondering what I would have to face when he came home. I wished he could see himself like I saw him—not as the abuser that he was but as a man screaming out for help with his traumatic childhood, with traumas that were not resolved and that were now reflecting in negative behaviours.

Deva had started ballet classes at the National Theatre, and even though she was not the best of ballerinas, it was something she loved going to. I walked her there and back most days. We went to movies, and whatever I did, I involved her. I could see that I was working hard to compensate for the missing parent. I was always trying to be both dad and mum to her because my immature brain did not connect with the fact that you can never replace the father in a child's life, whether he was dysfunctional or not.

Once she was ready to start high school, we considered a Catholic school again. Edward's family had all been buying in the suburbs. I hated the suburbs, but Edward wanted to get a bigger and better place so he could have more to show to his family in material possessions; our next house would reflect that for him. His family was very competitive with each other and always wanted to do better than the other. His eldest sister had bought a house in the South Eastern suburbs, and he was now set on the idea that if we sold, we would get something that was better than theirs. Our house inner city had doubled in price, so we ended up with a sizeable deposit with which to purchase our next place. Again, I thought that if he was close to family and if we had the house that he wanted, perhaps he would focus more on his family. I was sad to leave, as I liked being inner city and was not keen on living in the suburbs. I justified the move as being another way to distance him from pubs, as our next house was not within walking distance of any pubs.

Edward was excited about moving into the new house, as it was bigger and better and there was lots to show off. What had I been thinking? Very soon, he started bringing the drinking home; nothing had changed. I would come home from work, and by the time I got home on the train, I arrived to a drunk husband and a dysfunctional home. The penny had finally dropped. I began to see that there was no hope for change, because try as I might, he had no intention to change. There was some underlying unhappiness that drove him to drinking and gambling, and I could not save him from that.

It was a lovely house, but things did not get any better. I was starting to get my feet on the ground. We were getting a bit ahead financially. When Deva had started high school, I got a request from my family in India. They had decided to have a big family reunion, and everyone that was family was going to India for this event. I did not want to go, but Edward was determined to go. We arranged a flight and borrowed money, and Edward already talked like we were millionaires going to show off to the poor people!

I was not excited about seeing family, but I thought it was a good opportunity to show Deva where I grew up and a good chance to introduce her to the country of my birth. We arrived in India; nothing had changed. Or was it that I had changed? I saw more clearly the caste system, the racism, the disrespect for the environment, the way servants were treated, and most of all, the hypocritical group of people I had left behind.

Deva embraced the opportunity and had a great time with her little cousins, and she blended into the country very well. It felt very strange seeing family. Australia had changed me; my challenges had moulded me. I felt alien in the country of my birth. There was no feeling of excitement to see any of my family, even though I could see that they were happy to see me. Seeing my mum brought tears to my eyes. I had neglected to stay in touch with her. I was too ashamed that my life had not been working out the way that she would have liked it to, but more so that I could not share my feelings with her or tell her that I would be leaving Edward the moment I returned to Australia.

I also saw that she was no longer that arrogant and controlling parent I had known; rather, she was mellow. I got the feeling that things were not good for her while staying with Maggy. It was hard for my mother, I guess, after being queen of her own home and managing everything herself, to suddenly be limited to a room with my sister; everything was now in Maggy's hands. I could see that she was not happy, and that saddened me. It was not how I had seen her when I left India. She now looked frail and very subdued. She just loved seeing Deva and me, and whilst the whole party was happening around us, amid all that pretentious behaviour, I could see very clearly the dysfunction within the whole family, the whole environment. I could not wait to go back to Australia.

Australia was my country now. This was the country that helped me mature; this was the country that had the potential to make me the person that I wanted to be. I was more Australian than I was Indian, and if I did not look in the mirror, I would think I was Australian. I wanted to go back home. I did not fit here any more; I did not belong here. I was already an Australian citizen, and I seemed to have this country in my blood. India was the country of my birth, but Australia was the country of my rebirth.

We decided to travel around India, and we took the whole family with us. We hired a combi Datsun, and if there was any enjoyment I got out of being there, this was it. We travelled south, east, and west. I was so happy to see my little brother. He looked so disconnected from the family, and although there was still that very special love between us, not much was said. I often wonder if he felt guilty because he had to ask me for financial help; I felt awkward because I had to refuse that help at the time he asked me, because I had not been in a position to help him then. We seemed not to have lost the love we had for each other, but there was a sad distance. . I could also see that he was not included in a lot of family events.

Status has a weird way of excluding family members. My parents had high expectations of themselves and, consequently, the same expectations of us children. Failure to measure up to those expectations can sometimes exclude siblings, because they feel like failures and have to bear the consequence of the exclusion, which is indirect but very obvious. I did not have the courage at the time to discuss this with Lenny; I wish I had been able to, but the chance passed me by. I was just keen to enjoy his company for whatever time I was there and avoid the difficult conversations. Whilst the rest of the family looked like a unit, Lenny and his family lived a distance away from them and seemed to be very disconnected from all of them.

Edward took up the limelight with his big spending of what he could not afford, but it did not concern me. I knew that, on my return, I would be leaving him. That was very heavy on my mind, and it was hard to hide this from my family. My sisters saw how different I was, and there was an obvious recognition that I was not going to put up with their bullying, especially Maggy. She tried, but there was no way I would let her succeed now.

It was at this time when I was visiting India that Phillis asked me to sponsor her and her family. I was not happy doing it, but Edward had already agreed that we would do so when we returned to Australia. It was an additional burden I did not want on myself, but it was a request I could not refuse. I had started to put my efforts into my independence and my well-being in preparation for the time that I would leave. I was too busy to even brood over how I was being treated. I tried hard to keep things pleasant and avoided any conflict. I was absolutely worn out by the arguing and bad energy around the house. It was an uncomfortable avoidance, but that was all I had to work with. Edward was also playing the game. I did not know what was going on in his head or how he thought things would pan out, but he knew I was getting ready to walk out on him. He had suddenly started to mellow and become comfortable. with the idea that we would be separating. It was an excuse for him to fall deeper into the alcohol and sink into his own world. He also was anticipating that with the sale of the house, he would come into some money and would be able to spend it on whatever he wanted. But that was not my concern. I had now become the deserter, and he had turned the pity on to himself.

When you have the courage to take those fearful steps, divine intervention converts those fearful steps into courage. Suddenly, that Rubik's cube clicks, and everything starts to fall into place. I was not born into this life to be abused. Those eyes in the sky were looking down on me as they always did. We did not even have to go to a real estate agent; we actually stuck a 'For Sale' sign at the front of our home, and it sold in a couple of weeks. I then found a solicitor in town, who handled the conveyancing. It was not long before the house was sold, and I had already started to pack what was mine to take away.

We had enough furniture and essentials to comfortably divide between the two of us, so there was no need to fight over what we would take possession of. I started to pack, and that was a very painful experience. Everything financial and material was split into two shares for each of us, except for one agreement—that we would put an equal amount away for Deva, as she was still a minor and my responsibility. We did not use our solicitor for the settlement; I wanted to put as less stress as possible not only on myself but on Edward as well. I could see that reality had started to get to him, and he drank a lot more. But rather than getting aggressive, he was very quiet. I would wait for him to go to bed before I would start to pack things that I needed to take away with me. I did not want either of us to end up financially or materially disadvantaged, and that was what I was working towards. Edward had also promised that if I went for divorce, he would not oppose and would sign the papers without any challenge, which I hoped to do as soon as possible.

His family had now got the news that we had decided to split, and as soon as the house was sold, the whole family dropped in for a private conversation with Edward. They wanted to make sure that I was not going to leave him and take everything with me. Suddenly he became their concern when the situation was about money.

I had already signed up for a two-bedroom unit in Carnegie to rent, and all my belongings and Deva's were packed. Edward watched the whole process as I went through the packing, but rather than discussing anything with me, he continued to drink even more excessively. When he was drunk, he would then try to communicate. The conversations were pitiful and tearful, mostly about how much he loved me and did not want to lose me, but I had heard it all before. The words were slurred by the drinking, and it was not the sincerity but the drink talking. I was not interested in that because it was pathetic; it was too late for all that. I did not want that to cloud my plans. I was angry that, at this late stage, he was starting to voice his feelings. They did not mean anything to me any more. That made me sad. I did not love Edward, but I had committed to this marriage and had exhausted every bone in my body trying any which way to save it. I had given chances, I had begged for change, and I had cried my heart out. Now with my heart broken into tiny pieces, with only my little girl holding them together, I was ready to take my next step, not knowing what to expect, but going with courage.

It was the night before I was to leave. The removal truck was booked, and Edward was drinking in excess that night. I did not know what possessed me, but I just needed to ask one more time. I walked up to him and said I would take it all back if he would do as I asked and give up his drinking and seek professional help. I think I really meant it. I just wanted things to work for us, to work for Deva, but his words sealed the deal. He said that he would never ever do that and that I should go because it was all over anyway. I realised it was his pride talking, because his behaviour indicated to me that he was going to regret all this.

Pride—I know very well how damaging it can be. What the hell? Do we need to harbour pride in love? Shedding pride allows vulnerability to show through and makes one more human. It takes a lot of courage to apologise, to acknowledge your bad behaviour, to admit that you're wrong and to ask for help. I knew I was expecting what he just could not give me. I know how hard it is to carry a false sense of pride when deep down you are broken and vulnerable. I had no pride; this marriage had taken every bit of that, and I was happy for that. I was beginning to understand how much I would trade for love, but I also understood that I could grow to love someone yet not like them. Whilst most things are negotiable, it has to also be mutual. I learned to respect myself enough to not want to be treated this way.

The next day, I packed the car. It had been with him for a long time. Deva was a teenager now, and his abuse had started to flow on to her. He did not let her dress the way she wanted to; he did not like the friends she hung out with. She could see that she would be subjected to the same abuse I had been through. She was already getting a lot of unwanted verbal abuse; I knew if I did not make the move, she would move out of the home, and all would be lost. It was what I had been waiting for. There was no stopping me now.

As the furniture truck drove away, I felt my heart sink. Was this really happening? Was this the end of my 'happy family' dream? With Deva in the car with me and the rest of our personal stuff in the back, I was ready to drive away. I noticed that Edward hung around the house as if there was nowhere else he could be, and he was hugging our dog. I had wanted to take Hugo with me, as he was my dog, but I thought I had better leave Edward with some affection. Dogs were good at that. He used to always bring dogs home, and as soon as they got challenging, he would give them away. So I knew that before long, Hugo would be subjected to the same thing. I was aware that, at a later stage, Hugo would be back with me, as I did not want him to be given away like all the other dogs we had. As soon as I became stable and had the space to accommodate a dog, I planned to get him back.

Earlier in my marriage with Edward, I used to blame myself. I needed to make things better. I needed to become what he wanted to win his love. Perhaps he was the way he was because of me. But today, on the day of my leaving him, I was sure. It was not me. This was his baggage, given the circumstances of his growing up. However, it was not an excuse for his refusal to get the help he needed. We all get damaged by tragic circumstances at some stage in our lives. We can carry the baggage, or we can deal with it. The opportunity is there; we just need to seek the help we need. For me, it was the right courses, the empowering books, and all the positive learnings that came from my meditations and yoga classes that gave me the knowledge to respect and love myself. We just can't use our past to define us and consequently stunt our self-growth.

I said goodbye to him, and my feelings were that of sadness. I did not hate the guy, but yes, I disliked a lot in his behaviour. I had to stay strong, as I did not want my little girl to fall apart herself. I accelerated out of the driveway, my eyes on the rear-vision mirror, and I saw that as we drove away, he burst into tears and cried uncontrollably. I cried too as I paused. I looked at him for a few moments before getting on the road. It took a lot of courage to drive away, away from a life I had worked so hard to hold together. I kept going. To walk back and console him would be detrimental; there was no turning back now. The drive was very emotional, not only for me but also for my little girl. We both knew we needed to go, but we would have rather that it worked out so we could stay a family. I would never know what was going on in Deva's head, but we had no time to discuss anything. We were done talking. It was time to make the move and take the consequences when they came.

After all, this was her dad. She loved him. It was tearing her apart inside, but she had no option. She was just doing what I thought was best for her, and I hoped she knew that. But the damage was done. There would be a lot of challenges for her. It does not matter how much we try to protect our children; they will have their own challenges and sometimes have to face it head-on. In all my dreams, there was never a moment that I saw myself in this position. But I had walked away, finally. I had made the move, and I was sure that I had built up the strength this time never to succumb to his requests for a reconciliation. I wanted better not only for me but for Deva as well. Staying this long was long enough, but leaving any earlier would have been a bigger disaster, because I would not have had the mental strength to hold on to the separation. This time I was broken, but I was emotionally, mentally, and spiritually strong. I was going to make this work. I was a separated woman, a single mother, not sure of what the future looked like.

I now had a teenage daughter, dependent on me and totally confused with her life, and I had no idea how we were going to make this work. We just had to. This was my life, and I had the right to find my happiness. But it was not just about me.

WHO ARE YOU?

Relationships are a mirror of who I am. Most times, what I do not like in the reflection is something I do not like about myself, so the change starts with me.

Now I was on my own, with the responsibility of a teenage daughter. I was a single parent, but then that was what I had been for a long time. Yes, I had learnt that loving a man is not enough; I have to truly like him. I had grown to love Edward, but by the time I had decided to leave him, I knew I would never turn back, because I had given him every opportunity to want me to stay. I could have lived another lifetime with him, but I would never be able to change him. That was not my role. He had to want to change.

We had moved into the rental unit in Carnegie. I hated having to rent again, but I had not settled on a house and would review my situation when all the monies were in. This was only going to be a temporary arrangement. Now my challenges of being a single mother began. Deva had started to get a mind of her own and discovered that things were going to be different now that we were on our own. She would not have all the things that she could have with two incomes; we had to survive on just my income. I was determined to buy even a small place so we could have somewhere we could be permanently. I invested whatever small amount I ended up with after the sale of the house and the settlement of monies in the purchase of our own place when the opportunity presented itself.

Edward never came up with the money that we agreed on for Deva's education and did not contribute anything for her expenses after we left, but all that became of little importance. I was just happy to have my life back and to not have him crushing my spirit. To lick his wounds, he decided to blow all his share of the money on travel, which was his choice. However, I got to know this because, on his return, he called me. I was at work on the day he called. He was crying on the phone. He had spent all the money and was now broke and was asking me to lend him some money. No way was that going to happen. I had moved on and was not going to look back. He had had his opportunity and kicked it in the face. It hurt, but I asked him never to call me again. It was truly over; I had moved on.

I realised that I needed to get back into circulation and reach out to some of the mutual friends that we had. The last thing I wanted to do was to hide away and withdraw into a lonely solitary world. The harsh realisation I had was that some of them felt they had to make a choice; consequently, I lost some of our mutual friends. The sincere and true friends, whilst they did not cut contact with Edward, had the maturity to think differently and understand that we were friends irrespective of what had happened. I am so grateful for their friendship. I do not consider them friends any more; they are family to me because they treat me as family, and I love them very much for that. I also began to notice that some of the women that I knew were starting to get uncomfortable with having me around, because their husbands were at risk, and some of their partners were starting to look at me as free bait. I had no intention of getting into a relationship; I had just got out of one. I was going to enjoy my freedom and my life. I had no intention of stealing anyone's husband. I might have been broken, but I was not desperate!

I was starting to feel good about myself physically. I was now a size 8, and I was able to dress the way I wanted to. I have always loved clothes and the way I looked in them, and I had a creative way with the whole process. Getting dressed was now a ritual for me. I had to thank my mother for that. She always dressed well, and that was her expectation of all her children. However, even since I was a little girl, I had my own unique way I wanted to look. I created my own individual style. When I was a little girl, it was crushed, but I had control now and every opportunity to express myself in the way I dressed. I had a body I had worked so hard at and was not uncomfortable showing it off. It was not about attracting attention. For the first time in a long time, I liked the way I looked and the clothes I wore, and I was working towards feeling good about myself, with the empowered feeling that comes from walking away from what was not right for me. I had the freedom to look, speak, and act the way I wanted—to breathe without being accountable!

To wear the clothes I liked, I was conscious that I needed to be a size 8, even if it meant starving myself. And I did just that. I hardly ate. I wanted to show off this body that I had, and the more revealing the clothes were, the better, so long as it was not slutty, which I could not be. I had my own style of dressing and always attracted attention with the way I dressed. I remember the dress I wore a couple of days before I left Edward. It was a black dress and fitted me like a glove and tapered out from the waist to a few inches above my knee, and it had a loop in the hem, with little pink roses all around the hem. It looked so gorgeous, and more than that, it felt great. It felt so rewarding, as I was able to choose and pay for the dress I wanted, and irrespective of anyone else's opinion, I liked what I saw in the mirror. This was how I wanted to look at this time. It was the first night I had gone out on my own, without Edward. I loved dancing, and that was a big part of my social life.

I still had membership at the Anglo-Indian club. Whilst I was married, I never enjoyed going to their functions; they were not happy times for me. Things were different now. Now that I was on my own, with my daughter a teenager now, it gave me the freedom to go out and socialise. It was more important for me to stay in touch, so when my friends asked me to accompany them to a social dance night, I did not hesitate. We usually booked a table, and this time there were about ten of us at the table. I had an indication of who was going to be at our table, and I was looking forward to this night. I liked the idea of everyone dressing formally and looking their best. This time I could look my best too.

It had now been six months since I had left Edward. I had been getting a few phone calls from him, begging me to return, but I knew I could not and would not. I had no problem with keeping contact with him because there was no way I was ever going back. I did not want to give any indication that there was a chance to renew the relationship. I wanted that door shut, but I was open to Deva keeping in touch with her dad if that was what she wanted; she would have all my support to do that. I know Edward had not expected me to walk out; he did not realise that I had the determination and inner strength to do it, and his karma was that he regretted every minute that I was not in his life. Isn't it sad? When we have something in front of us that we love, we take it for granted. We abuse it; we make no effort to love and cherish it. And when it is not there, we miss it.

I felt really good as I sat at the table that night. It was as if I had died and come back in a different body. It felt different. I felt attractive for the first time in my life, and that was empowering. I was ready for this new life, even though I was not sure what it was going to look like. I had left my abusive marriage, but had I learnt all the lessons I needed to? I no longer felt that broken person and weak spirit. I was attracting a lot of attention, and this night, I was there on my own for the first time. It is amazing the energy you radiate when you feel good about yourself. I had a confidence that came from the decisions I had made and the person I had become, and that was the aura I was giving out.

Sometime in the middle of the night, I noticed a very attractive gentleman sitting at the table. We made eye contact a few times. He was the only stranger and person that I did not know at our table. I was surprised to see a new face and wondered what his connection was to our group. He introduced himself, and I was not instantly attracted to him. I was just intoxicated with the high I was on in being out for the first time in six months since my separation. I was happy to be this way. I had no idea at this stage that my life would change so much.

Relationships have a way of reflecting who you are. I was to start a journey of relationships, and even though I would misunderstand them because of my expectations, it would become very clear to me as I grew spiritually that the relationships I had were not meant to be about marriage and permanency. It was about growth and the universe bringing the right people into my life when I needed them, and every one of them had a purpose. I am forever grateful to all the men that have allowed me to see my reflection in them and make the changes I needed to. My relationships were never about attachment; rather, they were about spiritual growth.

I was to learn the bitter lesson of attachment. I was meant to make connections to enhance my life, and in this life, every time that I tried to attach myself—whether it was with family, friends, or relationships—I had a rude awakening. Some come into your life and stay, and there are others that stay for a short while. Everyone is precious and deserves to be there. Then there are some that leave, and as much as I may want them to stay, I have to let them go, because to hold on is futile.

Grant asked me to dance. He was tall, dark, and handsome, and he was very attracted to me. Did I say tall? He was six feet, six inches. He towered over me, but it did not seem to bother him, even though I felt a bit uncomfortable with his height. The added attraction was that he could dance, and more than that, he loved dancing. That was a tick in my box. We danced all night, and there were times on that floor that it got very erotic. I did not restrict him, as I was there for a good night and presumed that it was just a one-night thing and that I would never see him again. . Sometime during the night, in our conversations, he had worked out that I was separated and living on my own. I understood from his side of the conversation that he was divorced, had a daughter, and was house sharing with a couple of friends. At the end of the night, he asked if he could come by for a coffee.

Deva was now going out a lot with friends and would sometimes stay the night at their place. She was going through a 'not so cool to be with Mum' stage, so I was hoping that she would not come home that night, as I felt it was too soon for her to see me with another man. She was already going through a lot, and I was getting the brunt of all her frustrations. It was something I had taken on; after all, I walked out on her father. I would just have to cruise through it all.

I invited Grant for a coffee, so he drove me home. We sat on the couch at my place and talked, and before too long, we were kissing. It was what I had expected. His lips felt so good on mine, and I knew from that first kiss that there would be more. It was not awkward, and I felt very comfortable with taking this as far as we wanted it to go. My marriage had been so devoid of any good sex; this felt like heaven. Before long, we had our clothes off and were on the floor. Grant handled my body like he knew every part in detail; he was gentle and aggressive, and nothing was out of bounds. But there was one thing he could not achieve that night, and it was an erection. It must have been the excitement, or perhaps it was because it was our first night together. But it did not seem to bother him at all. I liked his confidence. We moved on, and I felt very comfortable sitting there naked with him. Although not much good conversation happened that night, I was happy to have him around and glad that I had asked him over. It was like having a big friendly giant around.

I was surprising myself with the fearless changes I was accepting in my life. I was going to give this night a go, irrespective of whether anything came of it. He had a lot of sexual confidence. He was comfortable in his own skin. I had already had multiple orgasms that night. He did not have to go all the way. I was glad that we did not have intercourse, because I did not have any condoms at home. I had not expected to get this far this soon. I realised then that I needed to equip myself with condoms, in all sizes, after this encounter. I was very particular about safe sex, especially as, at this stage, I thought it was a one-night stand. I was not prepared to meet other men and for things to move so fast. I was not ready for a full-blown relationship.

I was keen for him to leave my unit before Deva got home, so he left very early in the morning. Just as well, as it gave me enough time to tidy up before she got there late morning. I did not think it important to mention it, as I was not expecting anything to eventuate. I could not keep it from her for very long. The next day, when I returned home from work, there were a dozen of the most beautiful red roses outside my front door. I did not think it meant much except that he had enjoyed the night. It was meant to be; Grant was meant to come into my life. It was a time when my self-esteem had taken a battering, and I welcomed someone like him because he made me feel special. That was worth something even if it was short-lived. We would talk for hours on the phone, as he lived a couple of hours away from Melbourne, and when we saw each other, it was hours of sex. We just could not get enough. He said the right things and did the right things, and he put me up on a pedestal; it felt great to be there! I needed that. My ego was crying out for it at the time.

The first time I saw his penis erect, I freaked out. 'No way are you getting that up me!' But he had very gentle ways of introducing me to whatever he did, and I started to feel so comfortable with him. There was a purpose for having him in my life; it would build my sense of self. He had a way of making me feel beautiful and very attractive and, most of all, loved. What I thought was a one-night stand was now more than that. Grant wanted to hang around.

It was the best I felt and looked at the time, and I took advantage of every minute I had with him. Six months into my knowing him, he said he loved me and asked me to marry him. I could not define my feelings for him, as it was too early after my separation, and I wanted to experience life a lot more before I committed to anything. How could six months of a relationship give any indication of a lifelong commitment? I just could not believe I was hearing that, and I saw the disappointment on his face at my reaction. I had only just got out of a tough marriage. He knew that. How could he expect such a commitment from me? At the time, I did discuss with him that it was too soon for me to be making such decisions. We were less than six months into the relationship, and I was not even sure whether this was love or if I was just infatuated with the man.

Edward had killed my belief in marriage. If I could not make one marriage work, was it worth trying yet another one? I was not even ready to have a man in my space for longer. than I wanted him there. How would I be able to handle it 24/7? I became a challenge to him, and he worked on getting me to love him. . Grant continuously told me that he loved me, even though I could not bring those words to my mouth. Whilst it was nice to hear, I was not prepared to use those words unless it meant something. He treated me to expensive dinners, we went out dancing at nightclubs, and he showered me with gifts. It was as if I was the only woman around when he was with me. He treated me in a very special way. Was this too good to be true? I was not letting my mind go there, because I wanted to enjoy every moment of this feel-good experience. Was this the 'waiting for the other shoe to drop' syndrome?

I spent a lot more time with Grant and began to love having him around. I was settling into the relationship; we had moved from the honeymoon stage and were now in the middle of everyday things. I had introduced Grant to a lot of my friends, and he was liked by all of them. He had a charm that allowed everyone to believe that he was a great catch and a dedicated partner. We looked the perfect couple. There were some subtle behaviour changes, which I did not dwell too much on, as it is expected that you see the real person sometime into the relationship. There were times I would not be able to contact him; there were times that he would find some excuse to leave for no reason. His behaviour was erratic, but I had no reason to question it. I am not a jealous person. I gave every person that came into my life a time limit and then ultimate trust. He would spend some weekends at my place, but when he had night shifts to do, he would stay at his pad, as he would sleep for most of the day. I had absolute trust in him and had no doubt, based on the way he treated me, that he truly loved me and was a stayer.

There was an underlying concern about his strange behaviour. He gave me no explanation about it. I did not feel I had a right to ask, as I had not fully committed to the relationship. I wondered if it was because I had not accepted his offer of marriage, but it was not going to make me change my mind until I felt it was appropriate, until I felt I was ready. I did not want any more from him; I was happy to commit to the relationship but not to a marriage. If he did not tell me every day, he told me a million times that he loved me. I was not going to allow any doubt to creep in.

One day he turned up at my place with two tickets to Perth. His family lived there, and he wanted for me to meet them. We had a lovely holiday, but I noticed that he was a very different self when he was with his family. It was as if they knew something that I did not know. I had started to see some character changes, but I was not ready to face the facts. I loved my life and having him in it, and I did not want that to change.

We had been on a few holidays together, and these were always good times. It was no different to any new relationship. We started to spend a lot of weekends together, sometimes at his place and most of the time at my place. He had a strong interest in football, which I loved, so we started going to the games a lot together. I converted from Hawthorn, which was my team at that time, to Geelong, because he lived and breathed that team. Grant had a lot of influence with the team too; at the games, he would take me over to the change rooms, and I would get to see the players. He gave me a surprise at work and got one of the players to call me, and one of them invited me over to the change rooms for the next game. That was one offer I was not going to take up! He had a tremendous knowledge of the players and the history of the club, and it was nice being at the games because I was new to football and could rely on him for all the information I needed. For the first time, I was starting to understand a lot more about the game and developing my interest in the team and the game. I loved everything about football, especially in those days, as it was more about the game and there were no drugs or bad behaviour evident.

I had also moved from the unit, as it was too small. I had not realised that with Deva staying with me, there would at times be four to five of her friends hanging around and sometimes staying over. It had started to be crowded. I wanted her to have her own space, and I wanted to encourage her to bring her friends home and make our home theirs as well. I had friends living in Glen Huntly who told me of a house there that had come up for rent. They knew the owners and would be able to recommend that we get tenancy of the house. I took the opportunity to move out of the two-bedroom and into the four-bedroom house. It was an old house, but there was enough room for my life and Deva's without us getting on top of each other. It was a big house. I took a chance and asked Edward for Hugo, my dog, back. I had the space for a dog now, and I was afraid that if I waited any longer, he would be given away. I missed him. Edward agreed, so I had a companion to walk with and to have around me. I felt safe with him around.

It was possible to have Hugo whilst I rented the house, but I knew that sometime in the future, if I decided to purchase something, it would be only a unit or flat and it would not be possible for me to keep him. When that opportunity came, I would ask my sister's son, who had a great relationship with Hugo, to take him. I loved Hugo a lot, as he was a Mother's Day gift to me and came to me as a little pup. He followed me everywhere and won my love. I did not choose him; he chose me.

The only reason I agreed to let Zak have him was that he loved him very much and I would be able to visit him whenever I was able to. I watched Zak with Hugo, and I saw the connection between them; I knew that Hugo would be looked after. When I did eventually purchase a flat in Glen Huntly, I asked Zak whether he would look after the dog for me, and he was glad to. Unfortunately, not too long after, I was at work and got a call from my sister saying that Hugo had been in an accident. Zak had been walking him when two Rottweilers that were left on a property with no owners had grabbed him and dragged him under the fence and massacred him. He was torn open in the belly, bleeding very badly but still alive. That traumatised Zak as well. They had taken Hugo to the vet and called me to ask whether I wanted him to have an operation to close the gap in his belly. He had already lost a lot of blood and would not be the same after the operation. I asked them to request that he be put down.

I did not know how much I loved that dog until I got the news and got home. I sat in the kitchen, on a little stool, and wept my heart out. My dog was gone, and I would never see him ever again. He had been the closest thing to unconditional mutual love, and I would miss him very much. Sitting on that stool, I made a pact with myself that I would never have a pet if I was not going to be able to find the time to give him the attention and the space that a dog deserved. Hugo was no special breed, but he was a very special animal and loved me very much. He was my dog; he was always around me. I missed him for a long time after.

Deva was enjoying the vastness of the house; she had two rooms to herself, and there were always friends of hers over. They would lock themselves up in her room. I never knew what they got up to, but that did not concern me. I wanted her to be happy doing the things she wanted to and in her home. Grant had gone away on another trip to Perth to visit his family, and whilst he was up there, I did not hear from him. I decided to call him. He seemed a bit aloof on the phone, and I surprised him by saying that I was planning to take some time off work and join him there for a bit of a break. I missed not having him around and thought this would be a good opportunity to have a holiday and spend time with him.

He did not like the sound of that and said to me that it was no good for me to come up, as he was not going to be there but was going away with friends. I got that strange feeling in my stomach, the feeling you get when you know something is not quite right. I was starting to have doubts about his sincerity. Grant was a very attractive man. He had a charisma that any woman would be attracted to; all my friends were. The question in my mind was, had he found someone whilst he was away? Did he have the capacity not to be intimate with any woman whilst he was not with me, considering the high sexual drive that he had?

We were not very long in the rented house. I had started to get uncomfortable with money being spent paying someone else's mortgage. I wanted to get a little place that I owned because I did not want to be on the move all the time. The old house was starting to become like most rented properties, needing a lot of renovation but with nothing being done. I decided that if I was going to move again, it would be into a place that I owned. I also started to realise that with Deva being my responsibility, I needed to be careful with my money so I could afford the expenses that came with having a teenage daughter. I bought a two-bedroom flat inner city. It was very minimal, but it had a room for Deva and most of what I had fitted into the flat, even though it was a bit crammed. It was on the ground floor and had a parking spot for my car. It was much smaller than what I was used to, but it was central to shops and transport. Most of all, I could drive to work, as I had a parking spot at work as well.

Grant was certain that the relationship we had was permanent. I was always receiving flowers from him at work, and everyone in my circle of friends now knew that we were permanent partners. We went to a lot of work functions and social functions, and we were the most popular couple amongst our friends. We were a great couple. I had no further expectations and accepted our relationship for what it was. He moved some of his essentials into my place and settled in well; it was where he spent most of his time. He worked night shifts some weeks, and it made it very hard for us to function, as I had to softly tread about the flat when he was sleeping. It was challenging, but I accepted it as part of our lives and tried to make it work. I think what I learnt about myself at this time was that I could be flexible for the ones I loved, and I was beginning to love Grant.

And then one day, I came home from work, and all his furniture was gone. The flat was in a mess. I did not know what to make of it. He returned in the evening in a very bad mood and said things were not going to work out between us. He took the rest of his things that were there and left. I was devastated; it was as if my world had come to an end once again. How could this have happened to me? Why in hell did

I attract this behaviour? Hell, he had not even had a good reason, and if he did, he had not given me any indication of that. Yes, I cried that whole night when he left. But tomorrow was a new day, and I had decided I would be a new person. I wanted to explore the man's world. I wanted to get out there and treat men the way they treated me. I was not sure whether it was the right decision, but it was all part of the experience of finding out who I really wanted to be. I had to find a way to redirect this anger that I felt for Grant's unexpected treatment of me, but I was not going to waste my time feeling sorry for myself.

I started going out to nightclubs on my own. I had let Clyde know that I had separated and had my own place now. I always stayed in touch with him but got on with my life, as I had started to see very clearly what Clyde's purpose in my life was. He was the angel that kicked my arse to get me to move on with my life and become who I wanted to be. Grant was the person that revived the self-esteem that I had lost in my marriage. Yes, he was not in my life any more, but my self-esteem did not leave with him.

Deva spent a lot of time at her boyfriend's place, so Clyde was able to visit me as often as he wanted to at the flat. He was in the process of separating from his wife and was planning to purchase a place of his own. I loved the idea that he could now visit me at home. We picked up where we had left off. What I liked about Clyde was, he was not just interested in the intimate moments with me. We had truly deep chats. We had cleared it up in earlier conversations that I was not leaving my marriage because I wanted something permanent with him. We both knew that our relationship was on a different level. It was now nice to be able to see him more often and in better surroundings unlike motel rooms. I understood that my relationship with Grant was over; I was free to see others. I would not make my relationship with Clyde exclusive. We had that understanding. We were friends with benefits, and we were both happy to leave it at that.

I would work 9 a.m.–5 p.m., come home and have a bit of a sleep, wake up and get ready at 11 p.m., and go out, most times to mature nightclubs. I started to be very comfortable with going out by myself. I spent a lot on clothes and looking good but different. I liked the feeling I got when I walked into a club with no need to be in a group of people. It was empowering. I knew all eyes were on me when I walked into a nightclub. I was shallow enough at the time to feel empowered by the fact that men just could not take their eyes away from me. Women normally went to these places in groups, but I had the confidence to go on my own and leave on my own. I loved dancing and music, and I was never short of a partner on the floor. I had my favourite mature nightclubs I would go to, and I started to follow certain bands to where they played. I realised that I was doing these things much later in my life, but my marriage had deprived me of such enjoyment; life was going to allow me that, irrespective. I had put my life on hold the whole time I was married, and it was never too late to kick up my heels! There were a lot of exclusive clubs that catered to mature women, and these were the ones I frequented.

I had mentioned to Clyde that my relationship with Grant was over, and he seemed very happy about that because now he was free to call in any time he wanted to visit me. He brought me books that were all about empowerment and building up on self-worth. I had a chat with him about wanting to be sexually independent as well. I did not want a man to define my sexuality. I had attended a few sexually empowering courses and realised that women need to be sexually independent so they will not have to depend on a man for sex. I wanted to make men dispensable. I just needed to want them in my life, not need them.

I asked Clyde whether he would accompany me to an adult shop. I needed to do some serious sex toy shopping. I could have as much unemotional sex as I wanted. I could have orgasms at any time and any place I wanted. It was interesting walking into the local adult shop. That was an experience. I had not seen so many moving plastic objects, and it was no different from shopping at the local supermarket. There were shelves of so many gadgets, of every colour and for every purpose. Having Clyde with me for the first time made it less intimidating. Besides, he had a few suggestions which were helpful. Clyde purchased what I wanted, and I returned with a few sexual tools that were going to keep me satisfied and independent of men for my sexual needs. I had my very own sexual toolbox, which became a permanent accessory that I would keep updated and available for play any time I needed it.

I had a girlfriend who was single and found it very hard to get into relationships. She shared with me her desire to take her sexual well-being into her own hands. We were at a lunch together when she told us about her encounters with her vibrator. She could have as many orgasms as she wanted at any time of the day, and she said when she walked down the street and saw couples and single men and women on the streets, she felt like the cat that had got the milk. Had they had as many orgasms as she had had though it was barely eleven in the morning? I liked that story. It came in useful at this time in my life. It was what influenced my desire to buy my toys.

I also discovered that there was a female-only adult shop in the city. It was the most comfortable place for any woman to walk in and walk out with a bunch of goodies and feel like she had just walked out of a supermarket. The lady that ran the shop used to hold sex talks for women and have conversations and seminars on sex for one, along with other empowering sessions, which I went to a lot. I got a lot from them as well. I had my toolbox now, and it replaced men in my life. I just did not want to be hurt by another man ever again. The best thing Clyde did for me was give me a book by Louise Hay. He said it was a book that had empowered him to leave his unpleasant marriage and feel the love for himself. I stuck my head into it and did not look up until I had read the whole book. It was the book and the author that changed my life entirely. I read all her books and more of similar authors, and I used their techniques to bring positivity into my life. I started to feel a new sense of joy. This was the start of my spiritual self-discovery.

I started to read books that had meaning, books that I would learn something from, books that would inspire me. I did not want authors that wrote fiction; I read authors that had empowering stories to tell. I focused a lot on writing journals and gratitude journals. There was not a book I read which did not have something that I could learn from. I had another journal for copying interesting quotes from the books I read so I could touch base when I needed inspiration. I started to understand the person that I wanted to be. I had to discard the person that I did not like first. I had the realisation that this was a temporary me and that the day would come when it would all look ugly to me and I would not be enjoying it any more. For now, I decided to carry on regardless, until that day dawned on me. To get to who I wanted to be, I had to experience and then eliminate what I did not like about myself, and then I would be on that path of discovery. I was well on that path, but I wanted to pause and have some fun and enjoy that process.

I felt very empowered with the life I was leading. I was earning a good wage, I was very popular at work, I had a lot of friends, and my life was becoming exciting. I could buy anything I wanted and do anything I liked because I had the finances for that. I started phone dating. It was very different from today's Tinder and dating apps; nevertheless, it was available at the time, and I used it. Most times I would talk over the phone with intending suitors and realise I did not want to ever see them. I would talk to a lot of men and give them the impression that they had an opportunity to have a date with me. I had the greatest pleasure in not returning their calls, and sometimes I would call and be quite brutal about why I had no intention of going any further with them. I had lost myself there for a while, and most of all, I had lost respect for men. Why should I treat them any differently than how they thought it was appropriate to treat me? I felt indispensable and took advantage of that feeling. Not only did I learn that most of these dating sites were for desperados, but I also learned a lot about what I did not like in men and in myself.

There was, however, one guy that I agreed to meet. I had been speaking to him for a long time before we both decided that it would be good to meet. We decided to meet at a cafe in Elsternwick. I was walking up the street to meet him; he was wearing a suit and carrying a red rose in his hand. I had barely said hello to him before he grabbed me in his arms and started kissing me in the middle of the street. He was all over me, as if we had been together for ages. It embarrassed me; I had not expected this. It was as if he had decided that our conversations had entitled him to this behaviour. I had no intention of jumping in. I had a fair idea of who he was sexually, but that alone does not make a man. Whilst I was happy to continue seeing him irregularly, that was all it was going to be. It was becoming so obvious that most of these men were on these dating sites for one purpose only—what they did not want to pay a brothel for.

It took only a couple of times of us going out before I invited him over for a drink at my home. I was keen to find out a bit more about him; he seemed nice enough, but that did not tell me anything. I was sitting on the couch, having a conversation with him about his day, and what he said shocked me. He had spent the day with a woman. he had randomly met. He was obsessed with her. It was at this time that he went on to tell me that he was planning to rape the woman. I must have zoned out in the middle of his conversation, because I could not believe what I was hearing. He had done it a couple of times and always managed to convince the woman that she had agreed to it. I did not hear anything else after that because all I kept thinking was, was I the next woman? I had presence of mind. Or was it divine intervention in my life again? I walked to the front door, which was only a couple of steps away; opened it so everyone in the block could hear me; and in a very loud voice, asked him to leave and never contact me again. I did take a lot of innocent risks, but isn't that what life is all about? This could have gone in another direction, but it did not. I have always believed that I am protected, as long as my intentions are genuine, and this time it was no different.

I was in control, and despite his murmuring that he would never do that to me, my words were 'Get the fuck out of here before I call the police'. He slowly walked past me to the door and did not even look back at me. My heart was pounding because I was not certain of what could happen. I was not sure whether it was a fantasy or if he was for real. Why did he feel that he needed to tell me that? I sat back on my couch, my heart beating very fast, after he had left. Taking risks was my sure way of finding my experiences. I wondered, did I want to change that? How would I then get to experience people? Was this a safe way to do it? I did not make the decision right away, but it was not too long before I decided this was one risk I had to give up. There were two risks here: I could have been the next victim, or he had been looking for a safety net, as most rapists do to take the suspicion off them.

Grant had a way of appearing on the scene. He always had a convincing story. I did not believe anything he told me now; there was no trust any more. But I could not resist him. I approached my relationship with him this time with a lot more caution, sexually and personally. He had no convincing explanation for his erratic behaviour, so I was not going to commit to the relationship but would take it for what it was with a lot of caution and protection. He called me. We had a chat over the phone, and before long, we were in each other's arms. It felt good to see him again. We had had no closure and were happy to pick up where we had left off. There were no questions asked. The chemistry that we had between us was so physical we just could not resist it. I made it very clear to him that it would not be exclusive now and that my life would no longer be dedicated to him. I could see that he did not like it very much, but who was he to dictate to me when he was sporadic in my life?

I had accumulated some long service leave and decided I would do a bit of travel. I had made a deal with myself that I would travel as much as I could around Australia. I had started doing little bits of travel on my own, but my intention was to see as much of Australia as I wanted. This was my country now, and I wanted to see every bit of its beauty and its ruggedness. I was going to start ticking off every city, every attraction, every corner of this vast country until I had seen it all. I had no intention of going overseas until I had seen as much of Australia as I wanted. What sense did it make to travel to other countries when I had not seen all of the country that I lived in? I loved the outback, the colours, and the stories. Travel was my new drug.

I wanted to see every corner of Australia, but more so its outback. That is what its history is about. The people of that land were the true Australians. I needed to gain an understanding of that. Australia is such a vast country, and I had to split up my travel and see pieces of it between leave periods. I spent a small fortune on my travel within Australia. I could have travelled the world twice over for that price, but I would not trade that for anything. I saw such jaw-dropping beauty; I was in awe. I was spiritually and emotionally transformed by Australia's beauty. I could travel to any other part of the world; I am sure that I would see a lot and that it would be beautiful, but it is only just different beauty! The world could wait until I was satisfied that I had seen the country I lived in and learned all I needed to about it.

As I was growing up in India, travel was very minimal, and I did not have the finances to discover the beauty of that country. It was only when I went back when Deva was around fourteen that I travelled and saw a bit of the country of my birth. Being single, I found it challenging to see the country by car. I did not like driving on my own. I decided that I would arrange to do a tour to kick-start my trip. I had Central Australia in mind. Grant decided that the two of us should do it together by road. At the last minute, he cancelled, with absolutely no reason. But that had become repetitive behaviour; he would sway his commitment with some lame excuse. I was very disappointed, but it was what I had expected of him. I had taken the leave to go. I had become familiar with his instability and learnt not to depend on him.

I made other plans. A couple that were friends of mine at the time were going on a cruise and asked me to go along with them. It was not really what I wanted to do. Cruising had never turned me on. Why would I want to be stuck on a ship, surrounded by water, with a bunch of the same faces day in and day out? I was not keen, however, to waste my holidays. I decided I would go with them. They had plans to stay in Queensland for a while after, and I would be able to tag along with them if I wanted to. I was not particularly interested in cruising the New Zealand islands, but it would be an experience. I decided to give it a go.

They were also friends of Grant's. In a conversation they had with him, they mentioned that I was accompanying them on the cruise, and he asked if he could come along. They had booked a cabin for four, so there was room for another person. They asked me if I had any objection to that, but there was nothing I liked more. I just did not seem capable of shutting him out of my life, and I agreed to him coming along. It was a four-berth cabin, and there was room for him. There was every indication that Grant was cheating on me, but I just did not want to believe it. I loved him, and there was a glimmer of hope in me that he felt the same. I toyed with the thought that he might be losing interest because he had asked me to marry him and I had stalled. Even though the breaks in our relationship were frequent, it did not take even five minutes before we could connect as if nothing mattered. But it was not a stable enough situation for me to commit to anything permanent. What I did not know was not going to hurt me.

We met Grant in Sydney before boarding the boat, and we took off on a wonderful holiday together. It was the best time we ever had, because both Grant and I were party animals. We slept in and spent most of our day locked in the cabin room, as our friends needed to know that there was no access for the time that the door was locked. We took advantage of all the facilities available on the ship and partied all night at the many clubs on board. We danced, we got crazy, we drank a lot, and it was perfect. We got off at the islands of New Caledonia, Vanuatu, and another little island where the ship docked, and we made the most of all the sights to see and the adventures to experience.

It was in the very early hours of the morning, when we were at one of the bars, both of us absolutely out of our minds as we had been drinking and dancing all night, when there was a sudden feeling that the boat had become still. We were out in the middle of the ocean, and one of the engines had burnt out. All the emergency procedures started to fall into place. Just as well I had enough alcohol in me, because rather than panic like most of the others did, both Grant and I got another drink and walked over to the deck. I had resigned myself to the thought that if the boat went down, I'd want to drown rather than survive on a lifeboat, especially since I was not a swimmer. Besides, it seemed a better solution than spending more time in a lifeboat with some of the people who had been on the boat. I couldn't do that! I had had enough of them already, including the couple that we had travelled with.

Before commencing the cruise, we had all been shown the emergency procedure, but I was amazed how much panic had already spread amongst the travellers. Everyone was running around the boat aimlessly and running into each other to get to the lifeboats. I took a few deep breaths and sipped my cocktail with no concern about what could happen. We survived the cruise; the engine was fixed, and glory be, we carried on with the rest of the cruise. Today, if I won a free cruise, I would give it away, as it is not something I ever want to do again. But again, it was an experience.

Grant and I decided that we would do a bit of travel. We managed to see a fair deal of New South Wales and Queensland on bus tours, so it gave both of us the opportunity to see a lot more rather than having to concentrate on the roads. We returned to the Gold Coast. We had decided to share a flat there with the friends that we had gone on the cruise with. It was very hot in Queensland at the time; I would not have picked that time to be there, but it just worked out that way. We got a two-bedroom flat near the beach and shared it with the couple. but did our own thing. Grant and I did some very romantic travel together, and I wanted it to continue. I just loved this life in the sun, discovering such beauty in nature and doing so many exciting things with him.

I recall that on one of those hot afternoons, Grant was having a drink with a guy who apparently said that he was living in the block above us. We had the apartment on the ground floor. When I was introduced to him, I just did not like his presence. There was something about him; I had an intuitive feeling that he was not quite right. I mentioned this to Grant after he had left, as Grant seemed very eager showing him around our unit, which surprised me because he was staying in a similar unit upstairs—at least, that was what he told us. We returned from dinner that night and were so tired that we both flopped into bed. It was a hot, humid night. The door to our bedroom opened into the backyard; to get some air into the room, we left it open, as the fans were doing nothing to bring down the temperature. Fortunately, we had locked all our valuables away, and I had put the keys under my pillow. In the middle of the night, I heard a shuffle in the room and woke up to find a man sitting on the floor with his hands on our suitcases. It seemed like he was looking for something and knew exactly where to go.

I shook Grant. He had barely woken up when he saw the guy, and if he had not shouted, he would have been able to grab him. I hate to think what Grant would have done to his sorry arse! But Grant's shout enabled his reaction. He had oiled his body, so when Grant got a hold of him, he slipped away. I noticed he was the man that had been drinking with Grant earlier that afternoon—that was the uncomfortable feeling I had. I had sensed that he had a very negative energy around him. He had come prepared—oiled, with runners on, and wearing a pair of shorts—so he was able to get away quickly. Obviously, this was his night job! Chat up tourists, get a layout of the land, and come back to steal their valuables when they were not around. Grant gave chase, running behind him down the gravel roads, barefoot and totally naked. Thank goodness there was no one on the roads, as it was in the very early hours of the morning. Grant would have caught him if not for the roughness of the roads, so the guy got away. But I think that convinced Grant that my feeling about this petty thief was valid. . We had a great laugh because it was the funniest sight: this six-foot man running down the road. If it had not been at that ungodly hour of the morning, he would have been arrested for streaking.

As life dictates, all good things must come to an end. We finally got a Greyhound bus back, and we both felt very sad at the end of our trip because life would return to normality. With Grant returning to work, it would again be some weekends with me and a whole lot of time without, but I had accepted that that was how it was going to be. I just did not want it to end. It had been such a nice time away, and this long-distance relationship was starting to make me very tired. I also knew and had this nagging feeling that I needed to make some major changes in my life, but I was not sure what that was going to be.

I had managed to get a diploma in human services at Swinburne, master my yoga moves, advance my meditation, and keep it constant, as that was what my inner strength depended on. It was also fortunate that I kept my focus on my spiritual growth and registered some of the positive things that were happening for me in my gratitude journal. My physical body was doing its own thing, but my mental, emotional, and spiritual state was on track.

One of the most enjoyable journaling I took on was working on a discovery journal. It was a gift from my daughter, and I got so much enjoyment out of it. There were a lot of blank pages, pockets to put materials in, and some guidance from the author on what each segment required me to contemplate, reflect on, and write. I decided to use it very honestly, and as I worked through it, it started to reveal who I was at the time. It encouraged me to use collage, photos, and other information to excavate who I was, and it helped me confront the things I did not like about myself. It was one of the best journaling I have ever done and was also a catalyst for some massive changes that I would put in place so I could find the person I wanted to be. It took me a whole year to get through it all, and there will always be more room to add more and grow more, as there is always more room for change. I go back to this journal whenever I feel like checking where I have been and where I am now. There is always something I can gain from it. I worked through this discovery journal, which guided me through excavating my authentic self, and I began to discover who I was not.

I was on a train heading for self-development, spiritual healing, and mental strength. I started to see spiritual healers and mediums, and I started to get a clear glimpse of who I wanted to be. All my direction was coming from inside rather than externally. My spiritual guidance came from healers and mediums that connected with spirits from my past, and I took on their guidance. What the journal revealed to me was that I was shallow and focused on ego, and whilst I had a lot of men attracted to me and had a lot of friends, I had not much depth with any of them or with myself.

One weekend, after Grant and I had returned from our holidays, he was spending the weekend at my place. He spent most of his time at my place. I did not like going up and staying with him, because he shared a house with another couple, and I did not feel very comfortable crashing their space. His room was depressing; it was covered in black because when he worked night shifts, he slept all day, and he had to have the light shut out. So I was happy to have him hang out in my flat even though it was becoming quite crowded. I was totally physically in love with Grant, but I was not going to invest in the relationship because my gut feeling was that it would not last for too long. I was going to enjoy it for as long as it lasted, and I was confident that what I needed to know would be revealed to me when I needed it.

We had just finished lunch and were relaxing in the lounge room at my place when a call came through. He was sitting near the phone and answered it. He did not say much, and after he put the phone down, I asked him who that was. I need not have asked. I knew. It was the dreaded call that a lot of women may have experienced, the call that sits in your stomach and nags at your head; it never goes away because the curiosity has to be appeased. He said it was someone that he did not know. That was interesting; they had dialled my number! His expression said it all: it was a call that had surprised him too. I did not say much, and we spent a very uncomfortable weekend together, because that call sat in my stomach all weekend. It started to fuel all the thoughts I had in the past, and it was coming to a climax.

No sooner had Grant gone back than I redialled the number. Of course, the woman answered. We talked for an hour and realised that he was switching between the both of us because he could. She lived close to where he did, and he only visited me on the weekends that he was not on night shift so there was plenty of time to cheat with me. It had been going on longer than I had expected. I was devastated, and even though it probably happens to so many women, I could not help asking myself why he had done that. . It had been obvious to me that his sexual energy was very high, but I had ridiculously presumed that I was enough. I asked myself a lot of questions. Was it because he had asked me to marry him and that was him reaching out to me to make something of our relationship? Was the rejection part of the excuse for his behaviour? As he did not spend all his time with me, did he wonder if I was being unfaithful to the relationship? Or was he just so oversexed that one woman was not enough? I wanted to ask him, but if I was not exclusive to him, what was the point of hearing what he had to say? The woman on the line was sobbing and saying to me that he meant a lot to her and that she wanted me to know. She had seen photos of me, but he had said that I was his cousin. She had access to Grant's home and called in and had found my number in his phone book. She had a gut feeling, as he talked to her about me a lot. I admired her courage to call the number. I felt so much empathy for her. I just forced myself to listen to all that she had to say; I needed to hear it all.

The song 'Jolene' kept playing in my head. 'Please don't take him just because you can.' I felt such empathy for her, and I could not think of what to say to her. I was just as fooled as she was. I just assured her that I would not have anything to do with him; he was hers, and I would call him to tell him that. As I put the phone down, I wondered if he had planned the whole thing because he did not have the balls to let either of us know. Was he enjoying it because it was working?

When Grant left my place, he had known that something was not right, but he would not have expected that the two women he was sleeping with were mature enough to have a conversation about what was going on. I felt she needed him more than I did. She was so much in love with him. She was more committed to the relationship than I was, but I was also disgusted that he had put me in a situation like that.

As soon as I got off the phone with her, I did not give myself time to think or feel. I had to make this the end. I felt physically sick and wanted to call him whilst I was still angry so it would not get confused with my feelings for him. I did not say much; he did not ask me any questions. 'Get your butt down here. Pick up your things, which I will put in a bag for you at the front door. I do not want to ever see you again.' Those were my words. I said nothing else. He turned up and could not even look me in the face. I threw the bag at him and shut the door. That was the last that I saw of Grant, and I would never take another guy seriously after that.

How could I? I had come from a broken marriage, and he knew everything that I had been through. I open up very quickly in a relationship once it gets past the honeymoon stage. I can be strong, but I am an emotional person. I am an intelligent emotional person. I could not fathom why he would do that after all that he knew about me. Why did he not have the courage to call it when it was over rather than drag me along uncomfortably? However, the reality was, I had glimpsed that things were just not going right, but I had ignored it so I would not get caught in doubt and mistrust. I guess Grant needed more. We could not have been more anyway, as things had changed. What was once an exciting relationship now did not seem the same.

I have always believed in giving someone a second chance. But on the third strike, it is my call, and then you are out the door. Once I close that door, I will never open it again. There is no point in keeping the door slightly open, because there is the temptation to open it again. Close one door, and another will open. If a door does not open, it is not your door. Knock on another. What would the experience be like if the shoes were on the other feet? What if I started to treat men the same way that they thought it was right to treat me? What would it be like to play a man's game?

Not too long after that, I went away on a weekend with Clyde. He had now left his marriage and was settled into his own home. He arranged it all; we were heading to Daylesford for a few days. He had booked a cottage for us to spend the weekend in. It was the most beautiful cottage and was decorated like a doll's house. We had not tried spending a long time away ; it had always been overnight and same-day visits. I was ready for some uncommitted fun. Not too long after we had taken a walk after a bite of lunch, we returned, and he said he had something for us to share. It was totally unexpected. I had no idea that he had access to that stuff. It was a bag of ganja, which we were going to smoke together. I had never smoked pot in my life, but I was going to try it. I do not know if I would have ever tried it with anyone else, but I had so much trust and comfort in Clyde. I was going to do this with him. He obviously had explored this as well. There was nothing I would not try with Clyde.

We had a couple of glasses of champagne. Clyde lit the ganja, and we shared the whole stick. It did not take me too long, and things started to feel a lot different. When it hit us, we were both over the toilet bowls, vomiting our guts out. My whole world was spinning around me. All we could do was go to bed. We had the wildest sex ever and fell into a dazed sleep. When we woke up, I thought I was dying, and I kept thinking of no one else but Deva. *Will I see her again? I could die here with him, and no one will know.* I felt as if it was the end. My whole body was burning up, and I felt my blood pressure rise. For the first time, I was afraid of the risk I had taken, because I had no idea what the consequence would be. I was not in control, and neither was he. I felt my body getting hotter and hotter; it was like it was going to explode. I vaguely heard Clyde ask me if I was okay. We both knew we were not, as we were making ridiculous conversation with each other. We were not okay.

We must have fallen into a deep sleep. When we both woke again, we felt good and nearly normal but very hungry and horny, so we had some food first and another jump into bed. It must have been the pot, but we both just wanted to lie there and have sex all weekend. Then in the middle of an intense moment of ecstasy, I called out 'Grant', as if I was on top of him rather than Clyde. That put an end to everything. I guess I would not know how that felt, but Clyde took that very badly. Even though he did not show it very much on our trip back, he stopped coming around much. I did not think much of it. It was a moment of ecstasy, and it did not matter to me who it was with—but obviously not in Clyde's world. It did not bother me very much. It had not been too long since I had stopped seeing Grant; I was not going to be hard on myself. It was not intentional. It just happened. Get over it. Whilst I could understand his feelings, it was just the shoe on the other foot, and I was over it. That was how it turned out, and I was not concerned about how it affected him. I was emotionally disconnected from my sexual experiences for good reasons. To me, it was having sex like a man—unattached and unemotional.

I never expected him to be around permanently, but he had been a good influence in the time he was there. We had stimulating conversations that I would not forget, and he had a mighty influence on my life. He changed my thoughts with the positive books he lent me and with his words: 'Do not think that I am going to get you to who you want to be. Only you can do that.' 'I am not here to rescue you but to kick your butt.' I liked his honesty and his straight words. Clyde knew about Grant and all the intimate details because we shared a lot with each other; there was nothing we could not talk about. Even though he never actually admitted it, I knew he was jealous of what I had with Grant. The next time I heard from him was when he had another woman in his life. She had moved in with him and was obsessed with him, and he liked that. Whether it was his way of getting back at me, I would never know, because I just did not care. I was emotionally detached; that was the game I was playing. Do men always want women who love them more? Did getting it on with another woman heal the wound, or was it something to throw in my face?

I moved on very quickly from that. I may never see Clyde again, but I was happy for the legacy he had left me. I was on a journey of self-discovery, and any opportunity that would give me that chance, I would open myself to. Not too long after, I was on a train on my usual trip into the city for work. The train was packed, and if you did not have someone's groin in your face, it was an elbow in your back. Normally, this would be an invasion of private space, but somehow public transport broke all those rules. I happened to glance at a guy in a suit. He smiled, and I smiled back. Why did I feel that this was more than a smile? As he walked out of the train, he put his card in my hand. I'm not sure why, but I kept it. He was not the sort of person I would give a second glance to, but there was intrigue in his ugliness. I had to make that call.

I called, and the next thing I knew, I was driving to an address in Glen Waverley. I had no idea what to expect. It was 11 a.m. on a working day, and I wondered who in hell had parties at that time of the day. It was the most massive home, I noticed, as I knocked on the door. I walked in. The house was stunning but dimly lit. There was a locker to put personal possessions in, and everyone was wearing a mask and nothing else. I could not see the guy that I saw on the train anywhere, but I picked up a mask and put it on. I was greeted by a very attractive, tall, and almost unhuman-looking person, who asked me to follow him into a 'welcoming room', as they called it. You checked your clothes in and walked out with just your mask on. It was clearly indicated by notices all over the rooms that safety was very important, and there were enough condoms available, with more information on a table in the guest room about how to use the facilities and what was acceptable behaviour.

I had a few glasses of champagne and did not pay for it. At the time, I was not sure how this would be billed to me, but I was told that this was an introduction night, which was free, and that any further visits would only be warranted by a membership. I wandered through all the rooms; there was a great sense of eroticism and it seemed like the people there came from a corporate and professionalism background. There did not seem to be any sense of judgement, just enjoyment. There was no pressure to get involved; I could have just observed and left whenever I wanted. I chose a room. The whole venue was heterosexual, but nothing was out of bounds. It was my first experience of an orgy. I had never been touched by women in that way. I had never had so many hands on my body and so many people feeding off my body. But it felt so good. There was no kissing, and I liked that, as it would have made it too personal. Was this my experience of an orgy? It had a feeling of uncommitted enjoyment and no emotional attachment. It was raw, very sexual, and open to any kind of exploration in a safe space. I felt safe for the whole time I was there. It had always been a fantasy for me—not any more. It was my reality this time.

I loved every moment of it. I had wanted to experience it even just once—that weirdness of not knowing who these people were yet having such a sexual experience with them. I do not know how long I was there. When I decided it was time to leave, I walked into the massive shower, still keeping my mask on. It was communal but extremely clean and very flashy. . I showered, walked into the dressing room, collected my clothes, got dressed, and left, wondering if what had happened was real. There had been no judgement and no names. No one had cared what I did, who I was, or what I looked like. It was a place for pleasure, and that was all. It was not a place that one could wander into off the streets. It was strictly members only. Occasionally, a member would spot someone that they thought would fit into the scene, with the hope that they would take out a membership.

All the men and women were from the higher end of the job market—lawyers, solicitors, bank managers, and businessmen. The guy I had met on the train was a member, and I was his recruit. I never saw him again. I did not pick up the brochure for membership. I had the experience. I did not want to make it a habit, but I would never forget the experience. It was so not missionary! Some experiences are on/off, and others last a lifetime. Nonetheless, they are all experiences, and that is what life is about. Life does not judge me for my experiences; I can make the choice, as long as I take the consequences with it. I loved the experience. I wonder, would it have been possible for me to have such an experience if I had been in a committed relationship?

It was not soon after that I got a call from one of the guys I had been chatting with. He seemed nice enough to talk over the phone with, but I had no intention of having a full-time relationship. Every man was disposable as far as I was concerned. I felt a power. Sadly, it was negative, but I did not care about that. It was a power fuelled by ego, and for a short time in my life, I was going to afford myself that feeling.

I teased them; I never committed to seeing any of them, but I gave them the feeling that something would come of it. I partied a lot, and suddenly, I was in an arena where I was getting a lot of attention from men. I found that when I made myself unavailable, the challenge increased. It was all negative behaviour, but there is an aura that comes from a woman that has no need for a man. I was not afraid to go anyplace on my own; I looked very radical, both in my dress sense and the way I wore my hair. I enjoyed this shallow existence; it just felt good for the time. I had a lot of fun on the floor. I made a lot of guys feel that I was theirs during the night, so they bought me drinks all night. When it ended, I walked out the door on my own, took their numbers, and never called them ever again.

I decided that I would give into the calls from Julien and agreed to meet him one evening at my place. I was dating an Italian guy and an older Australian man at the time. I was paranoid about safe sex but never avoided sex if it was something I wanted at the time, and sometimes I never got back in touch with any of them.

I realised from my first meeting with Julien that he was obsessed with me, and I should not have agreed to see him any more. I did not think it would be a lasting relationship. This was one of the biggest mistakes I made, but it also came with a lot of change. I had seen Julien a couple of times, and he already wanted to spend more time with me than I wanted him to. I refused. He was someone I would never have even glanced at. What was it in this man that allowed me to have him in my life? I think I liked the fact that a man could be so obsessed with me. I was surrounding myself with such negative energy, but it made me feel falsely powerful. I figured if I treated him badly, he would get sick of it and walk away—not Julien.

Reflecting on my time with him, I think I was on the rebound. I had shut the door on Grant but had not dealt with the emotions that came from the break-up. I had not gone through the emotional process for dealing with the massive loss that came with Grant walking out of my life, even though I had orchestrated it. I missed him a lot even though my life looked good to me from behind those dark glasses. I was so much up my arse but was not focused on the lessons that I should have learnt along the way.

There was one night I told Julien not to come over to see me when he requested to, as I said I would be going out dancing. I knew he was not too happy about it, but tough luck. I just did not care, and I did not tell him where I was going. I went to my special nightclub. I was starting to be known there and would meet my favourites there that I danced with and flirted with. I hung out with the coolest guys at the nightclub. It was an over-thirties club, so it had some sophistication about it. There was one man on that dance floor that was interested in a dance. His name was Jean, he was French, and there was something about him I could not resist. We had a couple of dances. He was a very sensual dancer, but I moved on and danced with so many guys and girls that night. I went to the bar to grab my last drink before I left for the night, and he was there. He leaned over and kissed me, and it was different. I wanted to do it again. The French kiss—so that was the difference. It was a long, hard kiss, and there was so much sex in that kiss I could not wait to go back soon enough to meet him again.

We always met on the dance floor. Whether I was dancing with anyone or talking with anyone, he would walk up, and I would be his for the night. I wanted to be. If there was such a thing as sex on the dance floor, we took it one step further. We danced all night; he held me so close I could feel every part of his beautiful body, and he probably felt my closeness too. It started with a kiss on the floor. The song was 'Every Breath You Take' by the band The Police. We kissed right through the dance as we glided along the floor. Our bodies were so close, and before I knew it, I was moving into an orgasm, which I could not stop. I could feel my legs getting weak under me; I became like putty in his hands. Jean knew what was happening as he tightly held my shaking body close to him. I had not experienced anything like that before, and it felt so good. He held me so tight and so close; it almost felt like it was okay to let it happen. That was the last dance for the night. We said nothing, and like all the other time, we kissed and left.

I saw him the next time. I was almost embarrassed and wished he would not turn up that night, but he did. He walked up and sat next to me on the couch. I apologised to him for being so out of control, but before I could go any further, he said he was actually flattered that he was able to get me to that state on the dance floor. We continued to meet a few times, and that was all it was. We had no further expectations. Until one night I saw him there, and he was with another woman. I had my own circle of regulars that I hung out with, but I felt a bit flat that night, did not stay long, and left. I was okay with that. We made eye contact, greeted each other, and moved on. I never went back to that nightclub ever again. The connection I had with men was my choice, and like the choices I made, I needed to take the consequences. I was prepared for that to happen.

I had not realised that Julien would follow me to places. He would check up on whether I was at home or not. He would call me and accuse me of going out with other men, and it was as if we were in a relationship already. Julien was not a physically attractive person, but he had the most beautiful soul; some of the conversations we had were so deep. This was the first time in my life that I began to have a very deep connection with a man I barely liked, and I was attracted to him for the beautiful soul that he was. I had not been able to have conversations with a man on a deep spiritual level, but that came easily with Julien. Julien was Edward in another body and life, reminding me that I had wanted things to be different and that that was the reason I had left my marriage. But I was ignoring that., so it was manifesting in different people. I now started to acknowledge that men were repeating themselves in my life in different bodies. Obviously, there was a lesson here for me, but I was not yet ready to recognise that and reflect on a relative behaviour change in myself. I was just plodding along, with no specific requirement for who was in my life at the time.

I had decided that I would sell the flat I was in because interest rates were rising, and the mortgage on the flat was getting to be more than I wanted to pay. It sold for $10,000 more than I wanted, but I still did not get too much money out of the settlement. However, my priority was never wealth; it was experiences. I was more concerned about enjoying my life and living rather than having extreme wealth. I had enough to have the life I wanted. I was grateful for the abundance because despite what I earned, I was always able to save for the things I wanted, go on holidays, and buy the clothes I wanted. It was a universal purse that would cover the expenses. I never checked my bank account; I trusted in divine abundance, and that worked for me, always.

Julien and I started to hang out a lot, but it was when I had the time to give him. He was a man that enjoyed shopping, dancing, and nature. It was the most uncomfortable relationship, and he was the sort of person I hated introducing to anyone. We had a lot of similar interests; we were both passionate people, and whatever we did, we enjoyed. He had just come off a terrible break-up himself, which had left him with barely anything financially, and he was scraping by with odd jobs to pay his rent. But he was still very generous. He never spoke English as well as he spoke French, he was from the islands, and for the time being, he was good company. I was not going to take it for more than that.

As I had sold and had no idea whether I wanted to buy in the city any more, we decided to rent a house together. It was an old house, but it had a lot of room for the both of us. He had wanted to move some of his furniture in, and we had heaps of room for it all. He had got a job working for a contract painter, and it was bringing him enough money. I started to notice that he was now getting comfortable with the fact that we were together. I started to notice the excessive drinking but did not think much of it because it was harmless—until it started to get excessive. Julien was very keen to have a relationship with me, but I was not interested. When I was out living my life, which did not revolve around him, he got deeper into his drinking. I realised that it was his frustration at not getting things to work out his way, but that was not my concern. He hoped that at some time, he would be able to influence a change and progress to a relationship rather than be just house mates. He brought this up many times and would try on numerous occasions to make moves on me. I would always put a stop to his advances. I was happy to be housemates and to have him accompany me whenever I felt I needed a male companion.

One evening, after I had been in the house for a while with him, the conversation got heated. He was pressuring me to make something more of our friendship. It would always become an argument, but this time it was very verbal and it escalated. He was becoming very personally critical, and I was not backing off. We were sitting at the dining table. He moved his plate over to the couch and turned on the television in the middle of dinner and our conversation. I asked that he turn the television off and sit at the table. I barely finished my sentence before he was at my throat. It all happened so quickly, and I know he regretted it the moment it happened. In grabbing my throat, his fingernail made a slight cut on my skin, and it bled. It all happened so unexpectedly and so quickly, but that was enough for me. It was my past repeating itself. I had stuffed up this time, and I felt a deep sense of regret and failure. How could I, an intelligent woman, not have seen this coming? I was angry more at myself and the situation. He was too pathetic to even feel sorry for.

I had a friend that lived a few doors up the street from me. I picked up my coat and walked out the door and drove over to her place. I wanted to get out before it got a lot more violent, as I could see it could very quickly get there. Frankie was married to a policeman! She encouraged me to make a complaint and go through the procedure of an actual domestic violence situation. I was not even labelling it that. I was suddenly afraid and did not want to return to the house whilst he was there. I wanted him out of the house, or I would have to leave. I was prepared to do that. Her husband was away at work at the time, so she drove me over to the local police station. I made an official complaint against him. I did not expect that the police would take the matter seriously; there was an instance in the past when I reported a man beating up a woman in the flat above me, and they did not do anything because it was a 'domestic', as they called it, and would fix itself. I was surprised. Because Frankie's husband was senior police superintendent at the local police station, they could not ignore it.

That very night, the police went to the house and asked Julien to get a few of his things and leave. He did not have enough time to get all his belongings, which they said he would have to arrange to collect once they had arranged things with me. He only had time to grab a couple of things, and even though he had friends he could have gone to, he decided to sleep in his car. He presumed that everything would be all right in the morning and that he would return to the house, but he had been warned not to come anywhere near me, as the police officer had advised me to take out an intervention order against him. The next day, I went to the house and changed the locks. For the first time in my life, I was so frightened that he would appear at my front door. He called and asked if we could talk, but that was not going to happen. As much as he begged me, I asked him never to contact me ever again.

Neighbours told me that not even a week in, they had seen his car circling the street and watching what I was doing. I knew I had to put that intervention order in place, and I proceeded with that. We met in the court. I had a court counsellor to support me. I felt so degraded, as there were numerous cases all in the one courtroom and everyone was listening to everyone else's cases. It got to my turn. I said what I needed to say about the incident, and the judge ruled in my favour and slapped him with the order to stay away from me. I was escorted out of the court by a court counsellor. No sooner was I near the lift than I turned around and saw that he was standing next to me, asking if he could have a talk with me. Obviously, he had no idea what the intervention order was about. He was stopped by the court counsellor, who walked with me to the station so I could take my train home from the city. I was amazed at the way everything was handled and how protected I felt during the whole process.

I think I was able to very quickly get on with my life because I realised what I had got myself into. I had walked out of my marriage, but I had not dealt with the issues that were mine. It suddenly became apparent that I was attracting similar situations into my life. I had physically removed myself from the situations but had not been released mentally and emotionally, and there was yet another spiritual lesson. I had to eventually learn to forgive myself, forgive my family, and forgive the men that had hurt me, and only then would I allow positive things to come into my life.

I hated being in the house after that. It was around this time that my mother was on a short visit to Australia. She had never travelled on a plane before but made the decision to go around and visit all her children, wherever they were. Australia was the last stop on her list. She travelled with Laurina and stayed with Phillis and her family whilst she was here. Deva was a teenager by that time, and I took her over to visit my mum. It had been a long time since I had seen or spoken with my mother, because when I was leaving my marriage, I had a conversation with her about being unhappy and how I wanted to leave. Her words were that it was not about my happiness; there were no divorces in the family, and I was not to bring that disgrace on the family.

I will not forget my words—words I would have never had the courage to say to her at any time in my past. 'This is not about your happiness but about mine.' I just went on with what I had to do and never included her in what was happening. So when she arrived in Australia, I had been a single parent for a while. When the two of us dropped in to see her, she realised and could see that we both looked well, that I had got on with my life, and that, as most mothers would recognise, I was happy. I knew I would not see her again; that union with my mother was very special. We had realised on that visit that she had been diagnosed with breast cancer, and the cancer was almost visible externally when she made the trip. She returned to India, her mission accomplished, and would undergo an operation to have the cancer removed and go through the healing process. This was her journey to see and be with all her children and make her peace with them. For the first time in my life, I saw my mother for the person she truly was. What a courageous woman she was to take a journey like that when she had never been on a plane and to travel to a country that was totally alien to her so she could connect with her children. It was then, at that very moment, that my connection with my mother was restored, and I felt all was forgiven. I was loved by her and loved her.

I realise the medical profession sells cancer as a disease that is hereditary. We see so much about the disease on the media; sometimes it feels to me that they are selling the disease to people. There are advertisements that could influence vulnerable people into thinking they are the one out of ten that could be carrying the disease. In the minds of the weak, this could be a death sentence. I have always understood the brain and the mind's impact on inviting these diseases. I do not pay attention to any of that negative stuff; instead I focus on good health. More than that, I keep my mind positive and invite healing thoughts and deal with emotions, especially anger, and resolve resentment and issues. Every disease starts in the mind before it affects the body. Get your mind right, and that is your vaccination against anything that breaks down the body. The brain is the body's computer, so what we tell our brain affects our physical body.

My mother ended up in remission after going back to India. I am not sure whether it was her mission to reconcile with her children that healed her. The doctors were amazed. There was no need for the operation. I did get a call from Maggy that my mother had a relapse of illness, and the doctors suggested an operation this time. She had said, after the diagnosis, that she did not want to be operated on and instead wanted to come back home. She was quite prepared for the end of her life. She had resigned herself to the fact that she had had a good life and would rather die at home; an operation at her age would be challenging. Maggy insisted on the operation. I was not involved in the decision-making process, but I did not feel I had a right to that. I am not sure whether the rest of the family was consulted or whether it was a decision made by Maggy. My mother died in the hospital, against her will, after that operation. She did not die from cancer; her age could not withstand the operation.

I was aware when I saw her when she was in Australia that if she passed away on her return to India, I would not return to India for the funeral. I did not want to have to put myself through the drama of the family farewell. When she visited, I used my time with her to reconcile and say the things I wanted to say to her. I always knew I was very capable of saying goodbye to my mother in spirit. I wanted to remember her time in Australia and that feeling of coming together for the two of us as my positive experience with her. The feeling when she finally got that I could be happy being a single parent—that moment was very precious to me. I did not want to taint it by going back to all the negativity of my family in India.

When she eventually died, it devastated me. I guess part of my grieving process was reflecting. I could come to terms with the fact that she, whether dysfunctional or not, had always done the best for us with the knowledge she had at the time. I sat on the balcony, all alone, with her in my thoughts, and I cried until I felt I had got it all out of my system. I felt grateful for her visit to Australia. I wished I had been able to learn more about her. I think I would have realised that she was a very spiritual woman, trapped in her forced religious beliefs. I would have loved to have had more intimate chats with my mother about her feelings, her fears, her expectations for herself, and so much more; but this was not the time to have any regrets. There is something about a woman losing a mother. Even if the relationship is rocky, the loss is felt on a lot of levels.

I wrote a letter to my mother and said everything I wanted to say to her that I could not when I was a child. My intention was to ask a friend who I was closest to at the time if I could sit with her and light a fire. I was going to organise my own passing-away ceremony. We sat down in her backyard, which was very special, under the stars, and we lit the fire together. I was so appreciative of her for allowing me these last moments with my mother. I needed someone to be with me, and I was so glad I had asked her. She was the perfect person to ask because she understood the person that I was. We sat with the fire. I threw the letter into the fire and saw it rise in smoke, and I visualised the message going to my mum. I felt a tremendous peace engulf me. It was very special to have Anne with me in this experience, and we both just sat there, experiencing my mother's spirit, not exchanging any words. I had made my peace with my mother in spirit. I knew she would come to visit me in spirit. I expected it. I have always felt spirits; I have a great belief in their existence. And she did visit me. It was a few days after her death, and I was asleep. I had, in the past, always had conversations with my mother about my fear of spirits and not wanting to see them.

When we were young, my mother had a habit of putting a cross on our foreheads with her thumb before we went to bed, and she always said the words 'Bless you'. That was the fondest gesture I always held on to. A few days after my mother's death, I was woken in the middle of the night. I felt her presence right there, but instead of coming in front of me, she stood behind me and gently placed her hands over my head. She held it there for a while before she left. It was very special for me, and I felt nothing but love. That touch generated so much love; it brought such peace to me. It was as if all was well in her world and mine. There was no feeling of fear in me but absolute love, and that was good enough for me. I felt so much at peace with her. She had come to visit me, as a soul does before it moves on. I knew we were in a good space and would be forever.

Anne was one of a group of five girls I belonged to. We worked together and seemed to fit together even though we were of different ages and personalities. We started meeting for drinks after work, and nothing was sacred in the conversations that we had. This graduated to a decision to go away together on weekends around Victoria. There is nothing more refreshing than being part of a group of empowered women. Women have a way of validating who I am as a woman and have a very supportive yet keen sense of giving me a kick up the arse to be what I want to be. Every one of us were at stages of our lives that we were happy to be at, and we were very accepting of each other. Regardless of where we were in life, we had a sense of contributing to each other's growth in varied ways. It was uplifting to be part of this group.

We had been away on a few weekends together, and like with any group of girls, sometimes things would get challenging, as we were encouraged to do things that were not normally what we would choose to do. Some of those things would be having a spa bath together with no clothes on, watching a sexually empowering video together, or bringing anything that was of value to share and sharing it with the group. Whatever happened within the group stayed within the group. It was a lot of fun spending time away. Whilst most times we got on pretty well together, we also had our challenging times, and that revealed who we were as people. But for most times, we would relax, drink well, eat well, walk beaches, charter boats, and climb mountains. Everyone contributed to the planned weekends, and everyone was included in the planning and contribution to make it a success. Women have a way of lifting another woman to where she deserves to be.

One of our trips was a visit to a coastal town in Gippsland. It was quite remote at the time, and it was at that time that I had the realisation that I should focus on purchasing a country property. The job I was in was getting a lot more stressful. I was working for the general manager in the international division of the organisation, and it involved a lot of travel, long hours, and a lot of the city life. I needed a place to get away and find myself on the weekends. I was renting in Bentleigh at the time and wanted to invest in a country property. I was feeling the need to spend time with myself, to find myself. It was also important for me to eradicate stress in my life, as it had a way of infecting my life. I know a lot of illnesses are related to stress and our busy lives, and it is important to slow down and take stock of ourselves.

I loved this coastal town when I was there with the girls, and not too long after that, I drove up one weekend, booked myself into the caravan park there, contacted agents, and started looking for a simple home I could buy to be able to get away from my busy city life. Prices were very low at the time, and it was a good time to buy. It was close to a bigger town, but there was not much activity except for the beautiful, wild ocean. That weekend, I must have looked at nine houses, and then I walked into the one. It was just right, and I could see myself there. It was like Goldilocks walking into the home of the three bears. It was a beautiful two-bedroom cottage on a bit of lawn, with nothing in sight for miles.

I paid down the holding deposit to indicate my interest and to give myself time to talk with the bank. It did not take long before I had the acceptance of my offer and the bank's approval to purchase the place. It would not only give me the opportunity to spend time with myself but would also allow me to invest in property as well. Having more than the minimum 10 per cent deposit was also a good thing because it made a difference in what I owed, and that allowed me to manage the rental as well as have my weekender to throw myself on the weekends.

I never had it easy financially, but then again, my focus was never money. I had no big inheritance left to me; everything I achieved financially I had to work for and save for, so I had a sense of appreciation for all that I had achieved. I have always been a believer in abundance, and if I wanted something and put the hard work in, the universe would find a way for that to be achieved. Everything I needed has always come to me, so there was no need to be greedy or have too much.

The coastal property became my getaway, and in years to come, it would be my refuge. I jumped in the car whenever I got the chance on a Friday after work and went there and spent the weekend. That was where my spiritual transformation started. I had a lot of time to be on my own. I was the only company I had, so there was no excuse not to get to know myself better. I read a lot of books—not just any books but those that would change my life. I wrote for hours and spent a lot of time on the beach and in meditation. I had no need to interact with the locals, as I wanted the time I spent in my little house to be all about finding the things I did not like about myself and changing them. There was a lot about myself that I did not like. I knew all the answers lay within me; only I could make those changes. But I needed the quiet time to reflect on who I am not, which was who I was at this time, and to change it all into who I wanted to be and to feel happy with that person.

My life has been a series of jumping off cliffs. If I got an idea in my head, I did not think out the process too much. I just pounced. Sometimes it worked, and sometimes it did not. There were wings with which to fly sometimes and hard gravel to land on at other times. Looking in the mirror used to be very confronting for me, and the only time I gazed into a mirror was as a beauty requirement. But I started looking in the mirror every day with a different perspective. I would look into my eyes, and there would be times that I would cry because of the sadness I felt for myself. There would be times I would look with disappointment and anger. The idea was to look in that mirror and one day be able to look back in the eyes of that woman and say that I love and respect her. It took months, a lot of hard work, and a lot of changes and reflection before the day came. That day when I would look into that mirror and make eye contact with myself and look right into my eyes, it would look back at me with approval.

I hated who I was. I was shallow. I hung around with the wrong people. I treated men very badly. I was pretentious, and full of ego. I hated what my reflection was telling me about who I was. I had started all the groundwork, but all that was useless information if I could not bring that into my everyday practice. I was going to. I wanted desperately to look in that mirror and like the reflection in it.

Things were changing a lot at work. I had been in the organisation for over thirty years or more. The corporate world was changing, and so was I. For a long time, I had felt like I hated the job, but I was actually frightened of leaving it, as I did not know what I would do at that late stage in my life. I had become a qualified Indian head masseur and got my certificate in relaxation massage and was certified in Bowen practice. I had done two levels of Reiki. I worked in a clinic in Hampton to clock up the required free hours up and get the experience I needed. I worked on the weekends in therapy centres to add to my client experience. That progressed to my earning money once I had completed the required hours of free work. I guess if I had done this much earlier in my life, I would have probably made it my line of work, because I had a passion for it and a natural feel for healing. But I was afraid of relying on just that for an income; I needed to be getting a reliable and constant income. I had a lot of experience in corporate employment, and those were the skills that would earn me the income I needed. My healing skills were a passion, and I did not want to distract the dedication with the pressure to bring in an income from it. This would allow me to use my healing skills in my therapies as my passion. Working with my therapies would not be just about the money.

Property values had started to pick up. More people were starting to discover the sleepy coastal town I lived in, and what was once a mass of vacant land and extreme quiet was now becoming full of holiday homes. It was not as nice as when I had first bought there. It was changing in environment as well as population, but I had not noticed, as I had only been visiting. I decided to use the collateral that I had in my coastal property now to purchase a small pad for myself in the city rather than continuing to rent. I bought a one-bedroom unit inner city, which was more than enough for a city pad, but I was now paying a mortgage.

Not even six months after buying the inner-city property, things started to deteriorate drastically at work. The whole dynamics of the organisation started to change, and they were no longer employing staff for their capability but rather for purpose. I was well established at the time, which I had worked very hard for, and was executive assistant to the general manager of the international department of the organisation. I had employed a junior within our team, as I was starting to get very busy. My work also involved a lot of interstate travel with international groups, which I loved, but we needed someone to hold the fort whilst I was away. At the interview stage, I was a bit concerned that she was not the right person for the job. She seemed very immature and had no experience but was attractive and very young. She begged me to give her the job and said all the right things that I wanted to hear. She had absolutely no experience of working within a team. We did not get too many applications that were appropriate for the job, so I had a conversation with my manager. We decided that she should be offered the position on probation.

She was soon employed and sat at a desk very close to me so I could guide her and induct her into the position. I initially got on well with her but started to notice that she did not do very much work; instead she spent a lot of her time wandering around the office, talking with all the attractive men around. She would openly flirt with them and had no sense of office ethics, and there were times I had to awkwardly remind her that she had a job to do there. I could not give a shit about her behaviour; I wanted the jobs done, but they were not getting her focus. I was getting a lot of negative feedback from some members of the team, saying that she was not working well with them. She was rude and offhand and had a very poor attitude towards work and the women that worked alongside her. My position at the time expected that I would handle a lot of matters independently in line with my job description, and I had the support of my manager as long as he was updated on what was happening within the team.

I decided that it would be best to have a meeting with her, but I did the right thing and included her immediate manager so we could have a record of the meeting and there would be a witness to what we talked about. We had done a lot of work before merging two groups within the organisation to become a competent team, and her behaviour within the team was damaging the spirit of the team. I had noticed that she just did not seem to have any positive relationships with her female colleagues. Realising that she was young and had no office experience, I looked for ways to include her within our team. I was keen to discuss ways that we could make it work. This had been going on for a while, and she had frustrated not only me but every person she had got into contact with, most of them female. However, she had all the men in the workplace wrapped around her fingers.

It started to frustrate me that every day I came into work, there was some issue involving her. I had not had a situation like that to deal with in my entire career, and it was causing me extreme stress. I thought about it often enough to be worrying and took it home with me. Consequently, it did not surprise me when the stress manifested in a pain in my neck. Pretty relevant, as she was not only a pain in the neck but a pain in the butt as well! It must have been a combination of the situation at work and my working hard to get things done, but the pain was so severe that by the middle of the afternoon, I decided to call a therapist in the city to get a massage or some treatment that would ease the pain.

I made the call to a place I had got out of the Yellow Pages; it was posted under 'Massage', so I thought that would have to do. I finished my working day and headed straight to the place, which was upper city, for my treatment, feeling very exhausted from the pain. It was a new corporate building, and as I walked in, it was very impressive. It was a circular reception, and enclosed in glass all around was water, with plants growing and fish swimming. It felt totally relaxing. I was impressed with what I was seeing. I was already starting to feel relief, but that was not going to last very long.

There was a board stating the various organisations in the building. I found the one with which I had the appointment. It was on the fifth floor. As I got out of the lift, I was on a circular floor with a lot of doors, and I went up to the one that had the number I wanted. I had barely knocked on the door when a European woman opened it and welcomed me in and gave me a hug, which I thought was very unusual. I was expecting something more professional. I walked over to the counter to pay but was told that I could pay at the end of the session. A stunning Asian woman was waiting to escort me to the room. As I followed her into the room, I started to get a very uncomfortable feeling that I was in the wrong place. The decor seemed to not look anything like a therapeutic place should look like; rather than being relaxing and soft on the senses, it was loud, bright, and in my face.

She showed me into a room. I took a quick look around, and yes, it confirmed to me that I was really in the wrong place. The side table had all sorts of sexual objects and gadgets on it. There was a drink, presumably for me, on the table. The bed was a round waterbed and had red satin sheets and black pillows on it. The room smelt good. I had picked the wrong place; this was a genuine mistake. But the girl was there for a purpose, and she meant business. As soon as I realised where I was, I started to explain to her that I had gone there just for a neck massage and that I was in pain. She went on to reassure me that there were lots of women that went to that place, but it was in the few words of English that she knew. I just could not make her understand that I was there for a therapeutic massage. Any conversation I tried to make with her was lost in translation. She could barely string a couple of words in English, but I was determined to communicate with her.

I was making signs; she was ignoring them. Then I noticed a massage table in the room and felt a bit consoled for a while. Pointing to it, I tried to again indicate that I wanted the treatment on that table rather than having to hop on the bed. A large sliding door opened, and behind it was a massive shower. She signed to me to undress and take a shower. Again, not normal procedure. I stood there wondering how I had got myself in that situation. This was not the normal routine. I had been to therapy centres, so I was familiar with what should happen. I turned around, and there she was, totally naked and looking stunning. She had the perfect body, and with that long black hair, she looked perfect under that shower. I refused to get undressed, and for one brief moment, I wished I swayed towards women. This would have been perfect.

My persistence finally got the message through. However, instead of her understanding that I was not there to be serviced but to have a massage, she put it down to me knowing but being embarrassed over the whole showdown. She was the gentlest person, and I wished we had the ability to communicate a bit better. I finally got on the massage table, and she started to give me a massage. I had stripped down to my underwear, as you would do in a professional massage saloon, but then started the tug of war, with her trying to pull down my undies and me struggling to keep them up. She was all over my body, and it was like a body-to-body massage. Weird, but in another state of mind, I would have probably lain back and enjoyed it. Today I was not here for that. I was here to get pain relief, not sexual relief. This was turning out to be more stressful than before I had made the appointment, and the pain in my neck was getting even worse. I was getting angry instead of being relaxed. She was trying to assure me that there were a lot of single businesswomen that used the services, and according to her, women deserved nothing less than men. I agreed somewhere in that confused mind of mine.

She spoke her language. I understood what she was trying to say. There were more times of frustration than understanding, but in the end, I managed to get off that table and get dressed. I took another look at the whole room before I left. So this was what a massage parlour looked like—an upper-class brothel. I wondered how much this whole thing was going to cost me in comparison to a normal massage. I had by now worked out that I was in a brothel, and I started to doubt whether I had looked in the right section of the Yellow Pages. I was in so much pain I just could not think, and all I wanted to do was to pay for the session and leave. But when I got to the counter, I asked the lady for a business card, as that was one way for me to know what the hell I had been looking at when I dialled this number.

She said to me that they were a new establishment and had not yet had a card made, but there would not be a charge for the session. I was amazed that, after all that, they were not going to charge me. Understandable, as they had actually made my neck worse than when I had walked in. As I was standing at the front desk, I was conscious of some moans and groans that were coming from one of the rooms. As much as I did not want to believe that I was actually at a brothel, that was what it was, because a woman walked out of one of the rooms, and she looked like she would fit perfectly in a red-light district. Getting the message, I could not wait to get out of there. Fortunately, it was late and dark by that time. I rushed out of there and jumped into the first tram that came along heading for Flinders Street. I went on my way, hoping I was not seen by anyone that I knew. As for the ones that had seen me, I wondered what they were thinking.

Once I got home, sore but not damaged, I sat on my couch and actually had a good laugh. I had to come to terms with what had just happened. I had to share this news with someone, and fortunately, I had the perfect friend to call, who I knew visited brothels because he did not get the sex he wanted from his wife. When he used to tell me stories of his encounters at brothels, I would say to him, 'Why is it not normal for women to go into brothels to be serviced like the men?' I had mentioned that I wanted to know what a brothel looked like. Hey! Be careful what you wish for! I told him about the whole episode, and we laughed. Despite it all, I had to be grateful that I got my opportunity to have the experience and come out of it in much pain but not harmed. . The experience chose me.

That was not the end of it all. I went into work and told all my friends, the guy I worked for, and everyone else, because it was now hilarious that I had come out of the whole thing unharmed. . My manager's look was a combination of doubt, disbelief, and shock. He said, 'This could not happen to anyone else but you,' but I do not think he quite believed me. I did not give a shit whether I was believed; I had the experience. I bet there were not many in the circle that I was in that would have had a similar experience. I could tick that off my list!

I had worked very professionally with the general manager for a long time, but Kelly, my new assistant, had worked her web around him; he was starting to favour her a lot. The meeting I had called would cause more trouble than I thought. I said that she was not being a team player and asked her if there was anything we were doing as a group to exclude her. I saw a weird look on her face but thought nothing of it until the next day. It was as if she had been looking for an opportunity, and this was it. She made an official complaint about me. She was offended that I had called her out on not working as a team member. I guess it could have been anything. She was going to make the few of us within the team that had questioned her workings pay for it. She did not come here to do a decent day's work; she was the bunny boiler of the workplace.

My manager called me into his office the next morning and told me that I should not have called the meeting. Now I had done this on numerous occasions when I had to organise meetings between team members to discuss plans and get ideas as a team. I presumed that with my depth in the organisation and my experience, this was within my job description. I thought I had kept the meeting professional and respectful. It seemed out of character for him, because I would not have organised the meeting if I did not feel that it was within my capacity and role to do so. Obviously, something had changed, and I had not been brought into the picture. These were all the thoughts going through my mind. What a weak prick! Was he talking from his head or from between his legs? I could not help but let my mind wander to a time when we were away from location on a team-building exercise. I had left the group, as it was very late. We had an early start, so I decided it was time to call it a night. As I was working my way to my room, I noticed the two of them together alone. It looked a lot more intimate than it should have, but we had all had a few drinks and behaviours had become a lot more relaxed. Had they slept together? Was that the reason? Was she threatening to get him into trouble if he did not favour her? Did she have him by the balls?

During my talk with them, he indicated that I needed to apologise to her for what happened, because she had made an official complaint against the way I had handled the meeting. Her manager, who was present at the meeting, had supported her. He was male, of course! Like hell I was going to do so. I had done what I thought best to do in the interest of the team and felt that there was no need for an apology. I do not shy away from apologies, but I need to have done something worthy of an apology. Otherwise, it would be an apology just for the sake of. The pressure was on my manager to get an apology from me in writing; if not, Kelly had threatened to sue the organisation. There had to be more for her to be able to take legal action. It could not be just a meeting that would warrant that. I could see no grounds for that, so all I could think was that she had more on them than I was aware of.

Consequently, because I had refused to apologise, the organisation wanted me to attend forced counselling. To get to that stage, they used professionals to interview us and a few other staff members that she had complained about. The questioning was very discriminatory, and in the end, the report that they produced damned us and exonerated her. We were on notice to apologise and attend counselling. I was disappointed with the whole unfair process. I would be damned if I was going to apologise to her when I knew my intentions were in the best interest of all. The whole process was rigged to cover up someone's arse. We were the guinea pigs, and no procedures were followed. It was a harsh realisation that experience did not have any value. The dynamics of the organisation was changing, and it all felt very ugly.

I was working late that evening to catch up with work, and my boss came in after a meeting. He called me into his office. He seemed very stressed and was not dealing very well under the pressure of a new chairman desperate for this whole thing to just go away. The perfectly respectful and very good working relationship that we had ended that day. He asked me if I would apologise, and I said no. Without any warning, he jumped up. He had his face in mine, and I must have heard the work *fuck* a million times. It was at that time that I felt the most uncomfortable I had ever felt in his presence. It was as if he had no other word in his vocabulary. I had not experienced anything like this in a working environment. Over the time we had worked together, I worked very hard to develop a strong working relationship with him. He was a good man but did not handle stress and pressure very well. He was not a people person, so he was in the wrong job anyway and was trying very hard to swim against the current. That day, there was no regard for my loyalty and experience within the organisation and the thirty-odd years of service I had given them. It was as if something had to be done to cover up and get rid of the whole incident. The guy was absolutely mad. I understood that he was keener on keeping his job and that this was his pathetic response.

How many of us stay in jobs for all the wrong reasons? We may be qualified for the job, but if we do not have our hearts in it or if it is not working for us just as it should for the organisation, it can't be good to hang around. I would rather be cleaning dishes and love what I do than work for an organisation that makes out that it is reputable but does not value its staff. You have to be happy in your job, or it will show. My manager was there just for the money; they paid him extremely well, and he was not going to risk that.

When he first joined the team from Canberra, no one in the team liked him. He just did not fit in. He stayed in his office but always watched all the fun we had during our working day. We were a very close and upbeat team, and he was never going to fit in. I decided I was not going to let him be left out, and I found many ways of including and bringing him into our banter and fun. We used to have a lot of chats about work-related issues and discussed team building and how he could work better with his colleagues. He had no idea and presumed that sitting in his big office, behind a desk, was going to work. Obviously, that must have been a very Canberra attitude. I think he liked the attention I showed him, as no one else gave a rat's arse about him. If you did not fit in, you were excluded and left to your own devices to get through your day. I started finding more time for him and would wander into his office to talk and find out more about him. I knew he wanted to be included and did not know how. I invited him to join us for drinks after work and included him in our fun. He quickly fitted in and became very liked within the group. But this was all before he got the job of general manager; he was just a shitkicker at the time. He soon became a very included member of the team. Teams are like relationships; to make them work, everyone needs to make the effort.

But this day, I lost all respect for him. All the time and effort that we had put into discussions were thrown out the window, and I saw a very different person. There were not many people in the office that day, but one of my colleagues was in the office next door to us, in a meeting with another manager. He must have heard the drama next door; he popped his head around to see what was happening but soon disappeared. He definitely heard and saw what was happening. I excused myself from my manager's office and left. I got home, and I knew I could not stay in this job any longer even though I needed it more than ever. I was not in a position to change jobs, as I had a mortgage to pay, and I was hoping something would work out. I was in minor shock at the time as I kept going over all that had happened leading up to this day. What I experienced was bullying at work and verbal abuse, and I wanted to make him accountable for that. But would I stand a chance in this corporation?

The universe had already made up its mind that they were not deserving of me. I had received the kick, but I was still hoping I would have the opportunity to keep my job. No, the universe was not going to let that happen. I did not sleep at all that night. I cried my heart out, as I was so heartbroken. To think I had given this organisation good service all this time, and now I had become disposable. That was the harsh reality, but that was how the times had changed. We had moved from loyalty and good workers to who you knew and who was willing to play your game. That was the reality, but it was not my reality. I found it very hard to justify what had happened. I had all the material to take the matter further and could have made it a court case, but did I want that at that stage in my life? Was a payout going to change corporate behaviour? Definitely not.

I typed out a letter to my manager and copied it to the chairman; it was about the abusive language and the way I had been treated in the whole process. To avoid it being his word against mine, I decided to ask my colleague that witnessed and heard the abuse if he would support me and attend the meeting so he could tell them what he heard and saw. He refused to get involved. I had a lot of friends within the workplace, but there was not one person that could give me the support that I needed. I can empathise with that, because most of them were worried about losing their jobs if they got involved. We do sell our souls to the workplace and the money and lifestyle that it brings us. I soon realised that they were not friends; they were just work colleagues.

Suddenly came the realisation that I had no one on my side and that I had lost total respect for the organisation and now had to leave. I had to make the brave decision, irrespective of my financial situation, that my happiness was more important. I had to resign and lose a lot of superannuation and benefits I would have received if I had stayed for the rest of my working life. But there was no other option. I respected myself and was not going to apologise to satisfy an organisation's desire to shut down a case which they were not prepared to deal with fairly. Respect for myself suddenly became high priority rather than getting a high wage and being in a coveted position.

I ended up with half of my entitlements. I was so unhappy at the time; I was going to take whatever was offered and get out of there. I walked into the office and gave my resignation with a month's notice and allowed that to be on my manager's conscience rather than mine. He felt half the man that he was, because he knew I was nothing like what I was being accused of. This was a very wrong deed by the organisation, and as far as they were concerned, it was better that I left and this whole matter was erased. I saw some relief on his face, and I knew it was not because I was leaving. Rather, he knew he would be able to keep his job now. But with what conscience?

I had to decide what to do with my life. I had a mortgage and two properties to maintain, with no income. Did I need to stay in the city and try for another job, or make a total change and move regionally and experience something very different? The universe had narrowed down the decision for me. I was feeling so low and dejected, and I spent the night wondering what I should do. I was confused, let down, and feeling quite low. There are always massive lows that come before change. This was just one such time. I had good friends, but I did not want to reach out to them because I just did not have the words. This had been going on for so long ; I had lost the mental and emotional energy to deal with talking about the whole thing again. There were a lot of people that claimed to be my friends, but at the time I needed their support most, they were not interested. Of course, all of them wanted to keep the peace for the sake of their jobs.

After a meditation session that evening to calm my mind, it was clear—the decision that I should take in my best interest. I would have to sell my city pad and move over to my property on the coast. I had not thought any further than that. I decided not only on an employment change but a whole environment change. Two massive changes. Was I ready for it? I sold the inner-city property at a loss and decided that I would make regional Victoria my home. I had gradually moved most of my furniture over to this property, as I was visiting more often. I had minimal furniture in the unit, and my intention was to move all of what I needed into my regional property before settlement. Then an opportunity came for me to share a home with a very good friend of mine. I had only intended this to be short term, until I cleared up a few things I had to and finished some courses in preparation for a change in career. I thought staying with him would allow me the chance to sort out things with my job and pack up the unit. Or was I just stalling my decision?

Neville had become a very close friend. I met him through a girlfriend of mine, and he had become my backup to any function that I needed to take a partner to. I did not think anything of it because in all the conversations that we had, he always talked about being gay and being involved in gay activities. I felt very safe with him. We were just good friends, and he was the perfect person I needed in my life at the time. An uncommitted friendship with a man. Every girl needs a gay friend, and he was that to me. He related to women differently than other men. For me to have a base in Melbourne, Neville offered to share his house in the South Eastern suburbs. I decided I would take him up on his offer. I was not sure at that time whether I wanted to move totally away from the city, and I wanted this to be a kind transition for myself. I was going to have to leave family and friends back in Melbourne, and that would distance me from all the people I loved and the familiarity of the city. I got rid of a lot of unnecessary baggage in the way of possessions and moved some essentials over to his place, hoping to have the chance to take a deep breath and evaluate where I was before I made the final regional move.

Neville was a good dancer, and he was good at a conversation. There was a lot of wondering amongst his friends and mine if we were an item. I am not surprised, because seeing us together, it was easy to presume so. Him being gay was our secret. He had not revealed this to his family and was in a state of denial; he was embarrassed that it would not be accepted in his family circle. He was secretly a try-hard gay, but it was not working for him. Not being prepared to come out complicated his emotions. I just accepted that and loved the friendship that we had.

I trusted Neville with my life. There were times we would go out together, and he would drive me back after a few drinks. One time I had much too much, and he put me in bed before he left. Now that was very sweet. But that was the type of friendship we had. It seemed like he expected nothing more from me. He was a caring person and a good friend. Neville had his fair share of trouble growing up, which I understood from the conversations we had, even though we did not go into it in any detail. I respected his privacy.

He had a modest house in the suburbs. Neville slept during the day because he worked night shifts, and whilst I did not like softly treading around the house, I managed that very well. Then I noticed some signs of jealousy as I started to share with him the things I did in my day and the people that I was meeting. A lot of the conversations now became very unsupportive and very negative. I started to realise that you do not know people as well as you think until you live with them. There was a total character change, and it looked like his expectations were very different from mine. Was there a different reason he had offered to allow me to stay awhile?

I realised when I moved in with Neville that I had a couple of things that I had left with Julien, and I decided that even though I had no contact with him, I should follow up on the things I had left behind. They were not of much value, but I did not want to dump it with him. I wanted a clean move, and that meant collecting those things as well and getting rid of them. I wanted to go over and pick them up, and without thinking too much about it, I discussed this with Neville. I noticed that Neville's emotional reaction to me going back to Julien's was anger, and it was apparent that he did not want me to get in touch with Julien ever again. I thought it was a bit controlling of him to dictate to me that I should not return to the house. I was concerned that he was affected by it in this way. He began to show signs of wanting me to spend more time with him. As I occupied myself with doing things that I enjoyed, he started to feel left out and mentioned that I was living with him but spending less time with him. I thought he had a life, but obviously not. I started to get an uncomfortable feeling about him. Neville seemed to be more complicated than I had envisaged.

I was in the middle of doing a four-month course in Melbourne and was hoping to be able to stay with him until that was over, so I was treading softly around him and ignoring his erratic comments and behaviour. I tried to spend a lot of my time in my regional property so I would be around him less. Not long after I had returned after a weekend on the coast, as I walked into my bedroom at his place, I felt a presence. I have always had an extreme sense of energy. If someone had been in my home or in my space, I always felt the energy change when I returned. This was one such instance.

I had my inner-city unit burgled once. Even before I had entered the front door, I sensed the negative energy. Nothing in the unit had been moved or touched; the thief had come in through a slightly opened bathroom window and had taken all my jewellery. This time, when I walked into my room, I realised that some of my things in the room had been tampered with, including my underwear drawer. That was an uncomfortable feeling. I asked Neville whether he goes into my room when I am not there. Not that I would have worried if he did want to have a field day trying on my clothes; I knew he loved my clothes. But he became very angry that I would think that he would take the liberty of walking into my bedroom. I was convinced he had. The conversation became ridiculous. His reaction upset me and immediately ruined the perfectly good friendship that we had. I did not want to argue with him.

I had to think very quickly, as this was not going to work, and my only option at the time was to finalise things in the city and permanently move regionally. As scary as this thought was, it seemed like the only option I had. Yet another kick up the arse by the universe. I needed to move away, and I was stalling things.

This was so disappointing because I valued Neville's friendship. Masks—they have always fascinated me, for the simple reason that we all wear them. We are one person when we are at work, a different person when we are at home. We wear a different mask for different facets in life. Who are we really? I have masks hanging around my home, and there is a purpose in that. It is a reminder that I need to shed my masks as well and be as authentic as I possibly can. We wear masks to hold on to friendships; we wear masks so we can stay anonymous in relationships. We wear masks so we can be liked. Why are we afraid of being authentic?

I took whatever I could and disposed of some of my things. I had so much stuff it was beginning to weigh me down, and I knew that at some stage, I would need to get rid of it. I had inherited a lot of things from Deva. Some of the things were hers, for which she had no place to store; some of it were mine from my marriage; and some were unnecessary things I had collected over the years. I would only take with me what would comfortably fit into my regional property. I did not want to hold on to any unnecessary material possessions. I did not feel like I needed to hold on to all the things I had because they were sentimental; one item for that sentiment was okay. If I valued it, I kept it. If it did not have a purpose any more, I got rid of it. Decluttering has a very healing effect. It is an energy cleanser. Once you go through that process, it is very hard to go back to being a collector of unnecessary possessions.

I wanted everything in my home to be something of value to me, not materially but emotionally. I wanted it to bring happy thoughts to me when I looked at it. There was the opportunity to make a total change, get out of corporate work, and find employment that could relate to the person that I had become, opportunity to give up my pretentious city life and find myself in a regional town. I was challenged so I could make those humble changes. Could I do this?

Change is inevitable, but did I have to make it that challenging for myself? I was always looking at massive changes that looked unsurmountable, but again, the option was not to break it up into easy steps. Change has never intimidated me, but I had no time to think this through. I had to make a quick decision. I had to move all my furniture and connect all the services. Once this had all been done, I took a deep breath. What the shit had I done? I did not know where I would start to get employment. I had no friends close by, no family or anyone that knew or loved me. It was as remote as I could get. Considering I was a city girl who loved the city life, living regionally was totally alien to me. What the hell was I going to do in this remote town? I had moved into my coastal property. I had some funds, but no regular income. I could sit there and bludge for a while, or I could get my arse into gear and make this work. I had jumped off yet another cliff, and whether it was going to be rubble or wings was in my control.

The organisation that I had worked for in Melbourne, to set their conscience right, had offered me a working space in a career organisation before I left the city. I had refused their pretentious offers of a formal farewell or gifts, but I was glad for this offer; they owed me that. I spent a month there whilst I lived with Neville. It was at a cost of over $5,000 to them, for which I had an office space to work from and access to some of the best career advisers, courses, and workshops to attend. It was the best thing I did. Much better than a gold watch or any other gift would have done for me. I used the time that I was sharing with Neville to take advantage of this offer. The course also consisted of a lot of self-awareness tests, and one thing that came out of that was that I could take my existing skills and obtain a job within community services, as that was the area my new self was leaning to. The workshops had indicated that my changed interests lay in that environment. I was not really sure what community services actually encompassed.

I also had the skills from the therapies I had graduated in. I planned that rather than this being my main source of income, I would make a hobby business out of it and consequently allow my passion to rule the business rather than letting it be just monetary. The skills that I had gained from the corporate world would be what I would need to use to bring in an income.

I cried for a week. I needed to get rid of all the frustrations of why I had to make this decision, why the hell I made it, and what I was going to do from here. I arrived at a place of action. I did not want to sit in this isolated house in the jungle and wither away. I got my CV out—which was very impressive, if I say so myself. My career in the dairy industry had allowed me to become a professional executive assistant. I had a lot of experience, office skills, and qualifications because I had used every opportunity that was given to me to enhance my skills. I knew I would not find it hard to get a job.

I amended my CV and made a lot of copies. I drove to all the major regional towns around and walked into every corporate office and dropped it off, indicating that I was interested in getting a job. I was happy to take on anything that would use the skills I had. I also started looking at the local newspapers for anything to come up and hoped I would be able to get work so I would not eat into my savings.

Then on one of my visits to my daughter in Melbourne, I had taken the local paper with me, thinking I would glance through the job section when I got the time. Deva drew my attention to a job that was advertised in the paper; it was part-time and was a maternity-leave position. I had not thought to look a bit diversely. I was hoping to get back into full-time employment and had not considered that this might be a good opportunity to do things differently. After all, I had moved regionally, with no idea of how to find work like I was used to, so what did I have to lose? This was an opportunity to experience. Sometimes we need to be open to divine guidance. Do we manipulate our lives so much we fail to see the direction we had spiritually set for ourselves? Why do we set ourselves on automatic pilot? Why do we imprison ourselves when there are open doors?

I decided to put in an application. It was not the position I was looking for, but I have always been open to divine intervention and information coming to me from the universe in the voices of those around me. I would have to downgrade from what I was used to. It had very minimal hours and was not exactly going to be a financially supportive job. I would have to step down to a reception/admin position, and the hours were between 11 am and 2 p.m. Pretty awkward, but it was a relief position between two part-time positions. My position would be between the morning and afternoon shifts, to give them the opportunity to have lunch and run errands and have a short break from the front desk.

I expected it to be pretty straightforward, but it was more challenging than I had envisaged. Sometimes we land the perfect job, but without the perfect people to work with, can it still be the perfect job? It was stuck slap bang in the middle of lunchtime, so I had to virtually learn to rely on brunch before work. I also had to travel half an hour to get to the job. But I was not going to complain. It was a step into the regional employment door. I was not expecting to get the job, as my experience was way over what the job expected. However, my cover letter indicated that I was open to change and keen to try part-time work, as I was new in the region.

I started to get myself into a routine rather than holiday mode, as I did not want to lose the routine of a working life. Thank you, universe. I not only got a call for an interview, but it was in community services. I had the job, and even though it was barely part-time and did not pay as much money as I thought, I felt humbled but grateful. At least it was some money coming in, but more so, it was experience in community services. Sometimes it is not all about the money. My overheads were not that much, and I had to manage my lifestyle to fit in with my budget. It was also about where the experience would take me.

I turned up for my first day at work. There were two girls working at the front desk, one in the morning and one in the afternoon, with a three-hour break. The break was me. Pretty weird arrangement. I was not sure how it would work, but for where I was, it would. One of the girls just did not like me; the other was too condescending. But I was going to ignore all that. They were never going to be my friends. I did not want to have any contact with anyone and intended to keep my workplace separate from my normal life. The whole regional thing was so alien to me; they would not be able to relate to who I was, so I just decided I would walk in there, do my job to the best of my ability, and not make too many friends. I did not need friends. I did not need relationships. That was how I was thinking anyway, but the universe had other plans for me. It was a very different working environment than I was used to, so I was going to put my head down and focus on learning a lot about community services. I had absolutely no interest in socialising at work or after work; I had nothing in common with any of them.

I was still getting over all the hurt. I was grieving over having to leave the city, my family, and my friends, and I wondered every day if this was the right decision. I was totally out of my comfort zone. I felt totally betrayed by the men I had known.

But it was not them; I had betrayed myself. Why in hell did I attract such attention when all I had in mind was to treat people well so I could be treated well? This must be some karma I had not cleared. If I removed men from my life and focused on myself for a while, would that work?

I was taken around the office to be introduced to everyone. For some weird reason, the first thing I noticed was that I was the only dark face, and it made me question how multiculturally aware these people were. I have always known Australia to be a racist country, and there is no doubt about that. I do not want to hear one white Australian tell me it is not so, unless they have walked in my shoes. I have experienced so many racist comments and attitudes, I can't fathom when the day will come when we will see each other as who we are and not be judged by the colour of our skin or the country we come from. I do realise that sometimes it is not so much prejudice but rather total ignorance. Are we so afraid of difference? And what is the use of all that intelligence if we choose to stay ignorant? How long would I last in this workplace? My experience told me that just being who I was would be a mighty big challenge.

I noticed from the start that I was going to struggle to fit in with some of the staff, especially the ones I worked closely with. I did not plan to make friends, but I hoped to feel included. I pretty much got in, head down, and did what I was supposed to do for the three hours that I was there. I was always happy to return home. I was getting used to the silence and the stillness and the total darkness of the nights, and it took me a few sleeps before I started to feel comfortable and at peace at home. I also began to note that the coastal village I lived in was changing gradually and was nothing like it was when I had first bought there. I was starting to feel very isolated once I got home. There was not much interest for me in the town, except the beautiful, rugged ocean, which had attracted me to the property. The community had changed, and it seemed to be a place where most people came to hide from society.

There were a lot more houses coming up around me, most of them with no regard for the privacy of others that were there before, but that is the nature of change. My attempt to fit into the community soon revealed that unless I was a hard drinker, nothing happened. Socialising was always done around excessive drinking, and it was as if they were frozen in the seventies. Thank goodness I had moved on. It was not a good look. A lot of middle-aged people getting together not to have fun but to get intoxicated? Not for me. I had been there and done that.

Whilst the little house was my refuge for the years that I would escape from the busyness of the city, it was now becoming a place of isolation and a place for a lot of desperados. I realised that I would have to consider moving at some time. I had done a lot of renovations on the little home and had also extended a shabby garage into a beautiful room for my practice. I had started to get a few clients, as news had spread that I was a therapist.

Whilst I practiced in Melbourne, it was very safe to take in male clients, as I had always practiced in the safety of therapy centres. I started to realise that there were a lot of sleazy men around this town, and they were very curious about what this weird single woman was doing, living here on her own. I was amazed at the ignorance of some men. It was as if they did not know the difference between a professional masseur and a professional prostitute. When I last looked, I had not noticed a red light at the front of my place!

I started off doing treatments for everyone, being careful not to discriminate. Whilst there were a lot of men and boys that came through for treatment, there always had to be one idiot to stuff things up. That was my neighbour. He came in one day and asked if he could book in for treatment, which I was happy to consider. I booked an appointment for him. When he arrived, no surprise, the injury he wanted to heal was in his groin. Why did I not expect that? Rather than judge him, I was willing to treat him like any other client—except he was not. I had a lot of respectful clients come to me for treatment, but there had to be one bastard. This was him.

I did not think very much of it and proceeded to organise the treatment that I would normally do in my therapies to treat such an injury. He did not have a valid explanation for how he got the injury. It certainly was not from sport, as he was not an active person. I found it very hard to believe sex was the reason for his groin injury, or he would not have knocked on my door. Normally, the common understanding, as known by anyone that has any idea of what a reputable therapy session is supposed to be, is that you do not need to get fully undressed. But nobody told this dickhead that.

Obviously, this idiot had never had a positive hands-on treatment. Before I had time to explain anything to him, he took off all his clothes and jumped on to the table. I proceeded to cover him and started treatment. I noticed that he was very distracted and not relaxed throughout. Halfway through the treatment, I asked him to turn over so I could finish the treatment, and when he turned over, he proceeded to show me his groin and where the injury was. I ignored his advance; it was not as if I had not seen a limp penis before, and I had worked out that there was no groin injury. There was no injury at all—unless it was a brain injury! I completed the treatment and asked him to get dressed whilst I was out of the room, not engaging in any of this suggestive behaviour.

When he was ready to go, I told him that he was not to return any more for a treatment, as I did not like his attitude, and if he was so small-minded as to think that sex was part of the service I offered, I would have a chat with his wife. She visited their home on her breaks quite often, and even though we did not exchange any conversation except for a wave every now and again, I would have had no hesitation in having the conversation with her. That shut him up pretty quick. I continued to do a lot of treatments to subsidise my part-time work, but to keep myself safe and to not experience another arsehole like him, I changed my practice to cater only to women and children so I could safely continue to practice at home. I continued the business very successfully whilst I lived there, and I worked in my appointments in the evenings and around work hours.

The community services organisation had now offered me a permanent part-time position, as one of the girls had moved to another job. They decided to make it a job-share, so I would be doing Mondays to Wednesdays; Wednesdays would be a crossover, and the rest of the days would be attended to by one of the other girls. It resulted in a better salary and also justified the travel to work and gave me a lot more responsibility. I liked the idea of being able to work independently without anyone breathing over my shoulders.

For the first few years, I fitted into the job and began to like it very much. It was a totally different line than what I was used to, even though the skills were pretty much the same. I saw a lot of people in different situations of struggle, and being where I was felt humbling. I enjoyed doing front desk, as it was an opportunity to talk to and meet new people. It was also a big learning curve for me, and every day I could feel the empathy and humility creep into me as I found new appreciation and gratitude that I was in the position that I was in and was able to bring service to the community. Not only did the position entitle me to work independently, but there was also opportunity for self-development and career growth.

The first six years in the position were just great. It soon became obvious that what should have been an organisation with a service to the community in mind was changing. The structure was starting to look more corporate. It was getting very top-heavy, and there was very little staff at the bottom to attend to the deserving clients. It was now becoming a business engaged in fighting for funds rather than wanting to service the clients, and whilst they liked to give the impression that they were helping people, they were only scratching the surface. There should have been more lobbying going on with authorities for housing; funding should have been directed to services rather than wages and travel. People did not seem to recover even after a lot of counselling. How could they when most times, to receive this counselling, they were expected to get a doctor's certificate? When I was processing these certificates, I was shocked at the number of drugs some of the doctors had these clients on. General practitioners can be so irresponsible. They know full well that these drugs could make people dependent on them, and most times, it was pretty much for life issues, like death, separation, and abuse. How can anyone in that state of mind consciously make changes in their life?

Charities are a business. They advertise for help, but nothing ever changes. People continue to be poor. We have so much in this world and so many rich people; there is no need for anyone to be without a shelter or without food on their table. We have the money and the resources; we just have not got our distribution procedures right. The medical profession is a business. We sell sickness. We advertise drugs. We have all the ideas for treating sickness but not much on prevention and exercise. Why is there not much more on prevention or on strengthening the mind to take better care of our bodies? Do some GPs even know what they are treating, or are they playing a guessing game? Do they treat one thing and irresponsibly not care about the effects of that treatment?

Six years into being on the job at the community service organisation, I began to see them for what they were becoming. I was not able to deliver what I wanted from the front desk because most of my time was being dedicated to unnecessary administration work and useless meetings. There were more meetings that were a waste of time and a lot more food consumed at these meetings, which I have no doubt that donations were paying for. Money that was donated for one particular purpose was being used for what the organisation wanted it to be used, and the donor's request was ignored. We were actually starting to hide from our clients rather than service them. I started to lose respect for the organisation. The information I was trying to feed back to them in monthly reviews were received but totally ignored.

I could have stayed in this job for as long as I wanted to. I had sold my home on the coast and had bought a unit in town closer to where I worked. I wanted to be able to walk to work. However, whilst I was happy with my home, the town was the most depressing place I had ever lived in. There was also the realisation that some regional towns were very insular and excluded what was in their 'too hard' basket. I was tired of making the effort to fit in just because I had no depth in the town. If you did not belong to a sporting group, did not have children that attended the local schools, or were not born locally and did not live locally for years, you were not going to fit in and would always be considered a blow-in. I just had to make it work for the time I held the job, and that was not too hard to do.

I was fortunate that I had a lot of interests and never hesitated to do a lot of things on my own. I found a life outside of this miserable town, as I realised that it was not a place that I would like to spend too much time in. My time here was again temporary. The use-by date became obvious. I knew I needed to take the opportunity to move—not only give up the job, but move out of this town completely. The only two things that worked for me in the town were the golf course and the cinema; other than that, my life revolved outside the town. I had no friends locally; most of them lived outside of the town. The workplace was starting to become abusive. I could have stayed there and made numerous complaints about the way the staff spoke to me, but the managers would ignore conflict or resolve it to their benefit. It would just be a battle that, even if won, would not change very much. I decided it was time for a change. Staying any longer than ten years in such employment would only be at the cost of my emotional well-being. It was not the clients that were the problem; it was the dynamics in the organisation.

Leaving my corporate job in the city taught me that whilst the job might be bringing in a lot of money, it can never give you a lifestyle if you are not happy. I was starting to feel unhappy in this job, and from my previous experience, I knew that if I did not make the decision in my best interest, it would have a worse impact on me. And anyway, the universe would get frustrated and make the decision for me.

I made up my mind overnight. I was at the cliff again, as I had been numerous times in my life, and I needed to jump off and hope that it would all work out. I went to work the next day, gave my resignation letter and a month's notice, and requested that I do not receive any fake farewells, as I did not need that. I had used the opportunity to learn a lot about society and myself in particular, and it was time to see what else was in store for me. I had no idea what I wanted to do. I still had my work as a therapist, and perhaps I could focus on that a bit more. I had lost all faith in community services.

I do not waste too much time on decisions. If it feels right, I take the first step and trust that the rest will fall into place. If it does not, then I reboot and restart.

I wanted to live in a town that was community-focused so I could contribute to the community. I now had no need to even attach myself to a property or take life too seriously. I had done that all my life. The great Australian dream was not my dream any more; I was going to invest in my dreams, which were to experience life, as I can't take anything material with me at the end of my life journey.

All my life, I did not have the opportunity to live carelessly. I had too many financial commitments, which forced me to stay in jobs that did not do me justice any more. I had created the situation that forced me to stay in jobs just for the money. I wanted to focus my life a bit differently and to keep the focus on simplicity, abundance, and connections. I wanted to step out of the type of jobs I was doing and focus my skills on volunteering and more on doing my therapies, if that worked out. I could choose a town that I would love to live in, or I could put my things in storage and go and live in another country and immerse myself in the people, culture, and language there for a while.

There was a little coastal town not too far that I loved, and I already spent a lot of my time there socially. It was not only because of the idea of being close to the beach, but also because of the lifestyle and community that I could immerse myself in. I did not want, however, to invest in property again; it was too restrictive, and there was not much room to move. I wanted my life to be flexible and not stuck. I wanted to be able to pack up and go whenever I felt the need to, at universal direction. I had no intention of rooting myself in yet another regional town and realising that it was not where I wanted to be in a couple of years. I decided to rent in that coastal town for a short time to allow myself to decide whether that was what I wanted to do.

I decided that it would be for six months, and I would rent a good property. It would be a holiday and a time to think of where I wanted to be next. I had downsized a lot of my possessions in preparation for whatever decision I would make. The idea was that if I needed to store them at any time, that was what I would do. .

Settlement on my unit was a few weeks away, and whilst it was hard to leave the comfort of my little unit, I was glad to leave the town. It had nothing to offer me. I had a few garage sales, which I thoroughly enjoyed. There is nothing as therapeutic as getting rid of stuff I no longer need. Over a few years, I focused on bringing my possessions down to a minimum. I had mastered the art of dishoarding. The town house I was renting was aesthetically attractive, as most houses in this coastal town were. It was pretentiously large, but with no character. While the houses were big there were no backyards. It was not about comfort. It was my six-month holiday.

I have a simple but happy lifestyle. I want this time to be about being, about community projects, and about focusing a lot on the self and what supports who I am now. It is okay for now. It allows me to stay connected with family and friends and to enjoy a lifestyle that I love. I want to focus more on experiences as they present themselves, ones that I choose. I want to find a new love, but I have to stay open to that. If it does not come in the form of a human being, I have to acknowledge the form in which it will arrive. That is for now. Nothing is permanent; everything is temporary. Change is inevitable. I am that flowing energy that moves through change with courage. I trust in only one thing, and that is in universal direction.

I want to take a deep breath. Have I discovered who I am? I think so. I have had a lot of experiences and a lot of challenges. But do I love the person that I am?

EMOTIONAL RAPE

The stripping of a person's self-worth – Emotional rape, it does
not have the physical scars, but it cannot be ignored.

I intentionally use these strong words in this chapter. Abuse is talked about so much, but most times, there has to be physical scars—or sometimes even death—before it is recognisable. For the millions whose minds and, more so, spirits are being affected by emotional abuse, no candle is held for them.

I had moved away from the physical and mental abuse in my life. I had started on a new phase in my life, and I was slowly turning into a person I liked looking at in the mirror every morning. Every day I focused on being a better person than I was yesterday. I was giving a lot of love to myself and had no interest in attracting any male interest. I was aware that I still had a lot of work to do on myself, and if I was to have any relationship at all, it would have to be with myself. But obviously, I still had a lot to learn, and life had a totally different experience for me. I have never gone looking for intimate relationships; it has not been my desperate need. Most times, it was the men that found me and, as a result of that, allowed me to see who I was in their reflection.

Amongst the introductions I received on my first day of work at the community services organisation was a gentleman, and I say so because he was an absolute gentleman. I shook his hand. He had the gentlest face I had seen, yet it was a face that said he had been through a lot of challenges in his life. I did not think much of him at the time because I was not making any effort to connect with anyone of the opposite sex. I had a gutful of them, and I did not want to relate to anyone that was a man, gay or not!

His name was Jamie, and he sat in a little office diagonal to the front desk. The idea was that he would keep an eye on the front desk so there were no aggressive clients interfering with the normal running of operations. I realised that the experience of working in corporate and community would be miles apart. It was quite acceptable to tell a difficult client to fuck off if they were rude to me at my corporate desk, but there was a totally different expectation from this front desk. It started to change me as a person, even though I had implemented a lot of changes already. I liked the fact that I had to dig into my personal values as well and face the reality of other lives that were very different from mine. It was humbling to listen and talk to some of the clients that came to this front desk. It was a totally new learning for me, and I was going to get the most of what this position would offer me. The city and the corporate world can be so out of touch with the struggles of some, and there is very little opportunity to be confronted by such reality.

Without change, life is stagnant. When I was back in Melbourne, looking at myself in the mirror, I was approaching a decade in my life when most women were never seen out partying and dressing the way I did, but that did not concern me. What concerned me was that when I looked in the mirror, I saw a person I did not like at all. I hated how I treated men. I hated how I treated myself. I hated how pretentious I was. I hated the friends that I liked to be seen with. I hated the places I went to just because it was cool to be seen there. I hated how I avoided the not-so-cool people. I just hated everything I saw in that mirror. I was going to find who I really was. It may not be perfect, but I needed to find it and embrace what I wanted to keep and change what I did not like. I was already more than halfway through that process, and it would become my lifetime work plan.

I had to shed the entire fake personality. The focus was more on my inner self and being true to that rather than my external self. So whilst visually I might have looked like a lot of fluff, there was a lot of depth in this woman. I had worked very hard to excavate my true self, but there was not an end to this road. It was a work in progress, and I had to keep the focus.

Working in community services made me more aware of the struggles of others and their challenges to get through life. . The language that I had to use to communicate with them had to have a lot of empathy and compassion, which was very new to me, but I started to love the way I related to them. Every day, after work, I would go home and reflect in my journal about my day and how I could be better tomorrow or do things differently the next day and wake up a new person. It was empowering. I was becoming a powerful yet humble woman. I was not afraid of anything and anyone.

Sitting diagonally from me in an office was Jamie. Jamie gave me a lot of attention, but I only saw that he was a good man and wanted to help me, as I was new. He seemed to direct that attention not only at me; he was very helpful with other staff. Whilst I had those thoughts of him, I was totally disinterested in getting to know him. He was married, but I had no idea that he was in an unhappy marriage. I did not want to know. He looked after my interests at work, and I realised he was a very shy person but a very intelligent and capable man. If anyone at work did not treat me with respect, he made sure he had a word with them. He had a lot of respect from his clients. I hoped it was because he could relate to them rather than because he was in a better position than them. He was liked by most of the staff because he never gave them an excuse not to. I was not interested in getting to know him any better than what I experienced at work.

He was not a person that I would normally be attracted to, and I would not have made an attempt to get to know him any further if he did not make the first move. I saw Jamie as a work colleague. Yet I could not help but think that there was more to this meeting. My heart was so broken; I did not know it was visible until Jamie told me later that when he first saw me, I had the saddest expression on my face. When we shook hands at the introduction, he felt an energy, and he knew there was something there that he had to explore further. Yeah! We were both on the same page! I am glad he did explore it, because it would become the best relationship I had, even if for a short while. He was the only man I would ever love. It is interesting how love slowly creeps up on you but fails you very fast. There are some you fall in love with at first sight, and there is that one person you grow to love. I think we can sustain relationships with the ones we grow to love. . 'Love is just a word, until someone gives it meaning' (words from the movie *Book Club*).

It was the first Valentine's Day since I started this job. I felt so low when I woke up that morning. I had always received flowers and special gifts from my partners on Valentine's Day since my divorce. It was not the thought that I was not going to be remembered on this day, but it left me questioning what love really meant. None of those gifts mattered any more. Was love just a word commonly used, like *sorry*, with no honest emotion? That day, I found myself truly questioning: Am I loved? Do I love? Is there love? What is this word that is used so often, with no regard for feeling or emotion? How could we use the word *love* and not fight or change for who we love?

We love all the wrong people. We love people that we do not like. We use love as an excuse. We use the word without considering the meaning. We all want it, but we do not know how to give it. We abuse in the name of love. We use sex as a means of showing love. Yet it is a beautiful thing—*love*. It should be unconditional. It should be easy when you are with the right person. It has no expectations except to be respected and accepted. It can't be faked like an orgasm. It can't be given away if you do not have love to give; if you do not love yourself, you can't love another person. I know what love is, but am I capable of giving it unconditionally? If you can't change things, are you prepared to walk away from love, still loving? Is it a powerful emotion, or is it a feeling? Everyone wants it, but not everyone knows how to draw it to them or keep it. That is the magic of life—the discovery of love and the intelligence to keep it.

I was at my reception desk, waiting for my relief to come, and Jamie, like every day, went out for his lunchtime walk. He never walked out that door without asking not only me but anyone that was around whether anyone wanted him to bring anything. He seemed like he had a method to his life. He appeared to be the most generous person I knew, but I was seeing someone that was very set in his ways and frozen in the past. Did he have much life experience? I thought nothing would lift my feelings that day, but no one knew at the front desk because I was always professional. I left my feelings at home, and if I needed to be with my feelings, I would rather stay at home. Never mix profession with the personal.

Jamie walked in from lunch and walked up to my desk. He had picked a couple of white daisies from the street or someone's garden, and he gave them to me with the words 'A beautiful woman like you should never be without flowers on Valentine's

Day'. Those words are tattooed on to my brain, never to be forgotten, along with the feeling. It will never be replaced. That day, I thought it was the most romantic thing a man could have done. After that, any man could give me anything, and it would not have the same impact. He blessed my Valentine's Day, and I felt the love. He could have given me the world that day, and it would not have meant to me what those simple white daisies meant. It was simple yet given with so much love. I went home that afternoon feeling such a high. This small gesture meant the world to me. Why can't everything be this simple yet so exhilarating? Why can't the whole journey on the love train be this simple? I turned on my stereo, put on my favourite CD, and danced with joy for a couple of hours that afternoon when I got home. It felt that good.

From that day on, I would get home from work and there would be a message on my message bank. They were the sweetest messages, so non-sexual yet so special. It would be the flower I wore in my hair or the colour of my dress or the dress itself—he noticed every detail. He started to notice me, but how could he when he was living with another woman? I had to contain myself and not allow this to go any further. He would write love letters and put them in my hand, and they were not just words; they were verbally expressive of his feelings.

He came to know that I was a therapist. I was not sure whether he was keen for my touch or whether he wanted to heal the pain in his shoulder, but he asked if he could book an appointment with me. Perhaps he even wanted to know where I lived or how I lived. I trusted his intent and trusted that he genuinely wanted to heal the pain he had in his neck and shoulders. I had no expectations of him because I was used to married men having hiccups in their marriage and looking for something outside to distract them from actually fixing what was wrong.

He came over for a treatment. He had never had a therapist work on his body or had a woman touch him in that positive way before. It was a very professional treatment, and it did help him with his injury. I soon forgot about it and moved on, keeping my attention and behaviour with him very professional at work. He came back for a few more treatments, and it worked for him. I now had the understanding that he was very unhappily married; we discussed it briefly at times.

Jamie became frustrated because there were no advances from me. My treatment of him was no different than any of the previous times, so he had to take some drastic action. The next day, he handed me a very sensual letter detailing how he felt about the treatment. It was very clear that even though he was healed, he was also turned on by the feeling that came from that experience. In that letter, one of the things he said that triggered my decision was that he was in pain about his feelings for me. He had to know if this would go further, or he would have to cut off all connection, as he found it very challenging to deal with. He mentioned how he could not stop thinking of me. Was it manipulation? I did not see it at the time.

I did not read the note at work, but as soon as I got home, I read it. A certain seriousness began to grow in me. Had I turned so bitter with my experiences that I was no longer soft in my heart? I had to respond, and I was not sure how to. It was almost like the movie *Sliding Doors*. You choose one path, and the outcome can be so different. Ideally, I should have chosen not to get involved. Every bone in my entire body was telling me to stop this with a simple 'No, we can't do this' and to give him the reason for it. For God's sake, the man was married, and he worked with me. I had not wanted to cross those lines. I was not sure what I was thinking, but I made the very careless decision to invite him over for dinner. I was throwing all my promises to myself out the door. Perhaps having face time would help me clarify where I was or communicate how I felt about how this was spiralling.

I was flattered that he was attracted to me, I was touched by how he treated me, and I had no idea how the evening would go. I was expecting that we would just have dinner and a chat, but I was not at all aware of how this was going to turn my life upside down. There was something about him that I felt I needed to explore. It would be breaking all my rules for myself, but I was good at breaking rules.

When the universe brings someone into my life, I accept them with open arms, no questions asked. But the universe does this for a special purpose; it is possibly some soul lesson that I had not quite learnt. And here was yet another opportunity. Except this time, it challenged all my ethics of a relationship. I would never have commenced a relationship with a man unless he was single or divorced, and never with a work colleague. I had also decided not to get involved, as I was still getting over the hurt of previous relationships. I had moved regionally to have the time to do that, not to get into other relationships, so all the sense in me was saying not to take it on. But then I picked up that phone.

I called, and when Jamie answered, I invited him over to my place. My intent was to discuss the note and make it clear to him that this connection had no life. There was no way we could even consider this on a lot of levels. He said that he would come after he had finished work that day. I immediately felt so nervous because I did not want to be anywhere near a man, let alone get involved sexually. I was so nervous I just could not breathe. A few deep yoga breaths, and I was back to feeling relaxed. He asked whether he should have dinner before coming. I do not know what possessed me to say that I would cook for him, though I was not even sure what he ate. He seemed to have very basic tastes, a very meat-and-three-veggies person, with an occasional home-grown Chinese meal. There was no chance of cooking curry for dinner, or anything exotic.

He arrived. I gave him a hug and kissed him on the lips as he entered the door. I wanted to see how that would feel. He sat on the couch, and we had a chat about his marriage. I soon learnt that he was in a dysfunctional marriage and was keen on finding his way out of it but was not sure how to plan it all. She was still living at the property but had plans to move into her property in the Melbourne suburbs. It was very obvious that Jamie had feelings for me. I did not feel the same instantly, but I wanted to get to know him better. Was this his excuse to get out of his marriage because he did not have the courage to let her know that their relationship was so broken and he had no intention of fixing it?

I sat on the couch next to Jamie, and before long, we were kissing. The kisses became passionate. It was very obvious that Jamie was keen to take this further. I was keen to find out what having sex with him would be like. I had no intention of turning it into a relationship. That progressed to me walking Jamie into my bedroom. I had no hang-ups about sex; it had nothing to do with love for me, so I allowed him to undress me. He sat beside me as I lay there on the bed naked, and the moment his hands touched me, my body responded to his touch. It was the most honest touch I had felt, so gentle and so loving. I wanted more. I could see that he wanted it too. It had been a while since I had a man's hands on my body; my body was just responding to that. It was more a sexual need for me than love.

He did not even get undressed, but his touch was enough to make me orgasm a couple of times. However, whether it was his nerves or the fact that it was his first time with me in this intimate way, it was virtually impossible for him to get an erection. It was the least of my worries. He went out after we had those intimate moments, and he lit a cigarette. He was a smoker. He sat out on the balcony and was surprised when I lit one and went out to keep him company. We talked about everything else and avoided talking about what had just happened. But we were both happy that it had. There was no mention of a reoccurrence. I forgot that I had promised him dinner. I had not cooked anything, so I made him a couple of toasts. The poor guy went home happy but hungry.

This was the beginning of one of the most intimate, loving, yet challenging relationships that I would have, one that I was not prepared for emotionally. It would become a relationship that would last longer than its use-by date, but it was also the very first time in my life that I was in love with someone, more than I was willing to accept. We met a lot at my place. He had explained to me that whilst his marriage had broken down and his wife had moved into her city property, she still had access to their joint property; it would not be possible for us to meet at his place. I was happy for my home to be our meeting place. We were keeping our relationship low-key, as I did not want to make it public because of the impact it would have on the workplace and his reputation. He was still a married man even though they were separated.

I had no idea what I was doing. I was making all the wrong choices. It seemed like I was on the top of that cliff again, keen to jump off. Would I have the wings to support myself through this? *Life is about taking risks, not sitting on the fence,* I kept telling myself. Love is about my heart being broken, but there was a chance that it would not break. I had to find out. What I particularly liked about him was not only his love for food but his ignorance of all foods. One of the thoughts that overwhelmed me was 'I hope this guy never asks me to cook him a meal, because I would not know what the hell to make for him'. I am not a bad cook, but I am not a bland cook either. It was a weekend after our first intimate catch-up, and I did not know what to expect. Then came a call from him, asking me to put the kettle on and saying he would be there in a little while. I should have known—and not even he knew—but this was a booty call.

Jamie drank a lot of tea, black tea, and it amazed me that he did not drink any alcohol. It was actually music to my ears. A man that did not drink—that did not exist, as far as I knew. With the damaging experience I had with alcohol and men, this was a breath of fresh air. Jamie walked in, and we did have that cup of tea and also lots of sex that afternoon. It was as if we could not get enough of each other. We would have sex through football games and midway through conversations, any time and any which way.

We ate out a lot. At one such time, we were having lunch at a local restaurant. I have always loved art, but Jamie had a very different eye for it and a very different appreciation for it, which I found very attractive. On the walls of this cafe, there was some art that I loved because it was my style of art—bold, colourful, and unusual. I admired it. I was to realise that I just could not show appreciation for anything without it becoming mine. The artist had a few of her artwork on their walls; there was one big canvas that I absolutely loved but decided that I should not purchase at that time.

I could not look at anything with love; it could be a dress, a handbag, an ornament, jewellery, or homeware—anything that I liked, he would buy it for me. Was this generosity? Then why was it making me feel uncomfortable? I was not paying for anything. If we ate, he paid. If we shopped, he paid. If we experienced anything, he paid. Being an independent and self-respectful person, I just did not think it was fair that he should pay for everything without giving me a choice. I tried to discuss this with him, but he always had an explanation for everything. His only reason was that he loved me and that the joy on my face at the gifts he gave me was his reward. I did not doubt that, but I wished that he would recognise that it is also respectful to allow a woman, especially someone like me who has looked after herself financially, to hold on to some of that independence.

He had an appreciation for everything expensive. If he wanted something, he bought it, irrespective of whether he had the ability to use it or not. It was just because he could. But I loved that about him. After all, it was only money. I did not ask for that artwork, but my appreciation for it was apparently enough that I now owned it. He made me very happy, not because of what he bought for me but because of the way he treated me. He said the right things, he did the right things, and I felt that there was something about him I did not know. He was too good to be true, and I wanted to get into that before I was too deep into the relationship. After all, I had a lot of experience with things suddenly creeping up in the relationship and surprising me.

We were spending one evening at my place, and I think it was very early in our relationship. Jamie was still unsure about our relationship, as I had not given any signs of commitment. I was quite happy to take my time to allow who he was to grow on me. I needed to get to know this man better; it seemed that there was more to this package than I was aware of. Why had he decided to leave his wife? Who was he? At this stage, I only knew how I felt about him, and the rest could wait. But I wanted to put one question to him. I would hold him responsible for not speaking honestly with me at this stage. I got a good moment in our evening and asked, 'Is there anything about you that I should know at this stage?' Now this was his opportunity to communicate anything that could be damaging to a relationship. What was the reason your previous partner left? Are there any deep, dark secrets? If there was anything of relevance to the relationship, this was his time to speak. I did not need to know everything about him at this stage, but if there was a deal-breaker, I had to know. Without any hesitation, his response was 'Not that I can think of—nothing'. Regrettably, there were a lot of things I would discover as our relationship matured. I have heard someone say that before we get into a relationship, it is a good idea to have a coffee and chat with the previous partner. A lot will be revealed!

Every relationship has a honeymoon period, and then there comes a period when bits of the person you had no idea about suddenly start to reveal itself. The bits that you do not like or did not expect as normal behaviour. The bits that need compromise and the bits that need to be changed. The bits that reveal themselves once the relationship gets into a comfortable stage. The stuff you sweat and the stuff you let go. I was relieved to hear that response because that was what I wanted to hear. But it would have been better if he had used that opportunity to tell me what I needed to know. It was probably because he knew that if he was honest with me at the time, I would not have proceeded with the relationship.

He was intelligent. He was a smart liar; he was a charming manipulator. He was open with what he wanted you to know about him but very closed about the things he wanted to keep hidden. Most of the conversation I was hearing was about his wife's responsibility in the breakdown of the marriage. Not one time in the conversation did he ever take responsibility for what had happened, and that was a red flag waving right in front of me that I should have taken on board. At this stage, I was starting to feel invested in him and was hoping he wanted to use this failure to work at a better relationship. . Relationships, especially intimate relationships, have a way of showing us who we truly are as people.

We spent a lot of time at my place, and he loved coming over, as it was somewhere to hide this romance that was happening. We would go for walks on the beach and eat in local establishments, and it was his chance to disappear from the reality of what his life was. He now stayed over on weekends, and it was on one of the first weekends that he stayed over that there was the next red flag. Why was I not shutting the door on this? All the signs were there. We had a perfect weekend, and after a night of close encounters, I woke up the next morning and he was not next to me. It was a Sunday, and I thought we could lie in bed for a bit longer and take the day slowly. I was hoping for the intimacy of lying in bed a bit longer.

Jamie was not the best at sex, but he was a lover and knew how to make a woman feel. He was always concerned that I was happy sexually and felt satisfied. He put enormous pressure on himself to perform, so he would get very apologetic or concerned if he could not have an erection; he would almost be angry at himself. It was a man thing, I guess, but it never concerned me because I could see a lot of reasons for that. Just being close to him and feeling him next to me was the best thing ever, and that was enough for me. I had no doubt that the rest would come as he got to feel more comfortable and emotionally expressive. It gradually became clear to me that he did have an emotional blockage, which prevented him from connecting on an emotional level. He had numerous reasons for that, considering the life he had, but he did not have an excuse not to address it. We would need to address this at some stage if this relationship was going to become serious.

There were a few obvious flags popping up. It was still early, I had not made any commitment, and it was perfect for where we were. I was hoping that it would also give him an opportunity to pick up on who I really was, as he was now involved in my day-to-day life. However, I had already started to notice that Jamie did not show too much emotion. There was no emotion to indicate when he was angry, passionate, or sad. In fact, he was devoid of expressing any emotion. It was not that he did not feel the emotion, but it was as if something in his DNA deprived him of the right to show his true feelings.

I am energy sensitive; I easily pick up good, bad, and indifferent energy. This morning, after the first weekend he spent at my place, I woke up, and the energy felt different. He had already had a cuppa and was dressed, and I presumed he was ready to go home. I did not encourage him to stay. I felt that emotional detachment already, and it upset me because after such a lovely night, the morning felt empty—almost like a one-night stand. I think it surprised him because he must have been expecting to spend the day with me, and the behaviour that he was displaying was very normal in his head. I indicated that I had plans for my day, so Jamie decided to leave. I was ready for him to leave and needed to process his emotional detachment and what that meant for me. It did take him by surprise; as soon as he got home, I received a call from him, and he seemed concerned that I was a bit aloof and that he might have done something to upset me. I felt so reassured that he had cared to recognise the change in energy and had the intelligence to talk about it rather than pretend it was not there.

I was impressed he had sensed that and used the opportunity to discuss with him why it seemed a very cold experience for me that morning. We had a conversation about that, and whilst I knew it was part of discovering each other, I was keen to flag it as not normal behaviour. This was not just sleeping together. If we were going to make something more of this—and it was very clear that he wanted to, and so did I—we needed to bring some emotional investment into what was developing between us. Another red flag ignored. I was not prepared for how hard emotional detachment in a relationship could be. There were a lot of reasons that Jamie was emotionally guarded. I empathised with that, from all that we had talked about regarding his past, but there was no excuse to choose to get into a new relationship with no intention of changing that behaviour.

I started to realise that this would become a major issue for us. I invest emotionally in all my relationships. It is an expectation that I have of myself. I was prepared to invest in Jamie to ensure that he felt our relationship was a safe place in which to invest his emotions. I was hoping I had the experience to handle myself through this, and if the love between us was strong enough, it would overcome anything. This was the first time that I was experiencing an emotionally disconnected relationship. I was not going to allow that to happen. I was starting to develop feelings for Jamie, so I was keen to pick up and deal with those issues that were relationship breakers. I would have to find the strength to work through this, because I could be going against a brick wall. I wondered if he loved me enough to make the change. After all, I could not do it for him; he had to find the depth to draw on those emotions to bring depth to this relationship. Did he have the ability to do that?

Yes, he was married twice; he had had other relationships. But he had not been challenged emotionally. It was obvious from the conversations that we had that he always lived outside of those relationships. He had the charm; he had what it took to keep a woman interested. But if you are not prepared to invest emotionally, you do not have a relationship. I certainly did not want that. If he thought that he could repeat this behaviour with me, that was not going to happen. What had he learnt from his previous relationships? Jamie was not open to positive feedback about his behaviour. He seemed to take it all in, but it went into that part of your person that holds on to anything and everything rather than leave it open to conversation. This can sometimes turn into resentment.

I ignored my intuition, the advice of my soul wrongdoings. I would always get a feeling in my gut, like most women do, but I would ignore it for what I wanted. That would be my price to pay. I was not detached enough to see what was happening. Detachment allows me to see things a lot more clearly and actually nurtures connection as well. Even in love, we need to stay detached to see the relationship for what it really is to be able to make the changes that are necessary for the growth of the relationship. I was too in love, and I was ignoring the standards I had set for myself. This was the first time in my mature life that I loved someone.

We continued to spend a lot of time together. We were very different people, but our common interests made the time we spent together very enjoyable. We enjoyed football, golf, food, and movies. Jamie was a great golfer. We had enough common interests to keep it together, but to hold a relationship together, we needed more than that.

He was at my place one weekend. I mentioned that I had a passion for golf but had never thought that I would ever be good enough at it. I had friends that played when I was in Melbourne, and I always thought it was an exclusive sport and that you had to be born a golfer to play the game. Very casually, he said to me to come out and have a hit. He had a set of clubs, and we went out to a local course which was more of a paddock than a course. Jamie played it like it was a pristine course, and before long, he was guiding me through the game. It grew into a passion; I loved the idea of the little white ball, the open spaces, and the trickery, in my case, rather than the skill, of getting it through the fairway on to the green and into a little hole in the ground. I learnt about the putters, the wedges, flags, teeing off, and all the golfing terms and ethics. We would go out quite often to the local courses, and he would patiently guide me through the course. I just loved watching him play; he was consistent and was a master at the game. I will always appreciate the privilege of learning and playing golf with Jamie, because it became my passion and my salvation.

There is never a time that I tee off at the start of a game without him on my mind. I have never wasted an opportunity to learn, and I learnt a lot about the game from Jamie. I may never be a good golfer; however, it is not about being good but having enough passion to persevere. Passion. Every human being needs to be passionate about something in their lives. The more passion, the more living we do. I did not have to be good at everything; I just needed to have the passion. I was just happy to get out and have a game, and Jamie was more focused on getting me to play it well. That frustrated me a lot of times, but that was my baggage, not his.

He was now living at his place on his own most times; his marriage had broken down, and he had not heard from his wife. She had moved away, but there was a chance that she would return, as she still had some of her possessions at his place. Jamie spent a lot more time at my place. I decided to discuss with him the possibility of me staying at his place every now and then when convenience allowed that. He appeared not very comfortable with that at the start, and it was because he still had unfinished business with his wife. But I did not know the whole story, and I figured that if I was in his life, there was no reason we should not spend some time at his place. I was over hiding out at my place. I was ready to go public with our relationship, as I understood he was serious about his separation, and from what he told me, there was no possibility of a reconciliation. I was in this for the long haul.

I trusted my capacity at getting to the depth of people. I wanted to change this situation—not change Jamie, but challenge him to change. Because even though I had not experienced emotional ignorance in any of my relationships so far, I was to learn that this was not only frustrating, but consequently highly abusive in a relationship. But I was not about to give up on him. Jamie was special, and I was going to give it all I had. Being a deeply emotional person does not mean that I slobber all over the place; it is just that I am always more interested in how a person is feeling rather than in meaningless conversations. I have never been hesitant to show my feelings and to express them effectively, and this was a learnt habit I was not willing to let go of. There was a long time in my life that I did not have the encouragement to express my emotions, and if I was putting my vulnerability on the line, I wanted nothing less from a partner.

I know full well the consequences of holding on to feelings. My background and family history did not allow me to express my feelings without severe consequences. I went through an abusive marriage without anyone to talk to because I did not know how to discuss what was going on with me. I learnt to change that and be open with my feelings. Expressing feelings can be very daunting for those that don't or are uncomfortable with doing the same, but there is no way to build depth in any relationship without knowing what the other person is feeling.

Very early in my relationship with Jamie, I could see that he was so devoid of emotions ; there was no possibility of knowing whether he was sad or happy or whether he approved of what was happening in the relationship. The only emotion I got to witness was unexpressed anger, and that came out in negative behaviour. There was so much suppressed anger and no positive outlet. The negative response was to shut down completely; it was as if he was the only one in the room. I had never in my entire life experienced this kind of shutdown, and obviously, it came from not being able to trust and not trusting anyone enough to give of himself emotionally—that silence, that annoying silence!

The conversations that we had would mostly be about him being the victim and everyone being responsible for how he was treated in life. Whilst I can empathise that he did not deserve to be treated any less, we can sit and dwell on how people treat us, or we can make changes so they will not treat us that way ever again. It was hard having deep conversations with Jamie. I would get snippets of information from which I was able to understand he had a very challenging childhood, but most of us did in the decade that we grew up in. So did 50 million other people, and a lot of them were in worse situations. If you have survived and are able to tell your story, there is no reason to play the victim. Having a dysfunctional childhood is no excuse not to become the best person that you can become—the best version of yourself.

He had no faults but would have sarcastic digs at himself. He did not seem particularly interested in what my life was like before I met him; he always had something that he had experienced that was similar, so the conversation focused back on him. I did not have to know everything, but I always got to know what I needed to know. My weapon was to not only listen but to hear the message behind the words.

He invited me to dinner at his place for the first time. Imagine my surprise when I walked into his house. On an acre block sat this house, in a deadbeat town, with absolutely no soul in it—a massive house, with huge living spaces and a veranda that ran right around the house. It was fairly new and was designer built. It was the most beautiful house. Scattered about the house were some very attractive furniture, but not enough to fill the massiveness of it. It did not feel lived in and had a very cold energy about it, and I felt very uncomfortable. It just did not feel like a home; it was just a house. It had all the luxuries of a modern home but not the warmth, and I realised then why he wanted to spend a lot of time at my place.

There were the signs of a walkout, with remaining furniture that were not all picked up at the time. I actually started to feel empathy for Jamie. Here was this frail man, almost lost and occupying barely a bit of space in this house, calling it home. This just did not seem right, but there was more to this story. I noticed a restlessness in Jamie; it was as if he was expecting someone to walk through the door at any time. It was his home, but he was very uncomfortable in it. Consequently, I could not embrace the space as well.

It was my daughter's birthday, and I had asked Jamie to accompany me to Melbourne so I could take her out to lunch. It was also an opportunity to introduce him to Deva, because I had mentioned him. I noticed that Jamie was on pins and needles at any sounds that he would hear around the house, and he flippantly mentioned to me that his wife had said that she would be coming to pick up the rest of the furniture that was hers. I wondered what he would be left with; I was beginning to see the whole story unravel in front of me.

I was starting to get a lot more from him about his past and realised that everything that I was hearing was damning to her. I know very well that in a relationship, there are always two sides to the story and that both people in a relationship have to share a bit of responsibility when it falls apart. But I was not getting what part he played in all this. Things were starting to unravel, but I was also falling deeply in love with Jamie; I wanted to know what I was taking on. There were so many reasons to walk away, but that was never on my mind.

I am a 'three strikes' girl, and I will give it a fair go before I give up. I also know that once I decide that it is truly over and there is no hope for reconciliation, I will move on. We have to know how long to stay and when to go. To stay any longer than that would be to deserve what I'll get. We went to Melbourne. It was a happy lunch, and Deva was happy to meet Jamie. She has always been very accepting of the men in my life. I think she picked up that he was special to me, more special than anyone else she had seen me with, so there must have been a noticeable difference. I was so much more mellow with Jamie and so much more committed than I had been in relationships that I had in the past.

On our drive to Melbourne, Jamie had mentioned that he saw his ex-wife's car going past us in the opposite direction. I presumed that they had the keys and would be able to get into his place and get what they wanted and leave respectfully. What he had not said was that he had changed the locks. He had been aware that they were coming that day to collect the furniture, but he had said that he would not be there and that they should come some other time when he was at home. They had arranged to come that day and presumed that they could use their key to get in. His decision to change the locks came across as arrogant and extremely disconcerting to me. Why would he not want to hang around and give them access to what belonged to them? Had he agreed to accompany me to Melbourne because it was an excuse not to be around?

It was a lunch that I expected to pay for because I had arranged it, but after a very enjoyable lunch, Jamie walked up to the register and paid the bill for the four of us. It did not surprise me, but I was starting to get a bit concerned that he felt that I was incapable of paying for anything myself. How did he think I looked after myself before he had come along? I was used to buying myself what I needed and sometimes what I wanted, I always paid for my meals, and whilst I can accept generosity, it is totally disrespectful to ignore my request to let me hold on to my financial independence. He was more concerned about how it felt for him than how it made me feel. It would have been nice to occasionally be given the chance to pay the bill.

We left Melbourne and returned to spend the night at his place. It was late afternoon, and I was going to stay the night and go to work from there. I was immediately shocked on walking in. The place was an absolute mess. The locks to one of the doors had been broken, most of the furniture were gone, the house was left practically empty, and a lot of rubbish was on the floor. But what broke my heart was that the contents of the fridge had been emptied and thrown out on the bench tops, and some of the artwork had been grabbed off the walls. It looked like the rage of an angry woman. I was surprised at how calm he was; he was just devoid of any feeling. It was as if he was not surprised that someone would treat him in that manner.

He had just wanted to make things as difficult for them as possible. Was she betrayed by him? Had he treated her right? He would have had to have treated her appallingly for her to go to this length. I should not be with this man, but I could only see an emotionally broken man who had no idea that he was an emotional abuser himself. I was still not ready to turn my back on him—not now anyway, when I had seen what he had put himself through.

I insisted that he make a complaint to the police and that it be treated as a break-in. He did, but with it being a domestic situation, the police had no interest in pursuing it any further. No surprise! As our relationship was progressing, I insisted that he work on the divorce, as it was terribly unhealthy for me to be in this triangle. This was his baggage, and only he could deal with it. I wanted to start afresh and move on if we were going to commit to our relationship. This was not my issue; it was what he brought on himself. This was his karma. Take it on, deal with it, and let's move on.

Just before I met Jamie, I had a trip planned. I was travelling with a girlfriend of mine at the time, and we were going up to the Daintree and Far North Queensland. I was in the middle of my trip, getting ready to take the Skyrail at Kuranda to view the Daintree from the great heights when I received a message on my phone. 'Hand on my heart. Will you marry me?' Whilst it all felt very romantic, the reality was that he had already had two marriages that were unsuccessful. He had to prove to me he was capable of making yet another marriage work. Or was it just a case of locking it in so it would not go away?

We were constantly in touch whilst I was away. Then it happened—we were in the most remote part of the Daintree when I received a very expensive bottle of champagne and chocolates, delivered with a beautiful bunch of flowers. Now how can a woman view this as anything else but the most romantic gesture? This guy was giving me every reason to like him. It made me feel very special, like all his messages. He had the right words. In the back of my mind, this was unrealistic, but it was happening in my present moment; I was going to soak it all in. I was beginning to trust him wholeheartedly, and the only way to do that was to make some changes myself and take the risks, even if the signs were telling me to run. I was excited to return to Melbourne, and I was aching to see him again. I was falling more in love with Jamie. I missed him whilst I was away, and I was aching to be in his arms again.

Totally unexpected, when I arrived at the airport, there he was with another bunch of flowers to greet me and drive me home to his place. I believed that this man truly loved me and that this was what my life was going to be like. Flowers, lots of little beautiful gestures and gifts, and most of all, *forever*! It was no less than what I deserved, and I was willing to make whatever changes I had to feel secure and to allow him to feel secure in the relationship.

We had dinner and returned to his house. I stayed the night before I drove back home and returned to work. We were becoming a couple now. We had lunch together every day; we walked the streets hand in hand, unaware of anything and anyone. I was in love, and everything felt great. I wanted it to stay in this honeymoon stage, but the pressure was going to start. After the honeymoon stage comes the comfort stage. Were we relationship material? Would we be comfortable in each other's comfort zones?

Jamie had started divorce proceedings with his wife, and he enjoyed giving her a hard time over the settlement. For the first time, I started to see his obsession with money. Between the both of us, we had enough to keep ourselves happy. As long as he held on to her in our lives, it was not going to be possible for me to commit. I encouraged him to go through with the divorce and settle the best way possible so we could move on with our lives. I had intended that I would keep my place and he would his, and we would travel between the two. Jamie had traditional views about relationships, whereas I was happy to redefine it to suit our needs. Why do we feel the need to stick to norms in relationships when we have the ability to redefine our relationship so it is mutually accepting?

He was now keen for me to move into his property, and he talked about joining our bank accounts and bringing some of my things over to his place and using my property as our retreat. I had been in a few committed relationships before this, but there was not one moment in any of them that I would have been prepared to give up my home, my financial independence, and my comforts for love. However, I was prepared to do this for Jamie. I actually started to like who I was becoming. I was softening and bending my rules; I was as flexible as I could ever be and challenged my comfort zones all the time. The only stupidity was that I did not notice that he was not challenged at all. He was not making any changes, and his expectation was that I would fit into his life. Being in love can distract you from working out whether you like the person or not. I had not been able to tell any man that I loved him, until Jamie came along. It came naturally. It was sincere; it was honest. I had no hesitation to show him that I loved him in so many ways and to tell him in words how much I loved him. I was in love, and I would do anything for love. I will not beat myself up just for loving the man.

Our home was a loving environment. We cooked together. We cuddled on the couch and watched television. We went for walks at night. We made love any which way and anywhere. My world was sweet. I was beginning to nest. There were times I missed my home; merging homes did not feel the same, and his home did not feel like mine. There were too many negative memories, and the energy was not the same, no matter what I tried.

I discussed the conversation with Jamie that if we were going to live together, we should sell his property, which was ridiculously big for the two of us, and buy something else on the coast perhaps. I could rent out my property to make some additional money. It was only a conversation, because it did not matter how many houses we looked at or what plans we made; he had no intention of selling his property whilst we were together. He just expected me to fit into his plans.

It was when we decided to do a trip together that I first got a glimpse of what that mask was truly hiding. We had had a good day, and when we returned to the room, Jamie was restless. He wanted to go downstairs and have a play on the gaming machines in the hotel where we were staying. I had no idea that he had a relationship with gaming machines; it was a new discovery about his behaviour. I thought we had come to have a romantic weekend away, but apparently, Jamie only had to walk past a gaming room and the whole obsession thing would take hold. I decided to stay in the room whilst he went off for the rest of the night. I did not sleep much, as it concerned me that he could spend a whole night romancing the machines.

Now earlier in the relationship, when I asked if he needed to tell me something about himself that I needed to know, this was what should have come up. I would have probably made a completely different decision. I was so disappointed; there were no words to express that disappointment. Hell, he looked tortured himself, and that was punishment enough. The atmosphere between us was very quiet when we left, because when I tried to have a conversation with him about his gambling, he did not want to discuss it. He sulked all the way home in the car. We did not speak a word, and it was the most painful drive I had ever had. All the way home on the drive, which was a few hours, I kept wondering how something so nice could turn into something so rotten. He made no effort to discuss his absence or his obsession, and I had no words for him either. Could Jamie truly love a woman? Or was it just a need to have a woman in his life just like a cardboard cut-out? I was beginning to have my doubts about that.

This was only the start of his gambling obsession whilst we were together. Did he, in some dark part of himself, think that he could have the audacity to have a relationship with a woman and think that it would not surface at some time? Or was the plan that once he had her, it was something she would have to live with? I have nothing against gambling; most everyone does it. But a gambler is a totally different story. An obsession with gambling—now that was something I just did not want to deal with. Not at this stage in my life. Not in a new relationship. Surely most major issues should have been resolved by this stage of his life. This was not my baggage; this was not my problem. He would have to find a way to get this whole obsession with gambling venues out of my life.

I was so angry, more because I had allowed myself to already get invested in him. The penny had dropped. Obviously, any time that I was not around, he was creeping around gambling venues. That was a scary observation for me. I was so angry with

Jamie; I started to lose any trust I had in him. I had trusted Jamie right from the start, even before I got to know him intimately. I would have put my life in his hands. This was an absolute betrayal. And why was I not running for the hills? What was I waiting for? I started to see him through the eyes of his previous partners. Had he not learnt anything from previous relationships? Was he that arrogant to think that women would come into his life and just accept this dysfunctional behaviour? What I was waiting for was that he would love me enough to see the value in not hurting me and not hurting himself.

Most relationships have their baggage. This was not mine, but I was happy to unpack this with Jamie. However, he, and only he, could deal with it. I found the right time to discuss this with him. I was prepared, I told him, to stand by him and help him get over this obsession. It was only at this stage that Jamie admitted that he did have a problem, and in spite of his promises that it would not happen again, I was no fool. This was not something he could handle on his own. Did he have the humility and vulnerability to seek the help he so badly needed? Or would he control the behaviour to hold on to our relationship and consequently resent me for that? Sometimes love just isn't enough!

I began to feel very unhappy in the relationship and now started to see him for who he truly was. I was angry that I had allowed him into my life. I hated how I had allowed him to manipulate me into thinking that he was the one and that things would be different with me in his life. He had no intention of making any changes to his behaviour. Everyone else was trying to change him. Why did he have to be different?

That year, at Christmas, Jamie decided to host a breakfast barbeque for his workmates at his place. I had no connection with his work colleagues and had planned not to be at home for it, as it was his work Christmas get-together, but he specifically asked me if I would stay. I agreed. Sometime during the morning, after everyone had arrived, they stopped to exchange gifts with each other, and Jamie asked me to come up. I did not expect to be included in this process and was not expecting a gift, but I thought perhaps they felt that if I was not included in the gift giving, I would burst into tears. As if! No sooner had I walked up to the Christmas tree, presuming that Jamie had a gift for me as well, than he was down on one knee with a ring in his hand, asking me to marry him.

How ridiculous. In front of his workmates at a work party? This was planned so I would not have the urge to say no. This was a clearly thought-out, manipulated event. We had discussed the prospects of marriage many times, but I felt that it was too early to be thinking that way. Jamie had had two failed marriages and, from what I was seeing, not many successful relationships. Because I had no intention of rushing into a marriage without feeling comfortable in the relationship, he manipulated it. There was no way that I could hurt his feelings by refusing the ring, although that was exactly what I should have done. If I could go back to that time, I would certainly say *no*. I wonder what his reaction and that of his workmates would be! My fault has always been that I always put other people's feelings before mine, and I knew it would hurt me more to say no to him in front of this audience that he valued so much.

I did not waste too much time dwelling on it anyway. It was just a ring. If his behaviour did not support the commitment he was expecting from me, I knew where the door was. I loved the ring, and I loved Jamie. My intentions were right even though I was getting to know who he was and even though what I was seeing I did not like. 'Engaged' is a sign you find on toilet doors. Engagements have never meant anything to me; marriages were even less worthwhile if the two people in it were not equally committed. So what the heck, a ring was not going to mean anything else to me but just that—a ring, a beautiful gift, and nothing else.

I went back to my property that day to arrange with the local agent to put it up for rent. Jamie had left to go on to further work celebrations with his friends, and for a brief while, I allowed myself to feel excited that I was engaged. But the feeling soon deflated at the realisation that it was pretentious of me, because I had no belief in the word *engaged*. Commitment is a state of mind, an attitude, rather than a ring on a finger, which means nothing without the commitment. It was a beautiful ring, like all the lovely, exquisite gifts he often bought for me. Jamie had truly good taste for material things. I wanted to believe it was genuine, but there was something about the whole act that did not feel right. I wanted to believe this was true. I wanted nothing more than to have a committed relationship with Jamie, and I wanted it to mean something. But my gut feeling was not reflecting that. I was in flight mode now. Once the trust is filtered out of a relationship, it takes everything else with it. I did not trust him any more, and my subconscious had already decided not to make any long-term commitments with Jamie because I could already see the train wreck ahead.

It was as if a totally different person was emerging, and it was not the one I was first introduced to. I do realise that most relationships have a honeymoon period, when two people are so passionately in love that only the good in them comes out. Then it slips into a comfort zone, when they start to see behaviours that do not quite fit the relationship. Whilst there needs to be a bit of compromise, other behaviours can only be changed by the person themselves if they feel the relationship is worth changing for. It is impossible to bring your dysfunctional self and move it from one relationship to another without change. Why is it okay to think that the moment you get into a relationship, that person carries your baggage with you? They can hold your hand through it, but you, and only you, can do the hard work if you want to shed that baggage. Obviously, Jamie had no intention of changing. Why did he need to be different? Everyone else needed to come into his world and fit in.

I saw a lot of shallowness in him, and I could so relate to it. After all, I was there at some place in my life. But today I was looking for depth, depth in everything and everyone. I saw very clearly that most relationships, whether with friends or family, Jamie kept very shallow. He did not have the ability to build depth in any relationship he had. To find depth and build intimacy, you need to be prepared to invite a person into your soul. How do you build intimacy when you just do not know how to be real?

It may not be everyone that is entitled to that right, but the few people in your inner circle need to know the person that you are.

I had a conversation with Jamie about the shallowness of his nature and told him that if we were to be in a relationship, we needed to unpack that behaviour. I definitely hit the truth, because that was the barrier that would always stay between us and would continue to be the elephant in the room for the rest of the time that I would be in contact with him. That word settled somewhere in his psyche, and he was never going to forgive me for calling him shallow. It must have pushed a button, hit a real spot, if it hurt that much. But that was what he was. If the opposite of shallow is deep, there is no room to sit in the middle, not in an intimate relationship. If you do not want to find depth with friends and in intimate relationships, it is always going to be shallow. It is a choice to be shallow or to find depth.

I now had to see him as someone that was boring, pretentious, and very predictable, and being with him got very ugly. I was very unhappy, and when I felt that way, I knew I had to choose happiness. Suddenly I started to empathise with all his partners—in fact, with every single person that loved him or cared about him. I loved him with the core of who I was, but I loved myself too. I had put a lot of work into becoming this authentic person, and there was still a lot of work to do. As much as I loved him, I had to leave him. I kept thinking and rethinking, making excuses not to leave, thinking of the time and effort and the absolute trust that I had put into being with him. *Do I need to walk away again?* I wanted this to work. I came into this intending it to be forever. This was not meant to be forever; this was a soul journey, and there were lessons to be learnt. Learn or move on.

We now had a lot of arguments over minor things. I would express it verbally; he would express it in his silence. I slept in the spare room at the back of the house. I was once again at the lowest that I had been in a long time. What makes me allow abusive men into my life? Why do we ignore the signs and believe that they are going to change? Love has a way of allowing us to do that to ourselves. I now started to dislike him so much because of this emotional shutdown. He would escape to where there was no way of getting through to him. When I would approach to break the barrier, it would be another walk-away or walkout. Emotional rape! This behaviour had a name. This was a game he probably played all his life. Was this the reason he just could not sustain any relationships? He picked the wrong woman this time. I was not afraid to love, but I was not afraid to leave either. I can love, but in all respect for myself and him, I had to leave.

His way of dealing with anything that he did not like was with silence. He was absolutely devoid of empathy. Did I have to feel abuse on every level before I got the message? I had not realised how damaging emotional abuse could be. It quickly robs the soul of the person and creeps in slowly without the victim realising that they have the damage but not the scars to show for it. I was angry with him. I was angry enough to bring on some change.

And it came. I sat there always thinking of the other person's feelings. Was I going to hurt this person if I took the action that my heart was telling me to? I was making excuses for him that he had a troubled growing up, based on little glimpses through the pity stories that he would tell me that I got tired of hearing. People have been through worse in their lives but have turned out such beautiful human beings. What was his excuse? He had a beautiful woman who was willing to bring joy into his life, who loved him with every part of herself, and who saw so much potential in being with him. He just could not see that.

Jamie did not know what love was. He was surrounded by love but did not have the capacity to receive it. What the fuck was I doing there? Surely I had more spiritual sense to know that, and the universe was starting to get very impatient with me. It had to come soon, and it did. We had a confrontation before he left for work that day, and my day was pretty miserable. How could someone tell me every day that he loved me and, as soon as there was a confrontation, withdraw all those feelings of love? That was conditional love. I started to understand that Jamie had no idea what it was to love a woman. Hell, he did not love himself at all.

I waited for him to return home, hoping, but not knowing what I was hoping for. I realised it was not going to be a good night. He walked past me and totally ignored my presence. It was as if he had reverted to childish behaviour; obviously, it was something that had not been resolved in his younger years that was manifesting now. I walked up to discuss the issue. I was faced with aggression, and he walked out the door. He did not come back that night. Probably at some gambling venue, throwing his money away. But I did not realise that it was now my money as well.

He had already spent a great deal of our money on gambling venues and admitted to me at the time that he had a problem. But there was no way he was going to seek help. Was this his way of crying out for help to end the relationship? He never did have the ability to speak honestly about anything, and this always reflected in his negative behaviour. It was so obvious that a passion for gambling, whether one is a winner or not, can overpower a person's capacity to love. With not much words said, my mind was swirling with presumptions. I think if Jamie had got the help he needed and had been humble enough to know that he needed it, he would have been a very beautiful person. But he did not need to change. Women should come into his life and fit into his negative world. He did not have to get out of his comfort zone; let someone else do that. Yet he wanted it all—his gambling, his beautiful home, a lovely life, a woman when he needed one.

But I will not let myself off lightly. I knew it all, right from the first time I met him. Why would someone abandon his marriage at the first signs of things going wrong? Why was all the conversation about the part she played in the break-up, as if he hadn't existed in the relationship? Or did he? He had had relationships but was never present. What a sad man. But I was even sadder for staying until then. I was so tired of relationships being temporary and discovering that it wasn't like I had envisioned it to be, and I wanted for once in my life to have a near-perfect loving and respectful relationship. I deserved that. Now I was being the pathetic one. I was emotionally intelligent; I was spiritually aware. Everything I needed to know was being revealed. So what was I waiting for? My relationship with Jamie was not about nesting, but it was a journey of spirit. I did not stick to the agreed plan; the journey had its chance, and it had to end.

I had to make my move that night. I had tried to leave before but always gave in to his pleas to come back or to stay. This was my time to make a move. I called my daughter and told her I was leaving and needed some help to get my things, especially the larger furniture and other valued possessions that I had moved into his house to fill the vast spaces of the home. Deva's partner was more than willing to hire a truck, and I packed frantically all night whilst Jamie was away. I was not sure whether he would return that night, but the heavens were on my side—he did not return until the early hours of the morning. I cried the whole time I was packing, and I went to bed exhausted, with boxes and packed possessions strewn all over the house. I was up very early the next morning to get the rest of the stuff together before Josh arrived with the truck.

Jamie had come home sometime after I had gone to bed, and he would have seen all my stuff packed up. I was not sure whether he would have had a reaction. Was he even capable of a response? He was up very early the next day and, as if nothing had changed, walked up and asked not 'Are you leaving?' but 'Do you need any help with the packing?' Could this man get any worse? I had no reaction to that, and when Josh arrived, he went on to talk to him as if everything was in perfect order. When we had all the things in the truck and my things in the car, he walked up to Josh and asked whether he wanted any help at the other end to unload the truck.

I guess Josh would rather have not taken his help, but I was glad he did for his sake, as Josh would not have been able to move everything on his own. I wanted my things to be in the house, and I let the agents know that I could not rent the place out now. I wanted nothing else but some time to myself so I could sit down and give in to my emotions, curl up in my home for a while, and bring myself back to normal. I was smart enough to demand the joint account transaction card that he had, which I had trusted him with. He could not take any more money from our account. Now I had to go to the bank at the first opportunity and lock my accounts and separate all our joint accounts.

I cried through all my unpacking. I felt so angry—angry at myself, angry at him, angry at the waste of time, even though it was not. There was a spiritual lesson in this for me. But I was home; it was my space now. I did not have to tread around softly. I did not have to talk things over with him. I did not have to feel so unhappy. It was the hardest separation that I ever had to go through, and it was my confirmation to myself that I truly, deeply, and madly loved this guy. There was a quick feeling of gratitude that I had loved. I was capable of loving, giving myself wholeheartedly, and making changes for the person that I loved. I was just as capable of walking away if it was my self-love that was compromised. But I was also aware that I needed to sit down with myself and re-evaluate what changes I needed to put in place so I would not allow my heart to be broken any more.

I had also learnt that to love someone is not to change them. He was a grown man. If at that stage in his life he did not know the love of a woman—and more so the love of self—he was not going to make himself or anyone else happy. He could buy me the world, but he couldn't give me intimacy. He couldn't share emotionally. He had no self to share; he was empty. But I had loved him, and I had hoped that love would heal him. I also learnt that to love someone is to let them go, and so I did. I never wanted to see or hear from him ever again. I had to work through my emotions, and I was still so angry with him. I wanted to arrive at forgiveness, and that would be a long journey.

Then one day the phone rang. I expected that it would happen at some time, but I was hoping that when it did, I would be in a better mindset. I would have moved on from the anger that I felt at the situation and at him and at myself as well, and that would allow me to respond gently. And that I did. We made several attempts to resurrect what we had, but I had felt so betrayed; the trust was not there for me to want a relationship with Jamie. Whilst we could have been friends, there always seemed to be that blurred line—what were we really?

I thought I would be capable of offering Jamie friendship, but it was hard to ask that of myself when I had not resolved the feelings I still had for him. It would take me a couple of years of staying in touch with him before I would decide it was unfair to myself to give him my friendship. This was the man that I had allowed to break my heart into a million pieces, and he had no remorse for that. I was moving into a stage in my life where depth in relationships, family, and friendships were important, and I had no time for those that wanted to keep it shallow.

If I focus too much on the challenges, I take my attention to how much of myself I have discovered, the many changes I have been able to make, and the gratitude I feel for every single relationship. I am evolving because of the relationships I have had. I attract the right people, and it is not about them; it is about my self-growth. I have a clear picture of who I am now, what I want to change, and what I want to hold on to.

I AM

Silence—it confronts me with the self. I cannot hide
from the self. Wherever I go, there I am.

A relationship with the self can sometimes be intimidating. For the first time since my separation from my marriage, I had the opportunity to have a relationship with myself. I had been on that train, but it was always derailed by some dysfunctional situation. What have I learnt?

I will still give people chances. There are a lot of good, functional men in this world, but I do not need a man. I have to want him in my life. I can love a man but not like him. If what I do not like is something I can compromise on, I will, but I have my own dysfunctions to work on; I do not need his as well. I am imperfectly perfect, and my life is too, just the way it is. Travel will be my new love because nature gives back in every way possible. I want to seek depth in every person that shares my life. I want my inner circle to be made up of people that embrace and accept me as I will them. I have no room in my life for anything less. Frogs are princes in disguise; I just have to look for the perfect in the imperfect.

My intuition will now be my guide; it will make my choices for me. Sex will always be just another social act. I have absolutely no reason to attach it to a relationship, but if you are willing to bare your soul to me as much as you are willing to bare your body, then you deserve my full attention.

Every day I have the power to make a difference in front of me; I do not need to save the world. I can always be a better person tomorrow than I was today. Every mundane or glorious thing that I do is life giving me a chance. There is abundance in this world for everyone if I stop chasing greed. The only way I will connect is if I detach, because I then get to see the person or situation clearly, so I make a well-informed choice.

Love and *sorry* are just words if there is no action to support them. Respect is the new love. Violence is everyone's responsibility, especially the abused. If you are being abused, take a good look at your responsibility in all this, and only then can a change happen. Empowerment is everything. Humility allows learnings.

We die many times in this life, so death is just another transition. I am eternal. I am more spirit than human. Everything is a business—community services, religions, medical practices, charities, the lot. The biggest bludgers are our politicians. They get paid vast sums of money only to have little interest in who got them there in the first place. Voting is a waste of valuable time and funds. Royalty is a joke; they bleed the same as everyone else.

Everyone that has come into my life has made a contribution for my self-growth, and everything has happened for a reason. Everyone has good and bad in them as well as the choice to act from a lower or higher self. I am not afraid of conflict; I see it as an opportunity to make a deeper connection. Challenges are my opportunities.

I am here to be happy. If I do not feel happy at any time, at any place, or with any person, that is the time to make a move. Being alone is a better place to be than being lonely in company. I am tolerant, but I do not tolerate bad behaviour in my space. Do it in your own space. I welcome positive feedback, even if it hurts, so long as it is given respectfully. I am not religious; I do not need religion to believe in a higher power than myself and, consequently, to live consciously. I do not need to be attached to anyone or anything. I do not need to see to believe; I just have a knowing. It is all right if I do not know about something, but to not find out would be my ignorance.

Every day, in every way and in everyone and in everything, I see the reflection of who I am. I have the ability to change anything that I do not like about myself, but I also have the ability to embrace the things I love about myself and not let anyone change that. I love change; it can't be too hard for me if nature shows me that every day. My daughter and my grandsons have a lot to teach me. Children are our precious assets. We give life to them; we need to protect them with our lives. I strive for great friends. My friendships with women enhance my own sense of womanhood. My identity is not dependent on the approval of anyone; I strive every day to stand on my own womanhood by nurturing my soul.

I will always be that person that will get to the top of the cliff and jump off and trust life enough to give me the wings to fly. If I land on hard ground, I know I have the strength to get back to the top. When I do, life will be there to support me. I have learnt to conquer my fear with courage. Worry is a waste of my time on something that may not happen. I am limitless.

Family is a group of people with the same values. I am not my biological family. I can create the family I want. I do not sit on the fence because I cannot experience life that way. I do not wish any more; I have the will to do. Sensuality is sex for my soul. Meditation is growth for my spirit. All my answers have come from within me. I trust the universe, divine intervention, and the process of life, so I do not have to question life. I am a strong believer in karma, so I do not have to seek revenge. Affirmations have the power I give it. I will always forgive, but I will not forget, because to do that would be to open myself up to repeating the same mistakes. If I am an empowered human being, no one can treat me badly. I choose my battles. I find my passion. I create who I want to be. I strive to be true to my authentic self and unafraid of the consequences. I am brutally honest.

I am a work in progress, and that makes life interesting. Time to invest in myself.

That Glowing White Ball In The Sky

A bright white circle in the dark sky. Miles away, yet so close to the eye.
Mesmerising, mysterious, inviting me to watch.
Lighting the sky like a torch.

There is nothing more romantic than looking up into the night sky and seeing a full moon. It is mesmerising; I could stare at it all the time. Not a crescent or half, but an absolute full moon. Appearing in that night sky, it has a presence, and I just can't ignore it. I am fascinated with the moon. In the night sky, there is nothing more attractive than a full moon. It instils a range of feelings in me. I am lucky to have witnessed two amazing lunar eclipses in this life.

Today was one such day. I looked up through my kitchen window, and there in the sky was the first glimpse of an eclipse. It was a full lunar eclipse, and the shadow of the Earth was just starting to cover the magnificence of the moon. In a while, this white ball would be a bright orange. Isn't nature fascinating? It was a blood moon eclipse. I could not help but remember a previous experience.

The last lunar eclipse was a few years ago. My mind was taken back to the precious, sweet experience of watching this eclipse on the floor of the bedroom, naked on the carpet with my man at the time. We had just had the greatest sex ever, and we had lain on that floor absolutely in love, watching the eclipse from start to finish. It was the first thing that came to my mind with this new eclipse. Without putting too much thought into it, I wanted for him, wherever he was, to share this experience with me in our distance. I had to send him a message to see if he was watching it too.

Thank the universe for good memories and similar minds. He was thinking the same thing and immediately got my message. I received a reply reminding me of the last eclipse we watched together, and we both knew what the highlight of that night was. It became quite clear to the both of us that it was not just that beautiful moon that was our sweet memory; it was the intimate moments that we shared that were on his mind, as they were on mine. I had no expectations, only that we shared this moment once again even though we were miles apart. I was very surprised at the message I got back. It was a sext that said, 'I have just removed your red panties. .' That was all I needed. It came naturally, and the sexting was intense. I had done this before, but it still felt special. We could not stop ourselves, until it ended in a 'Nite beautiful . . . like to do this for real?'

It felt like an invitation, but I was not going to go there. Not expecting any further response, I woke up the next morning, and there was a text from him. 'When is the next lunar eclipse?' I should never respond without taking three full breaths, because my honesty allowed for softness rather than the harsh reality. 'It felt like a one-night stand . . . bring them on.' My intention in this message was to keep sex—even if it was a text—unattached and unemotional, just the way he liked it. There was no response, which was an indication that it was not the reply that he had been expecting. I had to rectify it and send a band-aid text. It read, 'Know that you can call this number any time you feel like having safe sex.' That was where I wanted to leave it.

I had no idea, but that opened the gates for a lot more. No one made me more comfortable in my skin than he did. Another message too sexual to mention, and before long, we had arranged to catch up. This was definitely a booty call. He put the challenge to me with his words: 'when and where'. We met, and it was very weird seeing him after such a long time, especially when we knew what we were there for. We locked ourselves up in the room and got room service. It was tense. was intense. It felt raw; it was just sex. I was not focused on his expectations. I had none. We slept deeply that night, had a shower together, and left. It was unemotional sex, no strings attached, no expectations. Just the way I liked it.

But it had to happen. That word, that elephant in the room. I realised that he had not forgiven me and had not moved on from that word. I had no need for any depth with him. I had no apologies for calling him shallow; that he was, and he had no intention of being any different. It was the very reason I had to let him go when I did. I wanted depth; he did not. He was a 'goals and post' person; I was a 'jump off the cliff and the wings will be waiting' person. But that word came up in our conversation after all this time, and I felt the dagger. It was that uncomfortable feeling that existed when we were quiet. That word. I decided I needed to clear this purgatory with him. I needed to sort out this elephant in the room so it would never surface again. I did not want him to change; I did not want him to be any different. My intention was to acknowledge to him that it was okay for him to be the shallow person that he wanted to be. We were not in a relationship, so it did not matter any more. I had no need for him in that way any more. I had moved on, and that was very obvious to me.

In my attempt to reconcile this, I sent him a text. 'If I asked you to dinner, would you come?' He said, 'That would be nice.' I then said that the purpose was to talk about that elephant in the room and put it to rest once and for all. I was very surprised by the response. 'Thought it was just dinner, now there is a motive and it is making me stressed and why do I always have to be different.' The guy would never get me; he never did. I felt totally misunderstood. There was the realisation that I had left this door slightly ajar, hoping for some resolution. But I got closure. I had to close that door and close it tight. My message said, 'You have made this all about yourself, it was me reaching out to close that gap with you, will take you off my contact list, you do not even deserve my friendship.'

I have closed that door. Life has its series of doors, but I know when I have finally shut one. This one was not my door. I guess this was unfinished business, and it needed to be confirmed and the file closed. It has been closed and archived. Why had I left this door ajar for far too long?

We were not meant to have a mundane relationship. We were not meant to have goals and posts. We were meant to connect spiritually so that we make our human experience a joy. We were meant to redefine relationships. We did not need to live together; we did not have to follow each other's paths or achieve each other's goals. We were meant to climb mountains and jump off cliffs and feel joy, with no expectations. We were meant to connect through our souls and form a union of bodies on that basis. I was a soul. I got caught up in a human existence, and eventually, we did not work together because we did not make that connection. I was not spiritually tolerant to allow that connection.

I have to move on from you; my wings are waiting at the edge of a cliff. I can't think of you, because it brings back the pain of my stupidity—not in loving you but in failing myself. However, the soul does not fear failure; it only allows for new learnings. And I will learn.

I see you behind the door that I have locked with love, but there is no reason to keep it open any more. Our journey together is over. We were soulmates. I would have loved for us to be life partners. I had to have this journey with you, but to hope that we would be life partners was a dream. For a short while, I will focus on the fact that after all the times we have shared, you did not truly know me at all. My mistake was that I thought no one knew me better than you did. For a short while, I will remember all those times I allowed you to hurt me with your behaviour; this will allow me to think of you less. I have spent too much time focusing on the good that came from knowing you. Then there will be a time I will look at the moon and think about you kindly and with gratitude. That is all I will allow for you. I have never loved anyone the way I loved you; no one has broken my heart into tiny pieces like you did. But you have given me a bigger gift—confirmation of who I really am. Whilst I may be very tolerant as a human being, I am not spiritually tolerant. My spirit needs to feel joy at all times, and to feel that joy is to grow as a human being. So whilst I can hold hands with those that are on their path of self-growth and walk the journey with them, I do not need to carry their baggage. I have my own.

I am spirit; I know I am. It is easy to forget that in a human body. I have to constantly remind myself. Does my spirit need some self-romancing?